Inter-Arab Alliances

Governance and International Relations in the Middle East

UNIVERSITY PRESS OF FLORIDA

Florida A&M University, Tallahassee
Florida Atlantic University, Boca Raton
Florida Gulf Coast University, Ft. Myers
Florida International University, Miami
Florida State University, Tallahassee
New College of Florida, Sarasota
University of Central Florida, Orlando
University of Florida, Gainesville
University of North Florida, Jacksonville
University of South Florida, Tampa
University of West Florida, Pensacola

Governance and International Relations in the Middle East
Edited by Mohsen M. Milani, University of South Florida

The University Press of Florida proudly announces a new, multidisciplinary series that explores the processes, structures, outcomes, and consequences of governance in the age of globalization in the Middle East. Governance is increasingly recognized as a critical element that simultaneously influences and is influenced by political, economic, social, religious, cultural, and global factors. Such factors include, but are not limited to, the nature and structural configuration of the state, leadership quality of the governing elites, role of non-governmental institutions and religion, the mass media, corruption, democratization, and foreign relations of the nation states.

Inter-Arab Alliances: Regime Security and Jordanian Foreign Policy, by Curtis R. Ryan (2009)

INTER-ARAB ALLIANCES

Regime Security and Jordanian Foreign Policy

Curtis R. Ryan

University Press of Florida
Gainesville/Tallahassee/Tampa/Boca Raton
Pensacola/Orlando/Miami/Jacksonville/Ft. Myers/Sarasota

14   13   12   11   10   09   6   5   4   3   2   1

Library of Congress Cataloging-in-Publication Data
Ryan, Curtis R.
Inter-Arab alliances : regime security and Jordanian foreign policy /
Curtis R. Ryan.
p. cm. — (Governance and international relations in the Middle
East)
Includes bibliographical references and index.
ISBN 978-0-8130-3307-5 (alk. paper)
1. Internal security—Jordan. 2. Jordan—Politics and
government—1999– 3. Jordan—Foreign relations—Arab countries.
4. Arab countries—Foreign relations—Jordan. I. Title.
HV6295.J67R93 2008
327.5695017'4927—dc22   2008033574

The University Press of Florida is the scholarly publishing agency
for the State University System of Florida, comprising Florida A&M
University, Florida Atlantic University, Florida Gulf Coast Uni-
versity, Florida International University, Florida State University,
New College of Florida, University of Central Florida, University of
Florida, University of North Florida, University of South Florida, and
University of West Florida.

University Press of Florida
15 Northwest 15th Street
Gainesville, FL 32611-2079
www.upf.com

For Alison, Sean, and Eileen

Contents

Acknowledgments

This book is based on almost sixteen years of research, and I therefore owe thanks to many people and to many organizations that made all the field research possible. Some of the earliest interviews for this project were conducted in 1992 and 1993, when I was Fulbright Scholar based at the Center for Strategic Studies (CSS) at the University of Jordan. I thank the Fulbright Commission and the Institute for International Education as well as all my colleagues and friends at the CSS, especially the Center's long-time director, Dr. Mustafa Hamarneh, who helped arrange the first interview in 1992, which soon led to an avalanche of other interviews. I later received a fellowship from the United States Institute for Peace (USIP), which allowed me to continue the research and publish initial findings in various journals and in book chapters. I am thankful that I have been able to return routinely to Jordan with the help of funding from both Mary Washington College and, more recently, the Office of International Programs at Appalachian State University. I also thank Christine Moore and the Jordan Tourism Board for allowing me to join a group of journalism professors and students from the University of South Carolina as they toured the kingdom. Since my many trips to Jordan have always focused on research, it was actually especially interesting and enlightening to view the kingdom from a media perspective and to once again tour Jordan's many sites for the first time in many years.

I have documented in the endnotes and bibliography some of the many political officials who were willing to give me their time and expertise on all matters relating to Jordanian domestic and foreign policy. I am thankful to all who consented to be interviewed (including the many who preferred not to go on record), especially since I was so often welcomed not only in offices in ministries and parliament, but also in homes. In addition to my fascination with Jordanian and inter-Arab politics, I am also continually drawn back to Jordan by the openness, kindness, and generosity of the Jordanian people. Since my first arrival in Jordan in the summer of 1989, I am indebted to countless Jordanians, from all walks of life, who have continued to make Jordan feel like a second home to me.

As the documentation for this book makes clear, I am also indebted to the excellent research of several scholars on whose expertise I have often relied.

Laurie Brand, for example, remains in my view the dean of Jordanian studies, and everyone who has worked on Jordanian domestic or international politics owes her a great deal. I have been especially fortunate to draw on the insights of the so-called Jordan mafia—Marc Lynch and Jillian Schwedler—whose expertise I value, and whose friendship is more important to me than I can possibly say. Within Jordan, there are several scholars and activists who have tolerated no end of questions and political discussions with grace, insight, and humor. Among these, I especially thank (in alphabetical order), Hasan al-Barari, Fares Braizat, Mustafa Hamarneh, Sa'ida Kilani, Muhammad al-Masri, and Ayman Safadi. In addition to drawing on the excellent research of the Center for Strategic Studies, I have also drawn extensively on the fine work of the al-Urdun al-Jadid Research Center, and therefore thank its director, Dr. Hani Hourani, and his excellent and dedicated staff. In the United States, I also thank Merissa Khurma, Press Attaché of the Jordanian Embassy and the Jordan Information Bureau, for her kindness and help.

This book has benefitted from the exacting analyses of two anonymous reviewers, whose very different additions, objections, and modifications were indeed difficult to reconcile at times, but which have nonetheless made the final product a much better book. I am thankful to Katy Godwin, for helping to rework the entire bibliography, and to several others whose insights over the years have helped to revise and refine this project, including Herbert Bodman, Timothy McKeown, Eric Mlyn, Bruce Kuniholm, Glenn H. Snyder, and Chris Toensing. I also thank my editor, Amy Gorelick—for her support, patience, and encouragement in bringing this project to fruition—and also Susan Albury and Kirsten Russell for excellent copy-editing and helping to make the overall manuscript clearer and a better read. Despite all the thanks to the many people and institutions noted above, all errors of interpretation are, of course, entirely my own.

Finally, I owe a great deal to my family—my wife Alison, my son Sean, and my daughter Eileen—whose patience and support, especially in the final stages of work, made this book possible.

PART I

Dynamics of Alliances and Inter-Arab Politics

1

Regime Security, Alliances, and Inter-Arab Politics

International crises in the Middle East have often led to shake-ups in existing patterns of regional alliances and alignments. Even in times of relative calm, regional alignments have long been characterized by fluidity and frequent change. Nowhere are these dynamics more prevalent, and more confusing, than in inter-Arab politics. Despite the high ideological premium put on pan-Arab unity in the rhetoric of Arab leaders, there are numerous alignments within inter-Arab politics at any given time. These alignments tend to be highly fluid, sometimes shifting in radical directions. Allies become enemies, and enemies allies, often with great frequency. What is perhaps most compelling about these regional dynamics, however, is the apparent contradiction between ideals of Pan-Arab unity and the reality of numerous different inter-Arab alignments or blocs.

For example, two of the most dramatic episodes of crisis and regional realignment occurred after the 1977–1979 Sadat peace initiative towards Israel and after the 1990 Iraqi invasion of Kuwait.[1] In both cases, few observers were able to predict the direction of realignment for key Arab states. Following Sadat's 1977 trip to Jerusalem and the 1978 Camp David Accords, Arab allies of the United States, such as Saudi Arabia and Jordan, not only opposed the U.S.-backed Egyptian-Israeli peace process, but also broke off diplomatic relations with Cairo and—along with Iraq—formed a key alignment against Egypt. During the 1990–1991 Gulf crisis and war, traditionally moderate and pro-Western Jordan maintained its alignment with Iraq, jeopardizing its long-standing relationship with the United States and the Arab Gulf states. Syria, which had long been the main regional client of the Soviet Union, not only supported Western intervention but also deployed thousands of troops to defend Saudi Arabia.[2] Events such as these have only added to the general mystique surrounding the machinations of inter-Arab politics, but the fact remains that—as in the two examples above—the alignment choices made by Arab states can have critical impacts on the prospects for either war or peace in the Middle East.

These fluid alignment dynamics, however, are not restricted to region-wide crises alone. Indeed, we can see similar patterns in bilateral relationships as well, where Arab alignments have not only tended to oscillate, but also have done so with great volatility. Consider, for example, how the Jordanian-Syrian relationship illustrates this tendency. In September 1970, the Syrian army invaded Jordan ostensibly to assist the Palestine Liberation Organization in its battles with the Hashimite regime. Yet in 1973, Jordanian troops were sent to the Golan Heights to support the Syrian military in the war with Israel. By 1974, recriminations and diplomatic hostility again marked relations between Damascus and Amman, while one year later efforts were underway to bring about political and economic integration between Jordan and Syria. But as early as 1980 the alignment had reversed once again, marked by Syrian-sponsored bombings in Jordan's capital and by allegedly Jordanian-backed opposition attacks against Ba'thist officials in Syria.[3] Jordanian-Syrian bilateral relations thus show the fluidity and volatility that can characterize inter-Arab politics.

But why are inter-Arab alignments so fluid? How can we explain why Arab states realign with such frequency? And most importantly, what explains the specific choice of alignment partners? This study provides theoretical and empirical answers to these questions, first, by examining the dynamics of inter-Arab politics and of shifting Arab alliances in particular, and second, by focusing specifically on how these dynamics have played themselves out in the case of one pivotal country: the Hashimite Kingdom of Jordan. Thus, while the first part of the book examines inter-Arab political dynamics at the regional level, the second and third parts examine the Jordanian experience in particular, from 1970 to 2007.

This study therefore explores one of the least developed areas of research in the international relations of the Middle East. Although numerous studies have examined the Arab-Israeli conflict, United States foreign policy toward the Middle East, OPEC and the political economy of oil, and the political development of individual states, there remain few systematic or theoretically-informed studies on inter-Arab politics. Given the dominance of the Arab-Israeli conflict in regional politics and of oil in the world economy, it is perhaps not surprising that the shifting alignments of inter-Arab relations have received so little attention. But the inter-Arab dimension to the international relations of the Middle East is not simply a sideshow. To the contrary, the alignment choices of Arab states can be critical to broader political outcomes in the region, and hence to prospects for either war or peace. Unfortunately, the importance of these dynamics far outstrips our understanding of how they work. This book seeks to provide at least a partial remedy to that situation.

In the discussion that follows, I evaluate the major approaches to alliances, alignments, and inter-Arab politics. Then, in the last part of this chapter, I present the regime security approach, which draws on the strengths—and attempts to make up for the weaknesses—of several earlier approaches to these topics.

Before turning to the literature on alliances and alignments, I will clarify briefly the meanings of these two concepts. While this study examines both alliances and alignments, there is an important conceptual distinction between the two terms. Put simply, alliance is merely a formal subset of alignment. Alliances are promises between two or more states, involving clear declarations of future intentions regarding mutual assistance in security and defense matters.[4] Thus alliances are bilateral or multilateral security arrangements that may involve formal defense pacts, such as NATO or the former Warsaw Pact. This more formal interpretation underscores the aspects of military cooperation involved in an alliance relationship, emphasizing that relations of enmity between adversaries are as central to an alliance as are the relations of amity between the alliance partners themselves. These definitions follow Liska's maxim that "alliances are against, and only derivatively for, someone or something."[5] The problem, however, is that Arab politics, while sometimes involving formal alliances, is characterized even more often by shifting informal alignments, and therefore the more specific focus solely on alliance can capture only a fraction of the dynamics of inter-Arab relations.

Alignment, therefore, is a far broader concept than alliance. Drawing on the work of Glenn H. Snyder, I define alignment as an informal relationship between two or more states, involving expectations of political and economic support that may include, but is not restricted to, security affairs.[6] Formal declarations of military support are therefore not a necessary condition for alignment, although they are central components of an alliance.[7] These conceptual distinctions are important because most of the existing literature has drawn on Western experience, and hence has tended to focus on *alliances* as formal security pacts between states, rather than on looser and less formal *alignments*. Yet, beyond the West, such formal alliances are rare. In the Arab world, and more generally beyond the West, one is more likely to find looser linkages between states in the form of fluid alignments.

Thus the stricter notion of alliance is a less frequent event in Arab regional politics, while the association of states in one or another loose informal alignment is a constant feature of regional political life.[8] Throughout this book, I will examine both alliances and alignments in an effort to capture the full array of behaviors in regional politics.

Approaches to Alliances, Alignments, and Inter-Arab Politics

Few scholars have examined the world of inter-Arab relations in any depth. Many of the most highly regarded studies cover only the earliest period of state formation in the 1940s, 1950s, or the 1960s at the latest—such as the work of Malcolm Kerr, Bruce Maddy-Weitzmann, Yehoshua Porath, and Patrick Seale.[9] Alan Taylor's work on inter-Arab relations provides an overview of historical events up to the regional realignments surrounding Anwar Sadat's peace initiative toward Israel.[10] Thus there remain few scholarly works on this topic, fewer that have a theoretical base, and still fewer that specifically explore inter-Arab politics since the era of Nasir or even of Sadat. A few welcome exceptions to this point, however, include the recent work on inter-Arab politics by Michael Barnett, F. Gregory Gause, Eberhard Kienle, Marc Lynch, Malik Mufti and Avraham Sela.[11]

The alliance literature in political science, on the other hand, has rarely focused on the Middle East at all; rather, it has been concerned mainly with alliances in European and Western historical experience. Nonetheless, there has been little cumulative knowledge generated by a voluminous literature.[12] Much of the writing on alliances has, in fact, concentrated less on generating generalizable theoretical conclusions and more on interpretations of specific alliances. As a result, we have numerous discussions of NATO, but very little knowledge of alliances and alignments in non-Western areas such as the Middle East. Many of the broader studies, while still maintaining a Western-centric bias, have tended to focus on statistical correlates of alliance formation and the outbreak of war.[13]

Since the literature on alliances and alignments has focused predominantly on the politics of "great powers," with scant reference to these phenomena in non-Western regions, the prevailing theories of alliances have too rarely been examined outside of the Western setting from which they were derived.

Neorealism and Its Discontents

It is in this context that Neorealism has remained the dominant approach to explaining alignments and alliances. This theoretical tradition focuses on system-level factors and security concerns, particularly as these are made clear through a balance of power.[14] According to this approach, states are expected to balance against threatening external powers, and thus alliances are the main tools utilized by states to regain equilibrium in the international system. These theoretical expectations strongly reflect their Western empirical basis. In short, the historical development of the Western state system has yielded correspondingly Western-centric concepts of national security, balances of power, and alliances. Yet these familiar aspects of international relations may be of questionable value outside their Western setting, unless they are modified to reflect the empirical realities of non-Western states such as those of the Arab world.[15]

While continuing to utilize a Neorealist approach to the study of international alliances, Steven Walt has made an important contribution to the literature by extending its empirical focus to include the Middle East.[16] In his book on alliances, Walt's main emphasis is on the regional alignments of the 1950s through the 1970s, with particular attention paid to the role of the United States and the Soviet Union, and superpower-client alliances in the region.[17] Although Walt moved beyond Western cases in his analysis, the specific issue of inter-Arab politics remained largely unaddressed.

From a theoretical perspective as well, there are limitations to Walt's framework, as his examination of Middle Eastern alignments remains rooted in the system-level approach to explaining regional alliances, largely ignoring domestic politics, while essentially dismissing the roles of both ideology and political economy. In doing so, Walt is drawing on the theories of Kenneth Waltz, whose work is seen by many as a cornerstone of the Neorealist paradigm.[18] In addition to giving domestic variables short shrift, Walt assumes that all Middle East alignments must be subject to the same motivations as Western security pacts. If one makes this assumption, then explaining regional alignment dynamics on the basis of balancing against external threats may have a certain appeal. Such an assumption, however, is not based in empirical reality. For as I have indicated above, most inter-Arab alignments do not correspond to the definition of formal alliances, since they do not necessarily include mutual defense pacts.

This simply underscores the difficulty of applying traditional theories of international relations to non-Western cases. One reason for the difficulty is that there are significant differences between the West and most post-colonial states—including those of the Arab Middle East—regarding even the most basic concepts in these theories. Notions such as "state" and "security" have far more complex and multi-faceted meanings for the countries of the Middle East. And the notion of a singular "national interest" guiding state policy seems even more dubious. If these concepts are largely inapplicable—or at least misleading—in their traditional forms, then doubt must be cast on the ability of dominant theories of international relations to explain the political dynamics of the Arab Middle East.

Furthermore, the preoccupation with system-level and structural explanations for alliances has too often led scholars to overlook the critical variables found within the domestic political realm. While external factors can exert powerful influences on states, they are not determinate. The foreign policy choices of a given state may indeed be severely constrained, especially if that state is a fairly weak institution, yet the decision-making process is in no way predetermined by the international system. In the final analysis, the political outcome must still be decided within the domestic policymaking process, taking into account the influences and constraints on decision makers from both the international and domestic arenas. For these reasons, chapter 2 is devoted entirely to an analysis of the two-level—domestic and international—security dilemmas facing Arab states.

The constraints of global and regional system structure are therefore but one of many influences on policymakers. Thus, regardless of the powerful nature of system-structure and external constraints, they are still similar to a road map; that is, they can be read differently by different sets of elites in a government, and hence the pivotal question turns on what elite is in power at what time, and what the main concerns of that elite are. System-level theories can tell us a great deal about tendencies of state behavior on the general plane of analysis, but only specific case studies of decision making can explain more specific political outcomes. And that is an issue requiring empirical study and field work—which is precisely the contribution of this study.

Of Balancing, Omnibalancing, and Budgets

Other approaches to alliance politics have expanded in theoretical sophistication and nuance beyond both Walt's and Waltz's approaches, by moving beyond system-level determinism to examine key intervening variables—such as offensive versus defensive military advantages,[19] domestic regime change,[20] and political costs of alternative policies.[21] Yet even these approaches suffer from the common list of problems: they examine only formal defensive alliances; they consider threats to be only of an external and military nature; finally, they draw only on Western historical evidence to support their analyses. As a result, we have ever more sophisticated approaches to the diplomatic history and formal defense alliances of the West, countless reassessments of European alliance politics in the First and Second World Wars, and not enough theoretical or empirical consideration of alignment politics among post-colonial states generally, much less within inter-Arab relations specifically.

In addition to this narrowness of scope and the lack of applicability to (or empirical evidence from) "Third World" or "Global South" cases, an equally important problem remains: the lack of attention paid to domestic politics. As this study attempts to show, inter-Arab alignments—and indeed alignments throughout the developing world—cannot be adequately explained without examining the domestic political arena. In his "first cut" at a general theory of alliances, Snyder emphasizes the powerful constraints that system structure imposes on political processes such as alliance and alignment formation. He also notes, however, that a full theory of alignments, or later "cuts" at such a theory, would have to incorporate other key variables, and among these are domestic politics.[22]

In contrast to most Neorealist studies, a growing body of work underscores the importance of domestic politics and internal political constraints on foreign policy decisions, including alignment choices.[23] The focus on domestic politics allows for theoretical understandings that can incorporate both domestic and system-structure influences on the decision-making process. Unlike purely system-level theories, frameworks incorporating domestic political factors have the potential to explain both process and outcome, rather than just the latter.[24] These frameworks provide for a more sophisticated understanding of national and international political behavior, an understanding that cannot be achieved if domestic politics, foreign policy decision making, and international relations are viewed as completely separate realms. This is especially true of precarious political regimes in the Arab world and other post-colonial societies, where internal security and political survival are more immediate and pressing issues than is the case for the developed post-industrial states of the West. In such a context, the Neorealist emphasis only on traditional security and threat considerations is too narrow, first because it tends to miss the importance of non-military factors, and second because it tends to see security threats as mainly external.

Steven David has also recognized that the precarious nature of Third World politics renders purely systemic theories, such as balance of power or balance of threats, of limited usefulness. Rather, the real balancing act is of an internal as well as an external nature. Third World politics, he argues, is characterized by "omnibalancing," in which states attempt to balance between internal and external threats.[25] In this, I argue, he is absolutely correct. But David's work, like that of Walt, is primarily concerned with the asymmetrical alignments between weak Third World states and their superpower patrons. The Cold War looms large in the works of both scholars, who justify their focus on the basis of the importance of the Third World to Western strategy. So much justification is offered, in fact, that it obscures the fact that regions such as the Middle East have dynamics of their own, quite apart from the machinations of "Great Powers." Harknett and Vandenberg expand on David's ideas by noting that internal and external threats can also be inter-related, leading to far more complicated and multi-level alliance decision-making than Neorealist explanations can account for.[26] My work, in turn, also emphasizes internal and external threats, but also expands beyond assymetrical alliances and also beyond these initial versions of omni-balancing. The regime security approach draws on the insights of these scholars while also incorporating explicit links to external threats, internal political economy, and domestic politics in understanding the politics of inter-Arab alliances and alignments.

In another challenge to Neorealist approaches, Barnett and Levy shift their focus even more squarely toward economic factors. They argue that international alignments, and especially those in the states of the "Third World," are more accurately explained as decisions made on the basis of economic needs and how these needs affect the stability of a regime over time.[27] Similarly, Laurie Brand also brings economic variables to bear on alignment choices by arguing, in contrast to most Neorealist approaches, that the domestic economy is the key element behind foreign policy choices, including alliances and alignments.[28] For Brand, the key is rent-seeking or "budget security."[29] Brand provides a strong and convincing case for the importance of economic factors in Arab alignment decisions.

Yet a problem remains. For although "budget security" is a compelling alternative to Neorealist explanations of alliances, particularly in developing countries, this approach may nonetheless also remain uni-causal. Either extreme, in other words, may leave us with an underspecified model. If the Neorealist emphasis on an external balance of threats tends to neglect domestic politics and political economy, too close an emphasis on budget security can concurrently leave out the original insights of traditional perspectives—such as the importance of external threats and military dimensions of security. Economic factors are indeed key variables, but they are not alone, and they must be examined in a broader context that takes into account the multi-dimensional influences on alliance and alignment in the Arab system and throughout the "Third World."

The discussion thus far has centered on various security and political economy approaches to understanding alliance politics. But while Realist and Liberal thinkers have challenged one another, Social Constructivists have challenged both as excessively "rationalist." In his study of Jordanian behavior in regional politics, for example, Marc Lynch has focused on changes in domestic politics and in particular on the emergence of liberalization, civil society, and the resultant expansion of a public sphere of dialogue and debate on Jordan's role, interests, and foreign policy decisions.[30] In doing so, Lynch challenges both balance of threats and budget security approaches as too uni-causal and too deterministic. Most importantly for Lynch and other constructivists, if interests drive policy, then these must be understood not as externally-generated, objective, and fixed, but rather as internally-generated, subjective, and variable. In sum, to adequately analyze the changing nature of state policies and interests, one must examine changes in the public sphere; one must examine, in short, domestic politics.

As the above discussion indicates, despite the differences in approaches between Neorealists and their critics, the growth of theoretical literature on non-Western alliances and alignments since the late 1980s has extended security studies and international relations theory beyond their traditional and limited Western confines. Out of this very strength, however, the danger arises of creating a false dichotomy, in which one must explain alliances and alignments as driven either by external military security fears or by internal economic motivations. Similarly, there is a tendency still in the international relations literature for the competition to center on levels of analysis—either system-level or domestic-level variables—to explain world politics. For those who study international relations in any part of the developing world, the idea of explaining foreign policy choices or international political behavior without reference to economics or domestic politics may seem ludicrous. But this does not mean that we must simultaneously dismiss entirely the insights of earlier approaches.

What is needed, I argue, is an approach that incorporates dimensions of both high politics and low politics to the security of governments, regimes, and societies. The question, therefore, may be how to bridge the gap between variables such as, on the one hand, system-structure and external security, and on the other hand, domestic politics and economic constraints. The link between these paradigmatic debates, I argue, is the ruling regime. And in the international relations of the Third World, many of these regimes are security-obsessive, to say the least, albeit with very different and broader conceptualizations of what "security" means. The approach offered in this book provides for a more developed understanding of the specific security-dilemma dynamics inherent in Arab politics (chapter 2), as well as the unique interplay between ideological and economic factors that pervade Arab regional politics (chapter 3). In doing so, and especially in the discussion of regime security (chapter 1, below), I attempt to carve out not just a middle ground, but rather a bridge that can link the external security concerns of Neorealists, the political economy factors favored by Liberal Institutionalists, and even the domestic political struggles, as well as the normative and ideological debates examined by Social Constructivists.

Regime Security and Shifting Arab Alignments

The above review of the literature has suggested the need to incorporate domestic as well as system-level variables, to expand traditional notions of security to include internal as well as external threats, and to account for non-military aspects of security. By failing to take these factors into consideration, the systemic theories that dominate the alliance literature cannot fully explain the dynamics of inter-Arab alignments.

The argument here, however, is not to abandon system-level variables in favor of an internally-focused theory of foreign policy dynamics. Instead, theories of foreign policy process and outcomes should examine opportunities and constraints presented by both the domestic and international spheres. This is possible only if domestic politics is seen as nested within the international sphere. Neither domestic nor foreign policy can be understood without recourse to the constraints presented in the other, overlapping, sphere.[31] The ruling regime resides at the intersection of these spheres, between society and the international system, and in making foreign policy decisions it responds to both. Therefore, the argument presented here is not for *either* a domestic or system-level model, but rather for one that recognizes the combined internal *and* external influences on foreign policy—in this case, alignment choices.[32]

In fact, the theory guiding this study is quite simple: that alignments are made and utilized by a ruling political elite in order to maintain its own security and survival. Among the costs of survival is external defense but also more immediately the costs of maintaining a ruling political coalition. If this assessment is found to be empirically accurate, then the unitary rational actor model of international politics needs to be disaggregated, in order to see that the state—while indeed a player in international arenas—is also a player in its internal relations with society, and society can provide constraints on foreign policy behavior as powerful as those imposed by the international system itself. Hence explanations that assume a priori that alignment behavior is driven by external changes in the level of external security threats will fail to capture both the purpose of, and the variables driving, alignment decisions.

The regime security approach to understanding alliances, alignments, and inter-Arab politics begins with the premise that even such central concepts as state, security, and the national interest can best be seen as having looser and more multifaceted meanings in post-colonial societies. The real question then turns on what the state really is, or more appropriately, *who* is the state? And this question leads to an equally important set of questions, such as whose security is really at stake in the making of state policy, and who is in a position to define "national" security in the first place. By answering these questions, this chapter offers an alternative to the Neorealist balance-of-threats approach to international alignments. Furthermore, it examines the conditions conducive to alignment in general, as well as the conditions conducive to particular alignment choices.

While the regime security approach is used, in this book, to examine Jordanian alignment policies and the politics of the Arab states system, it can also be applied especially to other post-colonial developing areas beyond the Middle East. In short, the regime security framework is specifically intended as a theory of non-Western alignments, and hence may be more broadly applicable to those developing states in Africa and Asia that are often collectively referred to as the "Third World." In terms of inter-Arab politics, the recognition of the internal and external nature of threats to regime survival opens the way for a more multi-dimensional understanding of Arab alignments.

The argument presented here is that states align and realign according to relatively narrow interests of regime security. The key interest is not the nebulous "national interest" invoked by political elites, but the specific interest of that elite in its own security and survival. I am arguing, in short, that no state, Arab or otherwise, has an objective or systemically defined national interest. Rather, the "national interest" guiding state policy is really an empirical issue to be investigated.[33] It is a function of what particular constellation of elites is in power at a given time. And security of the "state," particularly in authoritarian or semi-authoritarian developing countries, is achieved by thwarting threats to the continued tenure of the ruling regime, whether those threats are based internally or externally. Alignments are in this sense one set of foreign policy choices, deemed to enhance the security of the state-as-regime, which in turn equates its own security with that of the state-as-country. Policy outcomes in alignment and realignment depend not only on opportunities and constraints presented by the anarchic nature of the international system, but also on domestically generated policy preferences, which have pragmatic and material bases, rooted in the coalitions of elites that make up the ruling regime.

Why Ally? The Value of International Alignments

Alignments are external solutions to both domestic and regional security problems. Specific alignment choices will be made on the basis of the most pressing needs faced by a regime at a given time. Hence at times alignment decisions will be motivated primarily by traditional security concerns. At others, the most pressing need may be for economic support. These shifting priorities can explain not only the specific choice of alignment partner, but also the extent of alignment—whether a loose economic alignment or a full security pact. Thus, just as alignments may be prompted by external security concerns, they can also be responses to internal security fears caused by domestic opposition, economic discontent, or other threats to domestic stability and the government's survival. An external alliance can generate resources (economic and military) to counter domestic threats by stabilizing the economy, providing economic payoffs to key domestic constituencies, or strengthening the power of the state security apparatus.

Even the economic welfare component of an alignment has strong security implications. For it is the economic gains of an alignment, particularly through foreign aid, that lead to what Brand has called "budget security."[34] The economic cooperation and financial gains of close alignment with other states make it possible for poor states to meet their budgetary obligations despite their own scant resources. The economic welfare component of an international alliance may therefore not only be used to placate society at large, but also to pay the costs of maintaining the main components of the ruling political coalition. This includes the state bureaucracy and the security forces, as well as the acquiescence of key constituencies such as a commercial bourgeoisie. In short, for states of limited economic means and low tax bases, external alignments may be the only means to generate the revenue and resources to provide the payoffs necessary for the maintenance of the domestic support coalition, on which the regime itself rests.

Trade-offs in Ensuring Regime Security

Political regimes that wish to survive for long periods of time must be able to adjust to changes in their domestic and international security environments. The Middle East in particular is often seen as the most Hobbesian of the world's regions—where politics is expected to be "solitary, poor, nasty, brutish, and short." Yet even in the Middle East, while the politics of regime survival can indeed be nasty and brutish, a regime's life span need not necessarily be short. To the contrary, many of the regimes in the region have enjoyed long tenures despite seemingly precarious positions domestically and/or regionally. Survival may be maintained through draconian means, but in any case the key is the ability to adjust to changing conditions and security threats. Indeed, the use of force against one's own society is a sign of the weakness—not of the strength—of a regime's security position.

Ultimately the survival, stability, and longevity of a regime are a function of the state's ability to maintain a winning domestic support coalition. Changes in domestic and international circumstances affect the stability of these coalitions and hence affect the security of the regime, which in turn must adjust the makeup of its own support coalition in order to maintain itself in changing political environments and security constraints.

A key feature of an international alignment, therefore, can be to serve as—in effect—a transnational governing coalition, in which political elites collaborate with each other across borders, supporting each other's ability to govern and survive politically. For authoritarian regimes, political support coalitions may even be easier to achieve in international rather than internal politics. Thus, even in the interests of domestic political survival, governments can utilize alignments to internationalize their support base, thereby extending their ruling coalitions beyond even the domestic political arena. This unusual feature of regional politics, in which foreigners can serve essential support roles even in domestic politics, has led many Arab regimes to rely on external alignments for support, rather than relying on riskier strategies such as attempting to create a truly popular domestic support base through democratization.

In authoritarian post-colonial systems there remains little incentive for broadening one's domestic support base by reaching out to other groups in society, because reaching out to them would tend to require making some concessions to them. Rather, it is often far easier to draw on external resources and support, and to forego the risky alternative of substantial domestic reform. Indeed, political liberalization or democratization remain choices in domestic reform that few autocracies seem willing to pursue, since these reforms would be likely to result ultimately in the termination of the regime's continued tenure in power.

In economic terms, the possibilities of meeting the revenue requirements—or payoffs—for regime and coalition maintenance through domestic extraction are more limited the more economically dependent a state is on external sources of financial support. Domestic tax and resource bases, for example, tend to be minimal in many Arab countries. Revenues must often be accrued from outside, unless the state in question is subsisting on "petrodollars" rather than tax revenue. But even if a domestic revenue base exists, there remains the problem of taxation while continuing to limit political representation. In this type of context, the choice to draw on external sources of income through alignment partners avoids the need to make domestic political concessions. Such concessions may be required if the regime attempts to draw substantially on economic extraction from the domestic populace.[35] Greater reliance on external sources of economic support, therefore, can allow regimes to circumvent domestic demands for greater political participation. In this sense, theories of international relations can profitably draw on perspectives and debates within comparative politics, such as the extensive literature on the rentier state in the Middle East.

In addition to being politically difficult to achieve, policies of domestic economic extraction and political reform may even be less financially lucrative than an international alignment. Domestic economic extraction, in fact, is unlikely to offer the same level of resources that international alignments can bring in. In short, external alignments may offer greater rewards while also being easier to achieve than, for example, attempting to change significantly the conditions of state-society relations. Thus many Arab regimes survive across the decades by relying on extensive external support, while also resisting domestic change. What this pattern points to is a key paradox in Middle East politics: on the one hand, there is remarkable stability domestically, in terms of infrequent changes in predominantly authoritarian ruling regimes; on the other hand, there is considerable instability externally, as regional politics is characterized by constantly shifting alignments. Yet this regional instability can nonetheless be highly functional (if Machiavellian) at least for the ruling regime, for it provides the underpinnings of domestic regime longevity and survival. It also suggests the linkage between international alliances and changing domestic political fortunes.

The anarchic international system has few rules and roadblocks constraining coalitions, while the domestic arena has greater constraints, particularly in countries whose characteristics include a weak resource base, lack of national integration and social stability, and the persistence of authoritarian regimes. Indeed, the very nature of authoritarian regimes hems them in, leaving them few domestic alternatives besides changing their own authoritarian characteristics. Since such a domestic reform—even in the form of limited democratization—carries with it the risk of ending the tenure of the ruling elite, few such regime elites are willing to take this risk. For them, it is preferable to turn to the world of international affairs and diplomacy for support from abroad. Correspondingly, it is only when external allies are unavailable, or when their financial aid is not forthcoming, that economically dependent regimes find themselves reluctantly turning inward and initiating domestic reform in a defensive effort to maintain their own power.

Jordan in the late 1980s provides a classic example of this defensive maneuver. With the end of the Cold War, external aid and support declined, as the industrialized states became less interested in Jordan as a geostrategic asset. This decline exacerbated an already difficult economic situation, wherein the contraction of the global economy had led the Arab Gulf monarchies to cut back on their financial assistance to Jordan. Increasingly severe economic constraints soon affected the domestic stability and security of the Hashimite regime, leading to rioting and political violence. The government had no alternative left but to turn inward for support. But to gain this support required greater concessions toward the domestic populace, and required a renegotiation of the "social contract," in which greater political participation became the price of maintaining the long-term survival of the Hashimite regime. Conversely, by the mid-1990s, when Jordan had achieved stronger external alliance patterns, the domestic liberalization process began to regress, and authoritarian tendencies reasserted themselves. While this example underscores the importance of economic factors in regime security, it does not necessarily support the "budget security" argument. Rather, it may demonstrate at least one episode in which the attempt to shore up the budgetary basis for the regime actually undermined domestic security.

Why Realign? Explaining Particular Alignment Choices

The Middle East may be unique among the world's regional subsystems, in that almost every state is aligned at virtually all times. The specific sets of partners change, but alignments remain a constant in regional politics. The previous section discussed in detail the conditions that lead to this constancy of alignment. This section, however, turns from the conditions conducive to alignment in general, to the conditions conducive to particular alignments. This latter question is not simply one of "why ally?" but rather "why ally with this particular country rather than some other?" In short, how do we explain shifts in alignment and thus specific alignment choices?

Realignment occurs in response to shifts in the perceived domestic or systemic security situation of a regime. Security in this sense is defined by the regime's prognosis for its own survivability, and therefore the emphasis is on elite perception.[36] In this regard, I accept the constructivist critique of Neorealism by not assuming regime interests to be objective or fixed. They are indeed highly subjective and variable. They are also based on the *perceptions* of ruling elites. In a provocative study of Arab alliance decision making, Gregory Gause emphasizes the importance of threat perception and therefore disaggregates the very idea of security threats. In much of Realist and Neorealist analysis, threats are usually assumed to be self-evident. But Gause questions precisely "how states prioritize the potential threats they face in making alliance decisions."[37] In an examination of Jordanian, Saudi, and Syrian policy toward various conflicts in the Persian and Arabian Gulf, Gause concludes that "Middle East leaders view external challenges to their domestic legitimacy and security, based upon transnational ideological platforms of Islam and pan-Arabism, as being more serious than threats based simply upon a preponderance of military capabilities."[38]

Gause sees his argument as grounded firmly in the Realist tradition since it is concerned, after all, with such factors as states, power, security, and, of course, alliances. But I would argue that it is at the very least a direct challenge to the Waltzian *Neo*-realist paradigm, since the latter eschews the very domestic and transnational variables that Gause (and I) find to be so significant. Indeed, his argument, like the one I make here, is actually well suited to bridge the gap between Realist and Constructivist perspectives, since it links major concerns of both perspectives, by also bringing to bear not only the concerns noted above, but also those of domestic politics, regime security, and even transnational ideologies in threat perceptions. In Gause's words, "the threat trip-wire for these leaders was direct assaults on the legitimacy and stability of their ruling regimes. It was those rhetorical and subversive signals, not distributions of power, which were salient in how the leaders . . . prioritized among the potential threats they faced."[39] For these reasons, the empirical analysis in this book is not based on my own distant and third-hand perceptions, but rather on extensive field work and interviews with key decision makers, in order to develop a detailed explanation of threat perceptions and alliance choices in a narrative that remains both theoretically rich and empirically accurate.

It is important to note that changes in threat perceptions lead regimes to reevaluate current allies. If a threat to regime security is serious enough to warrant consideration of an alignment shift, then the specific choice of partner will be determined by the comparative value of new partners within the set of available allies. This point leads us to focus more closely on two sets of variables—one domestic, the other systemic—and to consider changes in the security context at either level. At the domestic level, the focus must be on the ruling regime and its perception of its own security vis-à-vis society. The regime is concerned with both maintaining a stable support coalition and thwarting threats from domestic political opposition. At the systemic level of analysis, the focus must turn to the regime's perception of its security vis-à-vis regional threats. The regime is concerned with not only political or military hostility from neighbors, but also the stability of a state's external economic partners, particularly its aid sources. Change in either the domestic or regional arena can prompt a change in alignments.

Even if the regime and its ruling coalition are unanimous in their desire to realign, however, the actual realignment still requires systemic opportunity. That is, the desire for realignment is a necessary but not sufficient condition for realignment. The ability to carry out such a policy is also a function of the availability of alternative allies. In most cases, however, there are some alternative partners available. If this condition is met, and if the regime desires to make a shift, then all the conditions are present for a realignment. The exact direction of realignment will be a function of the regime's assessment of its own security needs and of the comparative value between potential allies to meet those needs. This underscores the material and pragmatic function of alignments, in which regimes will ally with states that can best assist them in shoring up their security against the main challenges to their survival, regardless of the origins or nature of these security challenges.

Conclusions

In the sections above, I have discussed the regime security perspective mainly as an alternative to the Neorealist approach to alignment and alliance politics, but also to those of some critics of Neorealism. The former approach tends to focus on external threats and military aspects of security, and hence argues that alliances are driven by changes in the external balance of threats. In contrast, the alternative approach to alliance politics offered here—the approach I have labeled "regime security"—emphasizes the different empirical realities faced by states in the Arab Middle East and throughout the developing world.

I have argued that a focus on the regime, rather than on the state as a unitary actor, gives us a more realistic view of the country, and allows us to perceive more accurately the various sources of threats to the security and survival of a ruling regime, whether these threats are domestic or systemic, economic or military in nature. Alignments, therefore, are intended to thwart challenges from each of these areas, and are not driven by external military threats alone.

The discussion in this chapter has reexamined the relevance of key aspects of international relations theory in the Third World. It has made clear that alignments for post-colonial states are far more than simply deterministic responses to systemic security stimuli. To the contrary, alignment decisions depend on domestic as well as systemic variables; indeed, the domestic benefits of external alignment can be quite extensive—covering military, economic, social, and political affairs. Since few potential allies will be able to fill all these areas of need, it appears that alignment choices, most of the time, involve trade-offs. Yet, in any calculus of the costs and benefits of a particular alignment, the priority issue will be the ruling regime's maintenance of itself in power.

Such a calculus must consider both internal and external threats to regime security, involving a sometimes difficult balancing act, in which alignments are used to help alleviate pressures in one or both arenas. In sum, then, there are several characteristics of Arab alignments that are worth recapitulating and summarizing here.

First, internal security is at least as important a concern as external security, and security in this context includes non-traditional factors such as economic support for the maintenance of a ruling political coalition.

Second, internal/external security linkages are particularly germane for states that are economically weak and dependent, as they will have a constant need for external allies to help prop them up economically and/or militarily.

Third, alignments are outcomes resulting from a strategic calculus of regime security, a calculus made by the ruling elite and based on their perception of two factors: the internal and external threats to the regime's continued existence, and the ability of various alignment options to fill gaps in the current security situation. If a state is experiencing severe economic difficulty, it will seek allies that can address that need, particularly through foreign aid. Similarly, if a state is on satisfactory ground economically, but weak in military terms, it will seek allies that can bolster its military strength. In a constantly shifting regional and domestic environment, perceptions of the most salient needs will change accordingly, leading to fluid and shifting patterns of Arab alignments that are intended to fulfill these changing needs and priorities.

Fourth, while the above points have emphasized what alignments *are*, one last point is in order regarding what they are *not*. That point concerns an area that heretofore has not been addressed: ideology. There is, however, a very good reason not to have included ideology as a variable in the foregoing theoretical discussion, and the reason is that ideology is not the main causal variable in Arab alignment politics.

Even in the heady ideological politics of the Middle East, alignments are primarily pragmatic responses to real material needs, which are only later justified in ideological terms. The intensity of ideological undercurrents in Middle East politics cannot be denied, however, and for that reason I will discuss this issue in more detail in chapter 3. Nonetheless, the argument here is that ideology will not be the primary motive in determining external alignments, although it may tilt a state's alignment decision only if all other key variables are considered equal. But it is these other variables—external security, domestic security, and political economy—that are the primary determinants of alignment shifts.

In each historical episode of alignment and realignment decisions examined in the case studies of Jordanian alliance policies, the analytical focus is on changes (preceding the alliance decision) in each of three key areas: external security, political economy, and domestic politics. This serves to structure and focus the comparative studies, and underscores the need for an empirical analysis in order to tap into the subjective assessments of key decision makers. Throughout the book, the analysis draws on extensive field work (conducted in 1990, 1992–1993, 1997, 1999, 2001, 2005, and 2006) and interviews with policy makers covering the entire period under study.

Parts 2 and 3 of the book provide a detailed examination of Jordanian alliances and alignments from 1970 to 2008. Specifically, the chapters in part 2 provide an analysis of Jordanian alliances and foreign policy under the late King Hussein, while the chapters in part 3 provide an analysis of policy changes under King Abdullah II since the royal succession in 1999.

Before the book turns to Jordan's shifting Arab alignments, the next three chapters round out part 1 and examine more specifically some of the key factors raised in this chapter. Specifically, chapter 2 examines the unique regional feature of competing internal and external security dilemmas; chapter 3 provides an analysis of the relative influence of ideology and political economy in inter-Arab politics; and chapter 4 discusses very briefly Jordanian policy in domestic and regional context, with a short overview of the eight cases of alignment decision-making that comprise the empirical analysis in chapters 5 through 12.

Security Dilemmas in Arab Politics

A major theme in the literature on state behavior in international relations is that of the "security dilemma," in which states find that their attempts at ensuring national security through military build-ups can in fact lead to greater *insecurity*. The "classic" security dilemma refers to an external dynamic of arms racing and spiraling regional insecurity; but as I will argue in this chapter, in the Arab states system there is an internal dynamic as well. Arab states, in short, face not one security dilemma, but two. In the pages that follow, I demonstrate how and why this is the case, but for the present it is worth stating some of the implications of this different dynamic at the outset. For in addition to the heightened regional insecurity associated with the external security dilemma, this more multi-faceted security dynamic also yields profound domestic costs. These can include reproducing a domestic political environment conducive to bureaucratic-authoritarian and military regimes—a climate inhospitable to hopes for increased democratization.[1]

The central point of the security dilemma in its classic form is one of irony; that is, that state behavior can create consequences that are the reverse of those intended. The same holds true for the expanded security dilemmas explained in this chapter. Thus the real importance of this dynamic is in its ironic and inadvertent result: greater insecurity. I argue that Arab regimes, in attempting to provide for their own security and survival, have created an interactive internal-external dynamic—in short, a cycle—that too often provokes hostility and opposition not only from neighboring states but also from their own societies. In a region not short on real causes for conflict, such inadvertent provocation only adds to the security-obsessive mind-set of many Arab regimes. Yet it is in this very cycle that the ultimate paradox lies: specifically, that even as the coercive and military strength of Arab states steadily grows, so too does the domestic and regional insecurity of Arab regimes.

This suggests, therefore, that a better understanding of the internal as well as external security dilemmas facing Arab states will have implications for our corresponding understandings, not only of the international relations of the Middle East, but also of internal state-society relations, including prospects for political development, state-building, and democratization. In addition, this more multifaceted approach to the security dilemma of Arab states may therefore provide clearer linkages between domestic and systemic levels of analysis, between issues of military security and socio-economic development, between Western and non-Western conceptualizations of security, and finally, between comparative politics and international relations.[2]

As central as the security dilemma concept has become in international relations theory, ultimately its relevance and applicability turn on definitions of key terms as basic as *state* and, of course, *security*. Indeed, these concepts are central not only to Realism and Neorealism, but also to theoretical challengers such as Neoliberal Institutionalism.[3] All of these dominant paradigms in international relations theory, however, are drawn mainly from Western experience and may require modification in order to fit more appropriately the empirical circumstances of non-Western areas such as the Arab states system. It is necessary, therefore, to re-examine these key concepts in international relations theory and security studies, particularly when focusing on the Middle East and other post-colonial regions.[4] I will therefore turn first to a reassessment of state and security in the Arab system and the Third World (a topic that has received some attention in the recent literature), and then move on to address the heretofore unexplored implications of the multiple security dilemmas facing Arab states.

Rethinking State and Security in Arab Politics

A central theme of this chapter is to explore the proposition that the nature of the state, security, and the security dilemma are different enough in the Arab political context, and indeed throughout the so-called developing world, that each of these concepts needs to be reassessed for greater theoretical and empirical understanding of the international relations of states beyond simply those of post-industrial Europe and North America. While the issue of security in general has been reassessed in the recent literature on Arab or "Third World" politics, the specific security dilemma dynamics presented here have not.

It is necessary, however, to focus first on state security in order to make sense of the true nature of the security dilemma—or dilemmas—facing Arab states. In doing so, I am not arguing in favor of the myth of the wholesale uniqueness of Middle East politics.[5] Indeed, despite the fact that commonly used phrases such as "the Western world" or "the Arab world" seem to imply that these regions are virtually different planets, my intention in this analysis is not to argue for a separation of the Arab Middle East from mainstream international relations theory. To the contrary, by reevaluating and reformulating our ideas about states, security, and the security dilemma in light of the empirical experience of Arab states, this chapter seeks to integrate international relations theory to Arab politics, and not the other way around. For if even such basic concepts as state and security have tended to carry Western-centric biases, then only when we reexamine such concepts, and expand them accordingly, can they be usefully brought to bear on such key regions in global politics as the Arab Middle East.[6]

Unlike many of the present and former "great powers," most Arab states are relatively recent creations, forged during the decline of the Ottoman Empire and in the wake of European imperialism.[7] Among the colonial legacies for many of these states are artificial borders and weak legitimacy for both national boundaries and ruling political regimes.[8] In addition, inter-Arab politics is further complicated by ideals of pan-Arab unity and loyalty to a larger unit than the country itself or its ruling regime.[9] These larger loyalties and ideals have led to continual questioning of leftover colonial borders, and in some cases, even of the continued existence of some Arab states. The persistence of various non-democratic forms of government throughout the Arab world has only contributed to this crisis of political legitimacy, as the very nature of the authoritarian regimes in the Arab world serves to create and maintain a wide gap between the rulers and those whom they purport to represent.[10]

Although most Arab states are not as firmly established—either as governments or as countries—as those of the West, several factors still justify a focus on states as among the key entities in international politics even in the Middle East.[11] First, the European imperial legacy in the Third World extended the European state system across the globe, even if some of these newer states remain questionable as cohesive or integrated units. For despite the lack of social cohesion in many countries, the fact remains that foreign policy is conducted and alignments are established by central governments, even if these political regimes have only a tenuous connection to society. Thus although the state-as-country is often a questionable entity in terms of coherence, the political regimes that purport to speak for countries are left as the more salient units of analysis for understanding how states relate to one another, particularly in the "Third World."

Two additional factors have reinforced the state-centered process in the development of the contemporary international system: the development of a body of international legal norms and organizations upholding state sovereignty as a cardinal value, and the intense competition between the Western and Eastern blocs of states in the Cold War era. In the latter case, political conflict between the United States and the Soviet Union extended well beyond the northern hemisphere to struggles for dominance in the Third World. This global struggle, in turn, often reinforced ruling regimes and countries that were clients or satellites of the superpowers.

All three of the developments listed above—Western imperialism, the development of international law and organizations, and the Cold War—emerged from the highly developed states of the Northern hemisphere and later made their marks on the entire international system. The modern Arab states, however, had a far more compressed time frame in which to develop as nation-states than was the case in the history of the West.[12] Most achieved independence between 1932 and 1971. Many have a low level of internal social cohesion. As a result, there is often little identification between citizens and their governments. Political legitimacy is in short supply, and this shortage further weakens Arab governments not only in relation to the international system, but also in relation to their own societies. As a result, these ruling regimes are engaged in a perpetual and precarious balancing act in both domestic and international affairs.[13]

What all this suggests is that Arab states often have far more intense vulnerabilities and weaknesses than those in the West, and not surprisingly, they have different conceptions of national security, and hence different approaches to foreign policy and international interaction. The same can be said of many states in Africa, Asia, and even Latin America. Noting this disjuncture between theory and reality, many scholars have suggested the need to rethink the meaning of security in the Arab world and in the Third World in general.[14] These analysts emphasize the effects of lack of development, low levels of political legitimacy, impoverished and dependent economies, and weak state structures on the domestic stability and security of regimes. But what is most striking about the nature of security threats in post-colonial or "developing" states is that these threats are often far more immediate from *within* than from without.[15] And that political fact underscores the necessity to see the state-as-regime, rather than the state-as-country, as the key level of analysis.[16] The domestic weakness and vulnerability of these states make internal security considerations at least as vital as considerations of external threats. While these threats will be presented by the regime as threats to the "national security" of the country as a whole, they may more accurately be seen as specific challenges to the survival of the ruling elite itself.[17]

When examining the security policies of Arab states, then, the key questions to ask are these: security for whom? And security from what? The most accurate answers to these questions may therefore be, first, the security of the ruling regime (as opposed to that of the country as a whole), and second, the security of that regime against both domestic and foreign threats and challenges to its survival.[18] Security in the Arab world is therefore a multi-faceted issue, as threats to the regime are both internal and external. In tying this issue to international relations theory, then, the regime must be seen in its position at the nexus of the international and domestic systems.[19] Threats from the domestic society increase as regime legitimacy decreases, and this is clearly a perennial problem in the Middle East and throughout the "Third World."[20] And because the level of internal security threats tends to be higher in Arab countries than it is in the West, there is also a tendency for the military to be used as much for regime defense against internal opposition as for national defense against other countries.

Among the many empirical examples of this tendency, one of the most infamous may be that of the 1982 Hama uprising in Syria. In that year, Islamist militants had led a revolt against the Ba'thist regime and had taken control of the city. The Islamist seizure of power was followed by reprisals against Ba'th party officials and alleged sympathizers. These reprisals in turn met the resistance not of the police, but of the full weight of the Syrian armed forces. No reliable estimates are available, but at minimum thousands of Syrian civilians died during artillery barrages or later in the storming and retaking of the city by the Syrian army. While these events perhaps mark the extreme of such unrest (outside of a full scale revolution), nonetheless the use of the armed forces to preserve the domestic security of ruling regimes is not unique to Syria. Egyptian politics, for example, under Mubarak and earlier under Sadat and Nasir has witnessed repeated flare-ups of violence between Islamists and state security forces. And Sadat was ultimately assassinated in October 1981 by Islamists within his own armed forces. On an even bigger scale, the implosion of Algeria's brief experiment with democracy in the 1990s was followed by a virtual civil war between Islamist revolutionaries and state security forces, ranging from the police to intelligence services to the regular army.

While the use of the state security apparatus against a country's own population is, sadly, not at all unique to the Arab Middle East or any other single region, nonetheless, the fact remains that Arab military forces are as likely to be used to quell domestic "disturbances" as they are to defend the nation against invasion. Given that Middle Eastern militaries, then, play at least a dual role, it should perhaps not be surprising that Arab regimes are accordingly faced with more than one security dilemma. They are, indeed, subject to the vicious cycles not only of the more familiar external dynamic, but also of the as-yet-unexplored domestic dimension of the security dilemma.

Rethinking the Classic Security Dilemma

The concept of the security dilemma emerged from realist approaches to understanding international relations. Scholars such as Herz and Jervis emphasized the often unintended outcomes generated by state policies within an anarchic international system.[21] In particular, the logic of the security dilemma suggests that states will often find themselves tumbling down the slippery slope of escalation, arms races, and conflict even as they attempt to avoid these same outcomes. The idea that mutually belligerent states might plunge into an arms race or into violent confrontation is not in any way unique or surprising, yet what is more troubling is the tendency for non-aggressive states to find themselves in the same dilemma. It is to this quandary that the security dilemma refers.

Neorealists suggest that the source of this dynamic can be found in the anarchic nature of the international system, which in turn leaves states to fend for themselves in a "self-help" system stemming from incomplete information about others' intentions. The key variable is uncertainty. For example, if one state decides to strengthen its military defenses against attack from others, it may do so with the least belligerent of intentions; indeed, it may be seeking only peace and security. Yet the fact remains that in an anarchic world of uncertainty, what appears defensive to the first state can appear offensive to its neighbors.[22] If a neighboring state responds with even a modest and prudent military buildup of its own, then the first state is likely to read this buildup not as a legitimate security measure, but as confirming its worst suspicions of the other state's belligerent intentions. What may result, therefore, is a tit-for-tat cycle of armament and rearmament in which defense and offense are in the eye of the beholder.

Ultimately and most importantly, the greatest dilemma within this security conundrum is that now the various arms racing states, despite their greatly enhanced military preparations, are even more insecure than before the dynamic began. That is the crux of the security dilemma that so often takes place between adversaries in international relations. But as Glenn Snyder has explained, the security dilemma can even emerge between friendly states, in the form of the *alliance security dilemma*.[23] Allies may therefore fear one of two potential outcomes: either that their ally will not support them in a conflict ("abandonment"), or that the ally will drag them into an unnecessary or unwanted conflict ("entrapment"). Thus, even in addition to security dilemmas between adversaries, one can also find these dynamics among allies.

Yet this simple but insightful concept in international relations has heretofore remained confined to the parameters of Realism and Neorealism—with their emphasis on system-level analysis, states as unitary actors, external security threats and balances of power, and so on. But as the preceding section made clear, this chapter takes as its point of departure the reassessment of security itself in the Arab world and elsewhere in the so-called Third World. We cannot, therefore, speak only of a security dilemma, but rather of security *dilemmas* facing Arab regimes as they confront both domestic and external threats to their survival.[24] These threats—real and perceived—can be seen to emanate from any of several security complexes facing Arab regimes.[25]

But although the security dilemma concept pertains to unintended insecurities generated by state policies, this is not to suggest that all regional insecurity is simply a state of mind. The region is clearly not short on genuine hostility and security threats, but it is therefore that much more tragic that the internal and external security dilemmas may simply be adding unnecessary layers of insecurity onto an already difficult situation. Indeed, the external dimension of threats to the security of states has dominated analyses of international relations, particularly those from a Neorealist viewpoint, and Arab states have clearly been confronted with numerous real threats (sometimes from each other) in regional politics. The 1990 Iraqi invasion of Kuwait may have represented some of the most extreme empirical evidence of this level of threat, but one can look elsewhere as well to see inter-Arab conflicts and rivalries. These include, for example, periodic tensions between Algeria and Morocco; Libya and Egypt; Egypt and Sudan; Jordan and Syria; Syria and Iraq; Bahrain and Qatar; and Saudi Arabia and Yemen. Added to these inter-Arab affairs are various other conflicts, from the Arab-Israeli confrontation to Syrian-Turkish tensions to the anxieties of Arab Gulf states over Iranian ambitions.

In the Middle East, clearly, there is no shortage of external security threats to consider. One might, in fact, view this region as the most Hobbesian of the world's regional subsystems. But even here, and perhaps especially here, a focus on external security threats, including the dynamics of the classic security dilemma, yields an incomplete picture at best. As the above analysis has suggested, for Arab states and other post-colonial societies the internal or domestic dimension to the security equation can be at least as important as the external. And even within this domestic level of analysis, we might be mindful of at least two dimensions: state-society relations and intra-state or intra-regime relations. Threats to the regime can come from within its own populace (such as the threat of popular uprisings or even of smaller factions outside the state attempting to seize power), or from within the state apparatus itself (such as the intra-regime coup d'etat). Security threats in the Arab states system, therefore, can be more complex, more numerous, and from more sources than those facing most Western states.

At a minimum, then, we might consider the following to be summary features of Arab state security dynamics: (1) external threats may be more immediate and dire than those confronting Western states, but the problem does not end there, for (2) internal threats to security can be just as great as, or even greater than, those from outside state borders, and (3) economic dimensions of security can often be as vital as strict military security; for it is the economic underpinnings of these regimes and their societies that ultimately determines prospects for the domestic stability and survivability of ruling Arab regimes vis-à-vis their own citizenry.[26] There is a fourth point, however, that remains largely unexamined, and that is that (4) the interactive internal and external security dilemmas have yielded a dynamic in which authoritarian and semi-authoritarian governments remain dominant as heavily militarized regimes, but often with little organic linkage to their own societies. But given these heightened and more complex features of security and insecurity in the Arab states system, the questions remain: how has the high level of regional insecurity affected not only state-to-state but state-society relations in the region? And what are the domestic as well as international costs of the internal and external security dilemmas? These are among the questions addressed below.

"We Have Met the Enemy and It Is Us": The Internal and External Security Dilemmas

One of the distinguishing features of Middle East politics is the high degree of militarization in the region. High levels of domestic and regional conflict are also common in Middle East politics, although they are certainly not unique to that region. What is unique is the intensity and extent of security preparations in the area. The Middle East may in that sense provide the most classic case study of the security dilemma and its effects in global politics.[27] Indeed, the region has long been the most highly militarized region in the so-called Third World. This militarization may best be ascribed to both the unintended effects of the external security dilemma and also to very real regional threats to state security in the Middle East.

The states of the Middle East (including non-Arab states such as Iran, Israel, and Turkey) tend to spend far more on arms and the military than states in sub-Saharan Africa, East Asia, or Latin America. In addition, the results of this extensive spending have made the military itself loom large in Arab societies, occupying a much greater percentage of the overall population than is the case in the other regions of the developing world. Almost one in every five Arab citizens, for example, is a member of the armed forces.[28] This hyper-militarization of Arab and Middle East politics attests to the depth of regional and domestic insecurity perceived by Arab regimes.[29]

As noted above, the logic of the classic security dilemma suggests that the desire for security against external threats drives states to arm themselves defensively, forcing neighboring states to respond in kind.[30] Few states in the international system feel so secure that they will ignore an arms build-up across their border, and few would accept assurances that such armament is meant to be purely defensive. To the contrary, we have seen that one of the consequences of international anarchy and uncertainty is that governments often feel compelled to increase their armaments in response to perceived threats. And in the Middle East, longstanding conflicts over sovereignty, borders, resources, and national rights have added real material bases to the "insecurity complex" of Arab regimes. Hence it may be hard to believe that a neighbor's aims are defensive. Regardless of motivations, however, the development of vast military forces and the stockpiling of state-of-the-art weaponry is clearly a characteristic of regional security policies, and these policies have led to the seemingly inevitable outcome of the security dilemma—in which the effort to gain security through arms has only served to increase the insecurity of all states in the region.

From 1945 until at least 1990, the arms races of the Middle East were fueled not only by local conflict but also by the politics of the Cold War. No "Third World" region armed so extensively, or with such advanced weaponry, as the Middle East. To the superpowers, local states were often little more than proxies to a U.S.-Soviet conflict which saw the Middle East and its oil supplies as the "ultimate strategic arena."[31] But by the same token,

Middle East states themselves—particularly central Middle East states, or the "confrontation states," such as Israel, Egypt, and Syria—used the Cold War to gain advanced weapons systems and to earn extensive amounts of military aid from the superpowers.[32] Iraq and Iran also armed under these conditions, and eventually employed the full weight of their arsenals against one another in the first Gulf War (1980–1988). Even a small state such as Jordan was able to utilize its geostrategic position and centrality to the Arab-Israeli conflict to build up military forces and political power in great disproportion to its size and wealth.[33]

It is important to note here that the region's arms races, in the most conventional sense of that term, were rarely between Arab states, but rather between Arab and non-Arab states (such as Israel and Iran). Inter-Arab rivalries also included extensive militarization, to be sure, but were more likely to be rooted in normative forms of competition. In either case, however, arms racing and militarization were intended to ensure regime security. As Michael Barnett has noted, the inter-Arab dimension of regional arms races has often aimed at preserving government legitimacy and security by demonstrating a regime's commitment to Arab causes amounting, in effect, to "symbolic" arms races.[34] Regional rivals may use such external competition in an attempt to erode another regime's legitimacy from *without*, but thereby making it vulnerable to challenges from *within*. For that reason, Arab regimes have tended to be sensitive to such normative competition— but primarily for its domestic insecurity effects. Barnett's argument is therefore entirely compatible with (and indeed, complementary to) the regime security approach, because by engaging in either symbolic or material arms races, regimes are attempting to thwart regional and domestic challenges to regime security by enhancing symbolic credentials, and thereby shoring up their domestic legitimacy. Even regional normative competition, in other words, is treated by Arab states as a matter of particular importance to domestic regime security.

With the end of the Cold War, the most noticeable change in this regional pattern of militarization came with the collapse of the Soviet Union. For many states in the region, however, the collapse of the Soviet Union eliminated only one major arms supplier to the regional military-industrial complex, given the continued major roles played by NATO allies such as the United States, United Kingdom, and France, to say nothing of arms supplies from the People's Republic of China.[35] In sum, militarization and arms races in the Middle East have provided a classic example of the security dilemma in action, to the detriment of regional security.[36] Thus, *in addition to* the real threats that Middle East states can present to one another, hyper-militarization itself has in turn inadvertently added to regional insecurity and tension.

These external results, however, have corresponding internal costs as well. Just as the security dilemma leads to a vicious cycle of arms racing internationally, it can also lead to a cycle of increasing insecurity domestically. It can reinforce, in other words, a second security problem—that of the *internal or domestic security dilemma*. Massive spending on defense takes limited resources away from domestic economic development, perpetuating the internal economic and social stratification of Middle Eastern societies, and in many cases increasing it. This stratification, in turn, increases domestic dissatisfaction and dissent, and adds to the already-existing legitimacy crises of Arab regimes. Even the region's greatest military powers, therefore, are often insecure in their domestic state-society relations, and indebted and economically dependent in their foreign relations.

Syria may provide a useful case in point since it has long been one of the more powerful "players" in inter-Arab politics as well as a "front-line state" in the Arab-Israeli conflict. Yet, despite its military power, Syria has for decades oscillated between domestic and external conflicts. Syria's external relations, including its numerous wars with Israel, provided the context for the buildup not only of the Syrian armed forces, but also of a Ba'thist political regime whose firmest foundation was the military. President Hafiz al-Asad himself represented, after his coup d'etat in 1970, the triumph of the military wing of the Ba'thist Party in Syria. But that regime was frequently challenged by internal opposition, especially that of militant Islamists. The violent suppression of domestic Islamist opposition in the early 1980s, however, only heightened the wariness of Syria's neighbors: Israel (with which it clashed in Lebanon in 1982), Jordan, Iraq, and Turkey—to say nothing of its deep involvement in Lebanese politics, both during and after the Lebanese Civil War. In sum, the Syrian case underscores the domestic and regional insecurity of even one of the most militarily powerful Arab states.

When a militarized regime violently represses domestic dissent, this action only adds to the military-security nature of the regime itself, which in turn can lead to unease amongst the regime's neighbors and hence to the activation of the external security dilemma once again. There may be, in short, a spillover effect from the domestic to the external dilemma, in which internal repression may lead to further militarization, which in turn may increase fears on the part of the state's neighbors regarding its potentially aggressive intentions. This is not to suggest that a state would necessarily be uneasy with a neighbor's use of repression to crush internal opposition. Indeed, the state in question might even be relieved that its neighbor is preoccupied with internal events. But such "relief" might also prove naïve. For the neighboring state may be just as likely to foment external conflict in order to weaken its domestic opposition. States may, for example, seek to mobilize domestic support coalitions to "rally around the flag" in the face of external threats (real or imagined) and this mobilization may even involve provoking external conflict in order to consolidate the regime at home.

These security dynamics, however, and the ponderous military-security states that they have helped produce, are naturally quite costly and this discussion therefore must lead us back to the issue of political economy and how such burgeoning security forces can be subsidized. The financial support of most Middle Eastern militaries was only possible through external sources of income—from superpower patrons and oil producing Gulf states. The United States and the Soviet Union came to regard the Middle East and other regions as strategic arenas of their own global rivalry. But one of the costs of superpower attentions for Arab states and societies may have been the perpetuation or at least augmentation of the local and regional security dilemmas.

The oil states themselves, of course, were more able to draw on their own petroleum income to fill budgetary needs, and therefore tended to be less dependent on foreign aid or, for that matter, domestically-generated tax revenues. In most cases, however, it was the presence of external funding sources that allowed Middle East states to arm well above their own financial means and probably well above their needs. As a result, both major and minor military powers in the region tend to be highly indebted states. Thus, in addition to increasing regional military insecurity, these states may have only added to their domestic economic insecurity.[37] While wealthy oil-producing states such as Saudi Arabia were long able to draw on their own cash reserves to finance defense expenditures, few other states in the region could do the same. The ironic result, as noted above, is that among the more impoverished and indebted of the states in the region are the key military powers themselves, such as Egypt and Syria. Even a state such as Jordan, while not among the top military powers, has been as actively involved in the Middle East arms race as any state; indeed, its high defense expenditures may have helped to keep it within the ranks of the region's poor and indebted states.[38]

In sum, then, there are internal costs to these interactive security dilemmas as well as external costs, as economic underdevelopment (resulting at least in part from the cost of extensive militarization in an otherwise low- or middle-income state) leads to public disillusionment with Arab regimes and to calls for radical political change. Internal opposition then increases, resulting in still more domestic insecurity. Thus the weak or precarious political legitimacy of many Arab states—both as countries and as regimes—is further exacerbated by failed policies. The result is not just the standard "guns versus butter" trade-off, in which domestic social and economic development opportunities are squandered by excessive militarization. This trade-off is clearly part of the dynamic, but what is perhaps even more important, or at least more ironic, is the resultant domestic insecurity for these regimes themselves. The nation-states of the region may indeed be more deeply rooted as Westphalian states than ever before, yet paradoxically the domestic crisis of legitimacy has only increased for many Arab regimes. And the tendency of these regimes to use their limited resources for further development of the internal security apparatus as well as external defense, at the expense of lasting economic development programs, may serve only to perpetuate and even deepen this cycle. Militant Islamist movements may even be in part a direct response to these entrenched (and largely secular) security-states.

None of this is to say, however, that the security dilemmas or their internal and external consequences are in any way inevitable. To the contrary, such a dynamic can only result from the specific policy choices of Arab regimes. These security dilemma dynamics may be considered to be so prevalent in the Arab states system, however, as to be the rule and not the exception. But where might we find the exceptions? One might most reasonably expect to find such exceptions in the so-called hydrocarbon societies or rentier states of the Persian Gulf.[39] For these wealthier oil-producing states have the greatest means of obtaining revenue from sources other than a domestic tax base or foreign aid. Their very oil wealth might be utilized to make up for budgetary shortfalls, but even this wealth only feeds the spending habits of the security dilemmas, and merely postpones more difficult questions and decisions regarding the future of these regimes and their societies. Similarly, the aid provided to selected regimes by Western states can be seen as complicit in maintaining this ultimately dangerous dynamic. Even the wealthiest Arab states have shown signs of domestic unrest and opposition. Such opposition took violent turns beginning in the late 1990s and the early 21st century in oil states ranging from Bahrain to Saudi Arabia itself.

In sum, despite their wealth, the Arab Gulf states are in no way exempt from the security dynamic examined here. They are, in fact, just as likely as their poorer Arab neighbors to be victims of the same cycles of regime insecurity. Opposition charges against the assorted royal families and against the military-bureaucratic regimes of the Arab world range in terms of specifics, but in a broader sense they look quite similar: they all focus on what they perceive to be economic, political, and moral corruption. In short, internal opposition groups throughout the region, whether secular or Islamist, are tapping into deep reservoirs of domestic discontent. This discontent turns at least in part on anger over militarization taking precedence over socioeconomic development, on the self-aggrandizement and corruption of ruling political elites, on the regimes' economic and security connections to major Western powers, and on the growth of security states aimed at stifling domestic political participation or opposition.

The Rise of the Security State . . . and of Continued Insecurity

Given the interactive and cyclical dynamics outlined in this chapter, however, one might reasonably ask how long such processes can continue. For the mutually reinforcing tendencies of the internal and external security dilemmas suggest that the power of the security state might very well grow in tandem with economic underdevelopment, domestic disillusionment and opposition, and rising regional tensions. Even if this probability is seen as the worst case scenario, it remains to be seen if such dynamics can continue indefinitely. But, in this regard, it is worth recalling that perhaps the most powerful of the Middle East (although not Arab) security states was that of the last shah of Iran. One might even conclude that Arab states, whether in the Persian Gulf or the Maghrib or the Levant or the Nile valley, could profitably take note of the fate of the Iranian Pahlevi regime, not in order to replicate the shah's brutal attempts to hold on to power, but to perform the more daring task of reforming themselves. Hopes for reform, however, are in turn linked to the policies of external patrons and allies—particularly Western "great powers"—that continue to subsidize the prevailing military and civilian authoritarian orders in the region. Most of the Arab peoples, therefore, continue to live under varying degrees of authoritarian regimes, whether republican or monarchical. There is no shortage of grassroots activism or pro-liberalization sentiment in the region, yet examples of states embarking upon meaningful levels of democratization remain rare.

In sum, the regional tensions and recurring hostilities in the Middle East have been augmented by a classic case of the external security dilemma in action, with its resultant arms races and deepened regional insecurity. To this we must add the second dimension of the internal security dilemma. As this analysis has demonstrated, the domestic costs of these Arab regime security dilemmas may have been deep indeed. These costs include the missed opportunities for greater social and economic development that were sacrificed to pay for militarization, to maintain the arms races, and to build state security apparatuses designed to protect Arab regimes from their own societies.[40] And economic discontent, in turn, has led to greater political opposition. Thus the security state grows not just in response to the external security dilemma and heightened regional insecurity, but also in response to its domestic legitimacy crisis and internal opposition.

Ultimately many Arab states, and indeed states elsewhere in the "Third World," may actually have become less secure domestically as socio-economic development has lagged behind military prowess in many regimes' priorities. But the growth of the security state is one of the great paradoxes of Middle East politics. For are these then to be seen as "strong" or "weak" states? Surely, in terms of their sheer coercive strength, the multiple different intelligence and security agencies that support these regimes suggest that they are strong states. They are clearly strong in their coercive powers of survival. But in a deeper sense, outside of raw coercion alone, we might better see this coercive strength actually as the ultimate measure of political weakness. States such as these are weak indeed in terms of popular support, legitimacy, and organic linkage to their own societies. It is their very weakness and heightened domestic insecurity that leads them to build such powerful capabilities for repression against their own societies.

The more militarized the resulting security state becomes, the more detached it may become from its own society. This tendency is simply one among many reasons that the very notions of strong and weak states are problematic at best. But at the very least, even if one is tempted to focus on the cruder version of strength as coercive capability alone, one might be better served to note as well the more nuanced (albeit somewhat nebulous) measure of strength as legitimacy and genuine public support. Indeed, the paradox remains that the strongest coercive states are nonetheless often the weakest in terms of domestic legitimacy. This does not mean, however, that regimes created or imposed by Western imperial powers will have one iota more legitimacy or credibility.

While this analysis suggests that insecurity has actually grown along with state "strength" (when measured in terms of the coercive capabilities of the military-security apparatus), this does not mean that the current history of the Arab states system must be one of unmitigated chaos. Indeed, despite popular conceptions of the region as chronically susceptible to coups d'etat, many of the regimes of the Arab world have proven quite durable and long lived. King Hussein of Jordan (1953–1999), President Hafiz al-Asad of Syria (1970–2000), President Saddam Hussein of Iraq (1979–2003), King Hassan II of Morocco (1961–1999), and King Fahd Ibn 'Abd al-'Aziz Al Sa'ud in Saudi Arabia (1982–2005) each ruled for extended periods of time. And even these dates could be seen as conservative if one regards the "regime" in the broader sense of the domination of a particular party or family dynasty rather than focusing on an individual ruler. Thus King Hussein assumed the throne in 1953, but his Hashimite family has ruled since independence in 1932 and even before the period of the British Mandate that began in 1921. His son, King Abdullah II, inherited the throne and succeeded his father in 1999.

Each of the other examples could be similarly qualified, underscoring an even longer regime heritage. In Egypt, President Mubarak took power in 1981, but his regime traces itself to the Egyptian Revolution and the Free Officers Movement of 1952. Continuous Ba'th Party domination can be dated to at least 1963 in Syria, albeit under three different presidencies. But these include maintaining the presidency in the Asad family even after the death of Hafiz al-Asad (1970–2000), whose son, Bishar, succeeded him. In terms of many of the Arab monarchies, the period of continuous dynastic rule can be dated even earlier: the Saudi family has ruled at least since the independence of the modern state in 1932 (and one might even mark the beginning of modern Saudi rule with their 1902 recapture of Riyadh); the Alawi dynasty in Morocco traces its roots to the seventeenth century; and finally both the Al-Sabah and Al Bu Sa'id dynasties, in Kuwait and Oman respectively, can trace their dominance to the 18th century.

While many regimes of the Arab states system are long lived indeed, the fact remains that many of these have essentially become distant fortress governments, hiding behind their powerful police and military security apparatus. Worse still, some of these regimes have built their powerful fortress states against, and at the expense of, not only their neighbors but also their own societies.

Clearly, given the analysis above, it is simply not enough to examine the security relations of states from a systemic level alone, or solely with reference to the external dimensions of the classic security dilemma. Rather, this analysis suggests that, for a fuller understanding of security in the Arab world and perhaps well beyond, we must draw on the insights of comparative politics and domestic development in order to see the broader range of pressures and constraints on Arab regimes—pressures and constraints that they themselves add to by virtue of their own security policies.

The ultimate measure of the insecurity of these regimes, then, is not in rebellion and revolution, nor is it found in coups d'etat and other domestic challenges; rather, it can most clearly be seen in stagnating economies, regime resistance to political reform and liberalization, and finally, in the growing wall between the rulers and the ruled. By this I do not mean to suggest that any state has any moral imperative to follow along *Western* paths to democratization or economic development. Certainly there are many alternative approaches to greater political openness. But in the final analysis, the fact is that most political systems in the Arab Middle East remain either authoritarian or semi-authoritarian monarchies (Bahrain, Jordan, Kuwait, Morocco, Oman, Qatar, Saudi Arabia, and the United Arab Emirates) or single-party or dominant-party republics backed by the military (Algeria, Egypt, Libya, Mauritania, Sudan, Syria, Tunisia, Yemen).

One might reasonably object to the inclusion in this discussion of both Arab republics and Arab monarchies. But I argue that the regimes are indeed comparable, as all can be described as authoritarian or semi-authoritarian security states, whether they are led by a president, king, sultan, or emir. I would also argue that the traditional distinction in Arab politics between *mamlaka* (kingdom) and *jumhuriyya* (republic) is becoming blurred as many republics drift toward dynastic rule. The transfer of power from Hafiz to Bishar al-Asad is the clearest example of this point. It may be too early to know if dynastic rule will become a trend. But it appeared to be the case that, before his overthrow, Saddam Hussein had intended for one of his sons to succeed him. Similarly, despite protests to the contrary, both President Mubarak in Egypt and Colonel Qadhafi in Libya have at least established the groundwork for a succession from father to son. My point in this discussion, however, is not to dwell on regime type, but rather to focus more generally on how these regimes (republics and monarchies alike) maneuver between domestic and external challenges, and how this process affects inter-Arab alliances and alignments.

Meanwhile, achieving true security for state and society (in contrast to the rather dismal picture painted here) may require that regimes in the Arab world and elsewhere break from these security dilemmas at both ends—in their regional and domestic security policies. These must, in short, be seen as inextricably linked by virtue of their interactive nature. More attention to traditionally "non-security" or "low politics" factors such as socio-economic development and domestic political reform, then, may paradoxically lead to greater and more real security for both state and society than will the most dramatic augmentation of military-security capabilities.

Conclusions

This analysis has shown that the traditional focus on security as limited only to external military concerns is dubious at best for the Arab states system and perhaps well beyond, as there is more than one security dilemma at work. If the classic security dilemma suggests an outcome of greater external insecurity, broadening our conceptualization to include both the internal and external security dilemmas suggests an even more frightening dynamic. By being more specific about our notions of the state and focusing more acutely on the ruling regime (and hence on the link between the domestic and systemic levels of analysis) and by similarly expanding our notions of security to include socioeconomic dimensions, we are better able to see the interactive nature of these levels of analysis on security in the Arab world. In this way it becomes clear that the arms races triggered in part by the external security dilemma have internal costs, particularly in terms of economic development and the lack of meaningful domestic political change. The external security dilemma, therefore, can be seen to undermine domestic as well as regional security, but similarly this resultant internal security dilemma can have external effects. A severe domestic security dilemma may even lead states to ever more bellicose and risky foreign policies, in an effort to rally domestic support or at least undercut domestic opposition in the name of "national" (but really regime) security.

Iraq under Saddam Hussein may well have provided the best example of this type of predator-state, preying not only on its neighbors but also on its own population. Indeed, Saddam Hussein's regime typified the worst-case scenario of the development of the militarized authoritarian state, driven not only by systemic security fears but also by domestic insecurity to expand outward—preempting its opponents, diverting its detractors, and keeping its security apparatus constantly engaged in actions against real or imagined threats. This last point is especially important, for the very "success" on the part of the state in terms of building an expansive security apparatus does, in turn, produce yet another threat to the survival of a regime—that is, the security apparatus itself. Thus Saddam Hussein tended to ensure that the security forces were constantly active against domestic or external opponents, so that they could not direct their attention back to the regime itself in the form of a coup d'etat. In such a context, recurrent Iraqi policies of organized violence—against the Kurds, followed by invasion of Iran, then by invasion of Kuwait, and finally back to repression of the Kurds and of Iraqi Shi'ites—takes on a frighteningly logical if immoral appearance as part of domestic regime security considerations.[41] This is not to say that the regime of Saddam Hussein was typical, but it may represent the combined effects of the internal and external security dilemmas at their most extreme.

As we have seen, militarization, security dilemmas, and reliance on external allies all remain pervasive aspects of regional politics. The heavily armed feature of Middle East politics also underscores the region's divergence from the traditional arms versus alliances trade-off found in other regions. Put simply, many Arab and other Middle East regimes find their domestic and international positions precarious enough that they refuse to bank solely on either source of security (arms or alliances) and instead pursue *both* with intensity. This pursuit yields the overall dynamic not only of hyper militarization, but also of extensive external alignments and alliances, and of regime willingness to change these as threat perceptions change. It is also worth noting at this juncture that the military aid that can come from alliances is not just a function of external security concerns. Indeed, there is a key domestic function to be served by both economic and military aid: as these material aspects of alliances can serve as payoffs to the armed forces and internal security services which, in turn, tend to be key bastions of regime survival in the region. And here too, we can see yet another internal-external linkage in regional security politics.

What all this suggests, therefore, is that the costs of the internal and external security dilemmas include ever greater domestic and regional insecurity, just as, paradoxically, the actual military and security capabilities of states continue to grow in strength and intensity. In arming themselves at the expense of domestic priorities, regimes provoke internal opposition. And in building a massive intelligence, security, and military apparatus, they cannot help but provoke alarm in their external neighbors. Both the internal and external security dilemmas reinforce each other, and the cycle continues. In addition to heightened regional insecurity, then, among the domestic costs of these security-dilemma dynamics is the creation and perpetuation of authoritarian security states and a decidedly inhospitable atmosphere for liberalization or democratization.[42]

This does not mean that either liberalization or democratization are in any way foreign to Arab or Islamic culture. Nor does it mean that instability and coups must inevitably follow. To the contrary, as noted above, many Arab regimes are quite long lived precisely because of the fortress states generated in part by these security dilemmas. But in such an authoritarian context, of what virtue is longevity? Without greater attempts to understand these dynamics, and without greater efforts to break out of this vicious cycle, regimes and entire peoples will continue to languish in militarized authoritarian states, with ample insecurity—both regional and domestic—for all.

Ideology and Political Economy
in Inter-Arab Alliances

Too often pundits and casual political observers of the Middle East attribute the many realignments in the region to the heavy weight of ideology in the politics of the Arab world. Perhaps one reason for this attribution is that, during almost every Middle East crisis in the last several decades, the events themselves were quickly shrouded in a mist of ideological rhetoric. When this rhetoric is taken at face value, the fluid patterns of shifting alignments in inter-Arab relations tend to be seen as the result of ideological nuances that seem baffling in their complexity. But is ideology really the driving force in inter-Arab alignments and alliances? And if so, why do we so often see alignments between states that do not appear to be ideologically compatible? Indeed, why have so many regional realignments defied the predictions of Western observers?

This chapter explores two key dynamics of inter-Arab politics: political economy and ideology. The former includes the tangible, material interests of the states and societies in the region, while the latter is largely intangible, representing broad ideas and philosophical outlooks. I will examine how both ideological considerations and economic interests influence the foreign policies and alliance choices of Arab states. But in both cases these should be understood as variables *in addition to* other concerns of Arab states, such as external threats and the regional military balance, as well as internal security and domestic politics.

I will attempt to make two major points in the pages that follow. First, despite the pervasiveness of ideology in Middle East politics, alignments and realignments in inter-Arab politics are determined far more by elite perceptions of threats to regime security than they are by ideological concerns. It is essential to bear in mind, however, that just as an overemphasis on ideology in the Middle East tends to obscure the real material interests guiding alignment choices and foreign policy behavior, it is also true that a complete dismissal of the importance of ideology misses a key part of the dynamics of inter-Arab relations. And this brings me to the second point, which is to explain how Pan-Arab ideology in particular continues to matter in international behavior, even when it is not a primary causal variable in alignment decisions.

Thus, in response to the question of whether ideology drives alignment choices, one might be tempted to provide two opposite answers. Yet the paradox is simply this: ideology may not be the key independent variable explaining alignment choices; but it retains a remarkably durable utility as a marketing tool in state-state and state-society relations. Is it causal? No. Is it important in understanding domestic and international politics in the Arab Middle East? Yes. In this chapter I will explain how and why this is so, as well as how and why the material economic interests of Arab regimes are critical to understanding their behavior in the shifting alignments of inter-Arab politics. In the analysis below, I will turn first to a discussion of Pan-Arabism and ideology in Arab regional politics, second to an examination of the economic bases of Arab alignment politics, and finally to a brief analysis of some specific alliance choices in light of this overall argument.

Pan-Arabism and the Persistence of Ideological Politics

Many observers of Arab politics have long seen the Middle East as "awash in ideology."[1] The political development of the region has resulted in a "triumph of ideological politics" which often serves in place of concrete policy decisions aimed at remedying the many ills of the region.[2] These ideologies vary from the secular to the religious, from radical to conservative. Yet in general terms there are two major strains of particular importance to the international relations of the region—the predominance of Arabism, on the one hand, and the resurgence of Islamism on the other. In this section, I will examine each in turn, but with particular emphasis on the role of Pan-Arabism, since it is that ideology that has so deeply pervaded inter-Arab political relations.

Pan-Arabism rose in the late nineteenth century, predominantly in Damascus and Beirut and other urban centers of the Eastern Arab world.[3] With the onset of the First World War, Arab nationalism took on a more activist political role as Sharif Hussein Ibn 'Ali of Mecca joined forces with the British against the Ottoman Turkish Empire, in what came to be known as the "Great Arab Revolt." Among the goals of the Arab nationalist movement were independence and unity of the Arab peoples in a great Arab state. These feelings were fueled by a reaction to centuries of foreign domination, and were only increased further when Ottoman rule was replaced by European imperial domination under the political guise of the League of Nations Mandate system.[4]

Arabism was spurred on by the rejection of Western domination and the creation of the Jewish state of Israel in the former British Mandate of Palestine. The anti-Western, anti-colonial, and anti-Zionist components of Arabism led to its modern form, which came to be closely associated with socialism and aimed to bring about social and economic justice within Arab societies, to work toward the unity and even unification of Arab states, and to establish full political rights and statehood for the Palestinians. This is not to say that to be an Arab nationalist one must be opposed to the West, or for that matter opposed to a peaceful settlement with the State of Israel, but certainly it was this set of issues—Western imperialism, the Palestinian question, and ideas of social justice—that most deeply influenced Pan-Arab nationalist dialogue in its heyday in the 1950s and 1960s.

This modern form of Arabism was most influentially articulated by Egyptian President Gamal 'Abd al-Nasir and by Michel Aflaq, one of the founders of the Arab Socialist Ba'th Party (*Hizb al-Du'th al-'Arabi al-Ishtiraki*). This is not to suggest, however, that Nasir was one of the leading philosophers of Pan-Arabism; rather, as a well-known and influential political leader, Nasir served to popularize a somewhat watered-down version of a much richer philosophical tradition. Conflict within the ranks of the Pan-Arab nationalists, however, led to the "Arab Cold War" between Nasir and his Ba'thist rivals.[5] Perhaps ironically, Arabism had led to disunity as much as to unity. Inter-Arab relations shifted regularly in the 1950s and 1960s between attempts at formal unification, such as the short-lived United Arab Republic (1958–1961), and overt conflict.[6] The collapse of the U.A.R. was a major setback to Pan-Arabism, as was the Arab-Israeli war of June 1967. The six-day conflict was a disaster not only for the Arab armies but also for the political legitimacy of the Arab regimes, and it was a crushing defeat both for Nasir himself and for the cause of Pan-Arabism.[7]

A brief revival of Arab unity prior to the 1973 war was not enough to restore Arabism to its earlier potency. Anwar Sadat's unilateral actions toward the end of the conflict were soon mirrored in his post-war diplomacy, leading to the 1978 Camp David Accords and the 1979 Egyptian-Israeli Peace Treaty.[8] Sadat's Israeli initiative was yet another setback for Arabism, and a severe blow to the unity of the Arab world. Since the death of Nasir in 1970, the Arab world had moved from a period of alternating coordination and conflict centered around Egypt's virtually hegemonic power, to a period of extreme fragmentation of inter-Arab politics.[9] But with the blows to Pan-Arabism came a "pragmatic trend" in Arab politics, in which the ideological rhetoric of Pan-Arab unity was largely overtaken by a less ideological style of politics. This "new pragmatism" among Arab elites included efforts at more specific bilateral relationships and the preservation of individual state sovereignty, rather than broader multilateral efforts at pan-Arab unity.[10] Even the Arab governments most dedicated to Arabism—such as the Ba'thists in Syria and Iraq—came to emphasize territorial nationalism first and foremost as they consolidated their regimes. What began to emerge, in short, was an increasing emphasis on state sovereignty in the regional political order despite Arabism's anti-Westphalian origins.[11]

With the end of the Cold War and the collapse of the Soviet Union, Arabism suffered an additional blow. The state socialism and command economies of the Arab nationalist regimes appeared discredited, especially in light of the implosion of the Eastern European communist states and the mediocre performance of many Arab economies and political systems. In addition, with the fall of the Soviet Union, a chief source of economic and military aid was suddenly gone. Finally, the 1990–1991 Gulf crisis may have marked the lowest point in the life of the Pan-Arab movement. Yet the influence of Pan-Arabism continues and can be heard especially in the political dialogue of inter-Arab politics.

In this sense, social constructivist theorists have added greatly to our understanding of regional politics by taking inter-Arab debates seriously and noting the shifts in dialogue and even in conceptualizations of Arab identity.[12] Michael Barnett, for example, has traced the region-wide struggles and shifts in Arabism from the 1920s through the 1990s.[13] In his examination of these inter-Arab dialogues, Barnett argues that even Arab alliances themselves are responses to normative, rather than military, challenges.[14] Arab politics, in his view, is "symbolic politics," in which struggles are more likely to be political and even cultural, rather than military in nature. The changing fortunes of Pan-Arabism, especially since its peak in the 1950s and 1960s, have yielded a kind of "normative fragmentation," in Barnett's words, in which struggles now continue over the meanings of Arabism, national identities, and regional order.

Marc Lynch has extended this analysis by examining the impact of the media and information revolution on regional politics, especially as the region has shifted from the once ubiquitous state-controlled television stations to the far more popular satellite stations, such as al-Jazeera and al-'Arabiyya. Lynch argues that this revolution has resulted in nothing less than a new

Arab public sphere, as the new media has "conclusively shattered the state's monopoly over the flow of information, rendering obsolete the ministries of information and the oppressive state censorship that was smothering public discourse well into the 1990s."[15] Now, instead of the longstanding tradition of creating an "enforced public consensus," the new Arab public sphere includes, in Lynch's words, "an expectation of public disagreement."[16] Perhaps most interestingly for the purposes of this analysis, however, is Lynch's conclusion that, despite the many funerals given to Arabism over the years, "the new public has forced Arab leaders to justify their positions far more than ever before."[17]

Indeed, even approaching this problem from a Realist perspective, Gregory Gause has argued that ideology and ideas too can be read as threats to regime security. In his analysis of Arab alliance behavior during various Gulf crises, Gause concludes that "these states overwhelmingly identified ideological and political threats emanating from abroad to the domestic stability of their ruling regimes as more salient than threats based upon aggregate power, geographic proximity and offensive capabilities." The issue here, in other words, may not just be the ideas and worldviews of foreign policy elites, but rather how they perceive the ideas of others, and how they believe these might play within their own domestic politics. As Gause argues, "words—if it is feared that they will find resonance among a state's citizens—were seen as more immediately threatening than guns" to these Arab regimes.[18]

These perspectives, by prominent constructivist thinkers and by a particularly innovative realist scholar, are valid, accurate, and important. Gause hits on a key factor; that is, that inter-Arab ideological and normative debates can challenge a regime's legitimacy in its own domestic politics. In this sense, then, the regional dialogues over Arabism can best be seen as one of many considerations within regime security. Ideological and normative competition, in short, has regime security implications and hence these constructivist perspectives are complementary to—rather than competing with—the regime security perspective.

What, then, can we say about Arabism today? First, contrary to many claims even from within the region, Arabism remains alive, and various intimations of its death have been greatly exaggerated. It is no longer the zealous ideology of unification that it may have been decades ago. But this brings me to the second point: that the salience of Arabism does not lie in calculations of Arab regimes, which are more likely to be cynical in the extreme about Pan-Arabism. Rather, its salience remains in the hearts and minds of many in the general Arab public, whose attention to al-Jazeera, for example, suggests a broader identification with a pan-Arab culture, society, and nation. This broader sense of a region-wide Arab community and a collective Arab identity, may have even increased in the age of the new media, even as debates continue over the salience of country-level nationalism and national identity.

What is most striking about Arabism is not the overt contradiction between the ideology of unity and the frequently conflictual nature of inter-Arab politics; rather, what is most striking is the continued tendency of Arab regimes to resort to Arab nationalist rhetoric and symbolism to justify policy decisions and to rally public support. Therefore, rather than turn to the time-honored debate regarding just how alive or dead Arabism is, we might be better advised to examine not simply its degree of salience in contemporary politics, but also precisely *how* it is utilized as a political tool.

Regimes tend to draw on Pan-Arabist ideology in an attempt to enhance their domestic position and their regional standing. Arab nationalists tend to stress that, unlike Islamism, Pan-Arabism is a political force that is entirely unique and local to the region.[19] Ironically, Islamist movements see themselves as the more indigenous force, while viewing all forms of nationalism—Arabism included—as Western imports to the region. Still, Pan-Arabist rhetoric is invoked regularly to justify policy decisions, *especially inter-Arab alignment choices*. The skillful use of Pan-Arab symbolism and rhetoric can justify even the most unlikely alignments. Politics, it is said, makes for strange bedfellows—and Arabism can often serve to make ideological sense out of otherwise unlikely political marriages.

Pan-Arabism, in other words, may help to facilitate cross-border linkages and inter-state permeability. Rather than creating ideological limits to alignment possibilities, Pan-Arabism can provide an ideological justification for *any* inter-Arab alignment choice, no matter how seemingly unlikely, in a way that might be far more difficult in any other region of the world. From the perspective of a regime's relations with its own society, it must be remembered that Arab states are *expected* to have Arab allies, and to be working toward greater inter-Arab integration.

While this suggests merely the cynical manipulation of one of the most prominent ideological strains in the region, it is certainly also possible for avowedly Pan-Arab regimes to honestly pursue goals of Arab unity and even unification. Thus the question remains whether Arab regimes seek alignments with similarly-minded partners in order to bring about Arab unity in real institutional terms. In his examination of Middle East alliances, Walt has suggested that Pan-Arabist ideologies such as Nasirism and Ba'thism are more likely to drive states apart than they are to lead to alignments. "Birds of a feather," in other words, are more likely to fly apart than to flock together. This is so, he argues, with all "hierarchical ideologies," such as Ba'thism or communism, in which alternative interpretations of the same ideology result only in rivalry and conflict over the purer interpretation.[20] While I agree with Walt that ideology is not a primary determinant of alignments, this does not mean that it is without political salience or importance. For, as the discussion above has made clear, Pan-Arab nationalist ideology remains a key tool for regimes in "selling" their alignment choices to their own societies.[21] This ideology, therefore, cannot be dismissed as simply smoke and mirrors, for it provides a key variable—at times if only as a marketing tool—linking state-state and state-society relations.

Still, it has long been fashionable to declare Arabism in any form as finally dead.[22] But the critical question remains: for whom? With every regional crisis or inter-Arab dispute, new pronouncements are made by pundits and scholars alike that this event indeed marks the last gasp of an outdated regional ideology. Equally inevitable is the flurry of responses that Arabism is not dead yet. Perhaps it is merely resting. Or perhaps these arguments are missing the point, while still holding a grain of truth. For some in the Arab world, Arabism is dead in the sense that it is a conviction that is held sincerely by very few elites. For others, Arabism seems to be in critical condition, since it has so often been discredited or at least damaged by the actions of Arab governments in their conflicts with one another.

No event stressed inter-Arab divisions more clearly than the variety of responses to the 1990–1991 Gulf crisis. An Arab state had invaded and conquered another Arab state and an international coalition, led by the United States, began deployment of its own forces in the region. Arab League attempts at conflict resolution failed, and ultimately Egypt, Syria, and Morocco each dispatched troops to Saudi Arabia to defend it against Iraq. Surely this sad episode marked the low point of Arabism on the part of the governments involved; but what of their societies? At the level of "the street," rather than the ruling regimes, Arabism looked very much alive. It is not accidental that public opposition to any attack on Iraq was seen most clearly in those Arab states that had recently opened up their political systems—Jordan, Tunisia, and Yemen. In contrast, little opposition was heard, or reported, within the most authoritarian states such as Syria.[23]

In short, the Gulf crisis proved not that Arabism was dead, but that it held different degrees of salience at different levels of state and society. For some in the Arab world Arabism remains a noble goal of unity to be achieved. To others, it is an ideology that has been discredited many times over, and one that needs to be replaced with an alternative—whether that is territorial nationalism, Islamism, free market capitalism, or even democratization. What is clear, however, is that regardless of how sincere or cynical political elites are in regard to Pan-Arabism, few are above manipulating its symbols to justify their regional policies. And in Arab alignment politics above all, Arabism remains a legitimate and heart-felt ideology to some, a useful and cynically wielded tool to others.

But if Pan-Arabism is utilized as an increasingly cynical political tool, it is because of the triumph of territorial nationalism and state sovereignty over pan-Arab unity.[24] Since independence, efforts at achieving pan-Arabist goals have remained problematic, largely because both the goals and their obstacles have been institutionalized in regional politics. The main institution charged with achieving inter-Arab cooperation, coordination, and unity is the League of Arab states; yet the Arab League itself enshrines and preserves the state sovereignty of each individual Arab country.

There has long been, therefore, a contradictory pull between territorial nationalism and state sovereignty on the one hand, and pan-Arab unity on the other.[25] As the latter has suffered defeats, the former has grown and prospered. The difference is one between *qawmiyya* (nationalism associated with the Arab world at large) and *wataniyya* (nationalism associated with a particular country). The contradictions are felt both at the state level and at the level of society, where individuals are expected to maintain loyalty both to the state, and to an entity far larger than the single state. For most political elites, however, rhetorical flourishes are given to Arabism while real policy is more often dedicated to the preservation of state sovereignty and to the development of public loyalty to the state through country-based nationalist identification. Territorial nationalism has become the de facto ideology of political elites and ruling regimes. It is the ideology of the status quo.

The Islamist Challenge

In contrast to Arabism, Islamism has re-emerged as the ideology of the disenfranchised, of the opposition, and of those in search of radical change in the status quo.[26] Although the latter 1970s marked the beginning of a resurgence of Islamic political activism and even militancy, the origins of modern Islamic "fundamentalism" can be traced back far earlier. The first organized movement in the twentieth century emerged in Egypt, when Hasan al-Banna founded the Muslim Brotherhood (*al-ikhwan al-muslimun*). While it is not necessarily united from country to country, the Muslim Brotherhood remains the largest single Islamist grouping in the Arab world. As a result of its historical basis, the *ikhwan* were also the most well organized groups and hence were best able to take advantage of the Islamic political resurgence from the late 1970s onward.[27]

Like early Pan-Arabism, Islamism tends to be anti-Western and anti-Zionist. Unlike the Arab nationalists, however, Islamists tend to focus on establishing Islamic regimes in particular countries rather than attempting to achieve regional unification. In addition, Islamism has not been associated with socialism, as Arabism has. To the contrary, the Islamists tended to reject socialism, like nationalism, as yet another foreign import. The resurgence of Islam came on the heels of the failures of several alternative ideologies: nationalism, capitalism, socialism, parliamentary democracy, and so on. To these Western imported ideas, the Islamist response was simple: *"al-Islam huwa al-hal"* ("Islam is the solution"). Unlike these foreign ideologies, Islamists have argued, Islam is the only indigenous answer to the region's problems.

Yet, in contrast to the Islamic theocracy in Iran, Islamism has remained marginalized by the predominantly secular Arab regimes. At the same time, the increasing salience of Islamism in domestic and regional politics has also led these same regimes to play up their Islamic credentials and manipulate Islamic symbolism whenever possible. It is worth noting, then, that here too regimes have felt compelled to respond to public opinion and debates within their own societies by attempting to confirm their Islamic as well as their Arab identities. But, in general, Islamism has remained predominantly a force for political opposition to Arab regimes, rather than a force influencing the worldviews and policies of ruling regimes themselves. Indeed, Arab regimes in the old nationalist and "revolutionary" republics—such as Algeria, Egypt, Iraq, and Syria—all made extensive use of anti-revolutionary coercion and violence in their attempts to crush Islamist opposition movements. Each had its share of state versus Islamist violence in the 1980s and 1990s, with Algeria in particular degenerating into civil war in the latter decade. Even a state such as Saudi Arabia, with a royal family that viewed itself as practicing Islamic governance with the Holy Qur'an as its constitution, faced its main and most violent opposition in the form of a militant Islamist movement.

With the collapse of Iraq following the 2003 U.S. invasion and later occupation, and the rise of ever more militant and even jihadist forms of Islamist opposition in Iraq and elsewhere, Arab regimes have found themselves even more on the defensive. The greatest danger here, however, even beyond the challenge of al-Qa'ida and other jihadist groups, is that regime security is such an overriding imperative that even democratically oriented Arab nationalists and Islamists are likely to be swept away as regimes flail against real and perceived terrorist threats. The Mubarak regime in Egypt, for example, spent much of 2007 turning on Egypt's long-established and reformist Islamist movement—the Muslim Brotherhood—in the name of the ever-elastic war on terrorism. Yet in Egypt and elsewhere, coercive tactics against moderate forms of opposition are likely to lead more regime opponents to turn to militancy and perhaps even terrorism, thereby undercutting the security of both regime and society. Here too, in other words, even in the world of ideology, ideas, and identities, the domestic dimension of the regime security dilemma rears its ugly head.

The above discussion has made clear that—regardless of levels of sincerity—regional politics has long been pervaded by ideology, whether Pan-Arabist or Islamist in orientation. And this ideological flavor to regional interaction serves domestic as well as international purposes, as regimes attempt to enhance their domestic positions by stressing their Arab nationalist and Islamic credentials, as well as their contributions to Pan-Arab and Islamic causes, by playing activist regional roles.[28] From the perspective of ruling regimes, ideology plays a critical role in domestic politics and at least a supporting role in international relations and foreign policy. In fact, it may provide the critical variable linking domestic and international politics for many Arab regimes. Indeed, the clear implication of Arabism as an ideology is for governments to pursue activist regional foreign policies. And thus an active role in inter-Arab politics provides a certain legitimizing quality for Arab regimes, which make certain that the mostly state-controlled presses report every inter-Arab interaction in great detail, regardless of how trivial it is. Ideology, in short, may not be the primary causal factor in Arab alignments, but it is an essential marketing tool for regimes intent on justifying their foreign policy decisions, particularly their alignment choices, both to their neighbors and to their domestic populations. But, as I have suggested above, such ideologically based justifications may in turn simply veil the more tangible and material incentives underpinning many inter-Arab alliances. Having discussed both security dynamics and ideological issues, I will now turn to an examination of the regional political economy and its potential effects on inter-Arab alignments.

A Political Economy of Disparity, Dependence, and Insecurity

The most striking feature of the regional political economy, as it affects the international behavior of Arab states, is the high degree of economic stratification both between and within these states. High levels of economic disparity are not entirely unique to the Middle East, yet they are more extreme within that region than in any other part of the world. This disparity is due, in large part, to the effects of petroleum development on the regional political economy. The Middle East has been dramatically affected by several waves of change in the last few centuries, such as the impact of the colonial and imperial experience and also the rise of nationalist struggles for independence. These events reshaped the region and brought about the birth of the modern Middle East.[29]

Yet an equally important wave of change occurred far more recently in the form of the oil boom of the early 1970s. The political economy of petroleum changed the domestic and regional politics of the region, to the point that all states were affected—regardless of whether they were oil producers or not. This change is viewed by some as nothing less than a revolution, which brought about a new social and economic order, creating massive dislocations in domestic class relations as well as in regional state relations.[30] Almost overnight, tribal based sheikhdoms of the Arabian peninsula were transformed into economic superpowers, while previously powerful Arab states—politically and militarily—were suddenly "the poor relations of the Arab world."[31] There remain, therefore, vast differences in wealth between and among Arab states, creating a stratified political economy ranging from the very poor (such as Mauritania, Sudan, Egypt, and Yemen) to the very wealthy oil states (such as Kuwait and Saudi Arabia). Thus, by the mid-1990s, for example, the per capita GNPs of Gulf states such as Kuwait and the United Arab Emirates were more than twenty times that of even key military powers such as Egypt and Syria.[32] In short, the Arab states span the economic spectrum from among the wealthiest countries in the world to the most impoverished and indebted, and these economic issues must be kept in mind when viewing the foreign policy behavior and alignment choices of Arab states.

The petroleum-generated transformation of the regional political economy created vast new areas of opportunity, triggering demographic shifts as labor in poorer states migrated to the oil producing countries. Financial relations changed as great amounts of aid were available through petrodollars. States such as Jordan, Egypt, Sudan, and Yemen came to rely further and further on external sources of aid as well as remittances from laborers abroad. As early as 1975, for example, there were 175,000 Jordanian laborers in Saudi Arabia alone, amounting to 66 percent of Jordan's out-of-country workforce. On average, Jordan has since then tended to have approximately a quarter of a million of its nationals working in various Arab Gulf states in any given year. The net effect of this massive export of labor, from a country with a total population (at the time) of only 3.5 million, was an increase in remittances from U.S. $55.4 million in 1973 to U.S. $984.4 million in 1986.[33] New opportunities, however, also provided new lines of conflict and resentment, as economic stratification rapidly increased both between states and within societies.

With the contraction of the oil market in the 1980s, these lingering areas of resentment became more pronounced. Levels of dependency and demands for further aid increased just as donor states retreated from previous aid levels. Especially for the poorer Arab states, this increasing reliance on oil-generated foreign aid and on worker remittances from the Gulf created a deepening condition of asymmetrical interdependence and highlighted the increasing political importance of aid and labor flows in the region. It is interesting to note, however, that this interdependence does not extend to trade relations. By the 1980s, most Arab states had a greater stake in European rather than in inter-Arab trade relations. One factor that has hampered attempts at greater inter-Arab trade integration has been a degree of agricultural and manufacturing redundancy among many Arab states.[34]

Asymmetrical *inter*dependence, however, amounts to little more than *dependence* for the weaker partner in any economic relationship. In the case of the Arab states system, labor-rich and capital-poor states had become dependent on access to the oil fields and service sectors of Gulf states as key labor markets. Most Gulf monarchies, in turn, had become dependent on foreign labor—both skilled and unskilled—to keep their economies running. An important difference, however, and the one that marked the true asymmetry of relations between oil states and non-oil states, is that although the Gulf states were dependent on foreign labor, they were not necessarily dependent on *Arab* labor. Equally noticeable and growing with the level of interdependence, asymmetrical or otherwise, was the level of disparity and stratification. In short, the continuing gap between the "haves" and "have-nots" in the Arab world has, if anything, only increased in political salience over time. This is certainly a difficult issue to measure in any concrete way, but the class conflict implied by this rift was clearly one among many lines of contention underscored by the 1991 Gulf War and indeed later became part of the rallying cry of organizations ranging from Hamas to Hizbullah and even to al-Qa'ida.

But what does this rift suggest for regional alignments? Among other things, it makes clear the high levels of economic need on the part of virtually all Arab states, including even the wealthy oil producers themselves. The oil states tend to be the least populous, and hence have a need for foreign labor to exploit their own resource endowments. The non-oil states, in contrast, are considerably poorer and not blessed with such lucrative resources. They need access to the labor markets of the oil producers as well as to the oil supplies themselves. With increasing economic interdependence among Arab states, the politics of labor migration has become a central element in inter-Arab politics.

The same can be said of aid. The oil boom deepened the reliance of Arab regimes on external sources of income to fulfill their ever-increasing budgetary obligations. The size of military and defense expenditures alone are beyond the domestic means of most states, and this insufficiency has elevated the importance of outside aid sources to the status of a national security issue for most Arab states. One top Jordanian policy maker was particularly emphatic regarding the importance of aid and labor flows to inter-Arab relations, remarking that "there are two things that are essential: aid and labor migration. All the trade agreements put together are small fries . . . the most significant factors in Jordan's relations with the world are aid and labor flows. It defines the economy. It defines politics. It defines our relations with the Arabs. It defines everything."[35] Thus in inter-Arab politics, the economic dimensions of alignments cannot be separated entirely from issues of military capability; both are critical to the security of Arab states, or at least are perceived to be by Arab regimes.

Access to petrodollars and to foreign labor markets have thus become essential considerations in the calculations and policies of poorer Arab states. Once gained, these sources of financial assistance and labor remittances remain central to the stability of Arab regimes. Such political-economic dynamics have led to a cycle of dependence, in which economic reliance on allies provides more than economic relief for Arab regimes. Indeed, these issues now comprise the economic underpinnings of political stability. For Arab states, and indeed for many other states throughout the "Third World," the pursuit and maintenance of economically lucrative alliances can therefore be regarded by some policy makers as nothing less than vital to the security of the ruling regime as well as for the society that it governs.[36]

These economic dynamics are also important for the capital-rich and oil-rich states, since they have become dependent on foreign labor to extract their own resources. In addition, their small populations and smaller militaries leave them vulnerable not in the economic sense, but in the traditional military sense. To oversimplify, we might expect ruling elites to pursue alignment policies designed to fulfill their own economic and security deficiencies, and in the Arab context the general expectation would be for capital-poor, labor-rich states to align with capital-rich, labor-poor states. If the former states are also militarily powerful, they might have an additional appeal for an Arab Gulf monarchy, for example.

The symbiotic relationship between Egypt and Saudi Arabia serves as a case in point. The economic and security linkages between these two very different states have long since supplanted the earlier ideological conflict that characterized their bilateral relationship in the Nasir era, roughly from 1952 to 1970, and even the sharp break in their relations in 1978–1979 over the Camp David Accords and the Egyptian-Israeli Peace Treaty. In the 1950s and 1960s, the two states appeared ideologically polarized, with Egypt leading a socialist and secularist-oriented Pan-Arab movement of revolutionary republican regimes, while Saudi Arabia appeared steeped in the role of reactionary, standing firm behind ideals of pan-Islamic unity and conservative monarchical rule. By the 1980s, however, the economic symbiosis that is perhaps the more natural relationship between the two had emerged to the surface. This rapprochement may have been facilitated by the effects of the oil revolution in the region. But it is also important to note that the rapprochement had begun even before Nasir's death, and may best be traced to the disastrous Arab loss in the 1967 Arab-Israeli war. In a sense, Nasir's total defeat may have made him seem considerably less threatening to his Saudi neighbors, and certainly Saudi King Faysal had already come to believe that Israel was the far greater threat. Between that war experience and its successor, the 1973 war launched by Egyptian President Sadat with active Egyptian-Saudi collusion, the Egyptian-Saudi relationship had for all practical purposes reversed itself from hostility to alliance—based on common political goals vis-à-vis Israel, military needs, and growing economic connections between the two states.

Particularly from the 1970s onward, Egypt exported much of its substantial surplus labor to the oil fields of Saudi Arabia, thereby making labor remittances a major part of Egypt's yearly export earnings. Saudi Arabia, in turn, gained thousands of workers to keep its economy running, while also gaining the support of one of the largest military powers in the Arab world.

Egyptian labor and political support flowed toward the kingdom, while aid, investment, and remittances flowed back to Egypt.

Oddly enough, while the discussion above underscores the importance of economic factors, it does not necessarily make the case for the "budget security" model of alliance-making. For a critical intervening variable here is other, non-Arab sources of economic aid (such as the United States and the United Kingdom). The economic imperative is better seen therefore as imbedded within the broader concept of regime security. To put it another way, economic factors may be extremely important, but not necessarily deterministic, in the creation of inter-Arab alliances. There remain, therefore, several intervening factors that impact upon any pattern of economic influences on alliances. As suggested above, among these is the availability of non-Arab allies that might fulfill state needs. These alternative allies may be drawn from among the non-Arab states of the region—such as Iran, Israel, and Turkey—or from the dominant political, economic, and military powers in the broader global system.

This pattern can be seen in the alliance choices of such pan-Arab nationalist regimes as that of the late President Hafiz al-Asad in Syria. During the First Gulf War, between Iraq and Iran from 1980 to 1988, Syria elected to ally with the Iranian Islamist state versus its fellow Arab nationalist and Ba'thist republic in Iraq. Thus, even for Asad's Ba'thist regime, which saw itself as the most purely nationalist regime in the Arab world, did the logic of Pan-Arabism preclude non-Arab alliance partners? Clearly the answer to this question is no. Ever since 1979 Syria has maintained its close alliance with the Islamic Republic of Iran—much to the chagrin of more "moderate" states such as Jordan and the Arab Gulf monarchies, and especially to such non-local powers as the United States. Over the years, this alliance not only had the economic advantage of tying Syria into Iranian oil supplies, but also included the political and strategic benefit of holding in check a local Arab enemy—Saddam Hussein's Iraq—by supporting Iran in its eight-year war with Iraq. Ideals of Pan-Arab unity apparently were not enough to outweigh the economic and strategic benefits that Syria gained from its longstanding alignment with non-Arab Iran.

The other alternative for alliance-seeking Arab states is to go not only outside the Arab system, but also outside the Middle East regional system itself. With the struggle for influence in the Middle East between the superpowers during the Cold War, for example, alternative sources of military, economic, and political support were clear. And indeed the superpowers, regarding the Middle East as little more than an arena in a far larger strategic "game," actively courted local allies and client-states. In the early years of the Cold War, the Soviet Union may have appeared to be fairly successful in this regard, having established relationships with revolutionary governments in Egypt, Iraq, Syria, and South Yemen. But over time it became clear that the overwhelming victor in this competition was the United States. In addition to its strong alliance with Israel, the United States had longstanding relationships with Arab states such as Jordan, Morocco, and Saudi Arabia. To these early allies, the U.S. added an ever-increasing list of Arab clients, the most dramatic of which was the abrupt shift in Egyptian alignment under Sadat from the Soviet Union to the United States. Thus, in addition to the many alternative allies within Arab politics, Arab states have been able to maneuver in the broader regional and global arenas as well, seeking external support where they can find it—and the economic and military aid that flows from world powers such as the United States have held a particular appeal for most Arab states.

Unfortunately, however, this broad menu of alternative local partners or great power patrons may have helped consolidate the general regional pattern of authoritarian rule in the region, by permitting states to avoid internal pressures for domestic political or economic liberalization. It is not accidental, therefore, that the collapse of the Cold War confrontation and the contraction of the world oil market were followed by extensive campaigns of liberalization and democratization—both cosmetic and real—on the part of Arab regimes attempting to establish a new form of legitimacy and security in the "new world order." But for many Arab regimes, often painful economic adjustments and potentially dangerous political reforms were avoided in favor of a far easier path: the resort to external sources of economic as well as military support through international alignments.

It is still in the world of international politics that Arab states, like those elsewhere in the world, can find allies to enhance not only their military capabilities and external security, but also their economic well-being. It is in this context that political economy becomes clear as a key variable influencing alignment choices; and it is also in this same context that ideology re-enters the political scene. When domestic change is avoided, a high premium is placed on the role of ideology to justify, rationalize, and above all legitimize the actions of ruling regimes. New alignments and alliances can then be presented by member governments in ideological terms as strong and necessary steps on the road to greater Pan-Arab unity, and heralded by member states (mixing assorted gendered language) as making great strides toward "fraternal cooperation" or deepening integration and coordination between "sisterly Arab states."

Conclusions

This chapter has explored two key variables in inter-Arab and Middle East politics: the roles of political economy and ideology. I have argued that understanding the economic underpinnings of a state's security is critical to understanding its international behavior, including its alliance choices. The political economy of budget security can therefore best be seen as one of several components of the broader concept of regime security. Budget security is indeed important, but it is not alone sufficient to explain inter-Arab alignments.

I have also tried to demonstrate that despite the pervasive presence of ideology in regional politics, nonetheless these foreign policies are as rational and calculated as those of states anywhere else, regardless of the extensive use of ideological rhetoric in the Middle East. This is not to say that ideology is irrelevant, but rather that it is not itself a primary factor influencing policy makers. Alignments come and go in the Arab world due mainly to short-term regime security interests. The resulting alignment, even if it is with yesterday's enemy, is then justified in ideological terms. To miss this key dynamic, and to focus instead on the ideological rhetoric as determinant in itself, is to miss the forest for the trees.

It is perhaps true that Arab politics in the 1950s and 1960s was more likely to be influenced by ideological concerns, particularly pan-Arabism, but even at that time such an assertion may have been problematic. The great era of Pan-Arab nationalist ascendancy was characterized far more by conflict and rivalry between nationalist leaders than it was by cooperation and unity. In many cases even at that time, it was precisely the economic and security interests of the individual Arab regimes, and resultant attempts to preserve their state sovereignty, that got in the way of broader and even nobler ideals of cooperation, unity, and even unification.

And in contemporary politics, regional dynamics in the Middle East and especially within inter-Arab relations will continue to be characterized by ideological politics. But if anything the concerns of Arab regimes with the material economic and military bases of their own security have only increased over time. Economically dependent and indebted Arab states, and even rich but labor-poor or militarily weak Arab states, have a greater need than ever for local as well as non-regional allies.

It is in this context, therefore, that we find key economic and security considerations presented in ideological terms. Pan-Arabism can be used to justify even economic dependency between Arab states. This underscores the utility of Pan-Arabism to even the most cynical regime, since alignments driven by military insecurity or economic dependence, for example, can be made to look not like the actions of a precarious and insecure regime, but rather like the acts of a truly Arab nationalist state pursuing policies of regional integration and "fraternal" cooperation. Furthermore, for a regime that is truly committed to the ideals of Pan-Arabism, the ideological justifications for inter-Arab alignment choices flow even more naturally from government officials. The essential fact remains that to see a more complete picture of inter-Arab politics, one must understand the material regime security incentives as well as the ideological forces at work. But, like Dorothy in the Land of Oz, one must be willing to look behind the curtain.

The Case Studies and Jordanian Policy in Context

The first three chapters of this book examined the issues of security, political economy, and ideology in inter-Arab politics, while also presenting a regime security approach to understanding inter-Arab alliance dynamics. In this chapter, I provide a brief overview of Jordanian politics and policy in their regional context, as well as an introduction to the empirical case studies themselves.

The Hashimite Kingdom of Jordan has long played a regional foreign policy role that seems to belie its small size and its limited economic and military means.[1] That role in no way diminished even after the succession in the Jordanian monarchy from King Hussein to his son Abdullah in 1999. King Hussein had ruled from 1953 to 1999, and had long been regarded as one of the great survivors of Middle East politics and as a particularly skillful leader, guiding his state through tumultuous waters and countless domestic and regional threats to the regime's survival. But with the death of Hussein and the accession to the throne of King Abdullah II, leadership in Jordanian foreign policy shifted for the first time in forty-six years. The succession came at a particularly challenging time in regional politics, which would soon see the collapse of the Arab-Israeli peace process, a renewed Palestinian Intifadah, and U.S. wars in both Iraq and Afghanistan.

Yet, throughout these turbulent events, Jordan has continued to play a key role in the prospects for both war and peace in the region. Indeed, starting in 2003, the influential World Economic Forum began holding annual meetings at Jordan's Dead Sea resort, underscoring the Jordanian regime's determination to court the world's most wealthy and powerful economic actors, while also demonstrating the central role that these economic "powers that be" seem to attach to Jordan within Middle East politics. Similarly, the "Quartet" of officials from the United States, the United Nations, the European Union, and Russia met frequently in Amman, the Jordanian capital, in repeated attempts to revive the moribund peace process. For better or worse, the major powers of the early 21st Century seemed to regard Jordan as geo-politically far more important than its size or resources might otherwise suggest.

Yet Jordan is also a small country with limited resources and a weak economy, and it has historically been dependent on financial aid from various external patrons. The kingdom is also geographically situated in the very center of the Middle East, among neighboring states which are each more powerful in just about every sense of the term. As Jordan's former foreign minister, Marwan al-Qasim, has put it, "our borders make us more vulnerable even than Kuwait. And we are surrounded by more powerful neighbors: Israel, Syria, Iraq, Saudi Arabia, and even Egypt. As a small country, we have to be careful."[2]

The modern state of Jordan first emerged from the imperial machinations that divided the Middle East following the collapse of the Ottoman Empire in World War One. After the war Britain, under the League of Nations Mandate System, carved out Jordan's borders and set up the Hashimite regime under the Emir Abdullah. The Hashimite family had previously ruled Mecca in Western Arabia, before being defeated and expelled by the rising power of the Saudi family and their allies. Britain shortly thereafter established Hashimite monarchies in the newly emerging states of Jordan and Iraq. From that point onward, Britain maintained close strategic ties to the kingdom.[3] After World War Two, and with the onset of the Cold War, the United States also established stronger and stronger links to the Jordanian state, as the Western powers came to view Jordan as a conservative bulwark against communism and radical forms of Pan-Arabism, and as potentially a moderating element in the Arab-Israeli conflict.

From the beginning, then, Jordan has held close ties to powerful Western states and has in fact depended heavily on foreign aid from these countries to keep the kingdom afloat.[4] Jordan was therefore regarded as a client state—in terms of both military and economic aid—by successive governments in both London and Washington, D.C.[5] The U.S.-Jordan relationship might best be seen as a structural factor running beneath all of the inter-Arab alliance decisions addressed in this book. It has also been a mixed blessing for the Hashimite regime. On the one hand, the Jordanian monarchy has benefitted from extensive military and economic aid, but on the other hand the close relationship to the U.S. government (and therefore to its unpopular policies toward the Middle East) has been just as constantly a liability to the regime's domestic legitimacy. In that sense, close alliance with the U.S. has both helped and hurt Hashimite regime security over the years.

In terms of regional politics, Jordan's strategic concerns are very real, as has been underscored by three major wars with Israel since Jordan's independence. The kingdom was an active participant in the first of the Arab-Israeli wars in 1948. In that hard-fought campaign—a defeat for the Arab forces—Jordan's Arab Legion held on to East Jerusalem and the West Bank. Following the war, then-King Abdullah I made the controversial move of annexing the West Bank to the Hashimite Kingdom. Abdullah was soon thereafter assassinated by a Palestinian nationalist, who also took a shot at the king's grandson, Hussein. Amazingly, Hussein survived the attack. After a short period in which his father, Talal, ruled the kingdom, King Hussein ascended the Hashimite throne in 1953. From the moment when an assassin's bullet bounced off of him, Hussein—like his country—began to develop an international reputation as a survivor. In the years that followed, Jordan under Hussein was in some respects caught between the Arab-Israeli conflict, on the one hand, and the Arab Cold War, on the other.[6]

As a conservative, pro-Western monarchy, Hashimite Jordan fended off numerous attempts by Nasirists, Ba'thists, and later Islamists to undermine or transform the regime. Jordan also managed to survive not only the 1948 war, but also the even more disastrous 1967 war (in which Israel took East Jerusalem and the West Bank) as well as a brutal civil war in 1970–1971. The empirical examination of Jordanian policy and inter-Arab alignments in this book begins in 1970, in what amounts therefore to the "post-Nasir" era.[7] With that in mind, a few words are in order regarding the contextual background of the new decade and its implications for Jordan.

Entering the 1970s: Domestic and Regional Security Challenges

Jordan's entrance into the 1970s was anything but smooth, as it began with a bloody civil war which threatened to topple the ruling Hashimite regime. While the decade would end under the threat of war with Syria, it had also begun with pronounced hostility between the two countries. Yet the clash that marked the beginning of the decade was the more dire of the two conflicts, since it involved not the mere threat of armed hostilities, but rather an actual Syrian invasion of Jordan, as the regime in Damascus attempted to support the PLO in its conflict with the Jordanian state.

Thus in 1970–1971, King Hussein's Hashimite regime withstood the greatest single challenge ever to its survival, as the guerilla forces of the PLO clashed with the Jordanian army, while Syrian armored divisions invaded across Jordan's northern border. Within Hussein's regime, East Bankers urged decisive action against the Palestinian forces, to eliminate them as a domestic threat to the Hashimite monarchy once and for all.[8] The battles that followed were indeed ruthless and have since become known as "Black September"—particularly for the Palestinians.

The Hashimite victory was achieved in September 1970, but the destruction of the Palestinian forces continued through the following summer, culminating in the expulsion of thousands of Palestinian fighters and refugees to an already-precarious Lebanon.[9] In Jordan, the civil war was seen as far too close a call for the Jordanian state. And so it came to purge pro-Palestinian, pan-Arab, and leftist dissidents, and to reinforce the positions of more traditionally loyal domestic constituencies such as the bedouin-dominated armed forces and the East Bank business and government elite. The reinforced domestic coalition was distinctly conservative in character, and hostile not only to the PLO but also to the Syrian regime of Salah Jadid, which had invaded Jordan in support of the Palestinians.[10]

In addition to this extreme domestic crisis for the regime, Jordan's domestic and regional economic situation changed dramatically as well. As was discussed in chapter 3, the regional political economy of the Middle East underwent radical changes from the early 1970s onward, tying the Arab states of the Middle East into an ever more interdependent oil-based economy. While oil dominated the political economy of major petroleum exporters, such as the Arab Gulf states, even their more resource-poor cousins, such as Jordan, became intimately tied to the economics and politics of oil.[11]

For Jordan, the oil boom added petrodollars to its national economy and to the state's coffers in two major ways: through direct aid from Gulf states and also through remittances from Jordanian workers in the Gulf. Jordan's main export had become its people. This came to include not only unskilled laborers, but also even greater numbers of professionals—engineers, bankers, teachers, and so on. Both Jordanians and Palestinians carrying passports from the Hashimite Kingdom had long been essential parts of the development of the infrastructure of the Gulf states, but from the early Seventies onward this process expanded rapidly, giving the Jordanian regime a stake of its own in Gulf stability, which was intimately tied to Jordan's domestic political economy.[12]

The rise in Arab aid came just in time for Jordan, as Britain continued its withdrawal from the Middle East "east of the Suez" by 1971.[13] In addition to assistance from the Gulf monarchies, United States aid helped to fill the gap left by the decline in British financial commitments to the Hashimite regime. The American connection soon replaced the earlier British ties in another important way, as the Jordanian armed forces began to adjust from British to American arms and materiel.[14]

Jordan's entrance into the new decade was thus marked by significant changes in its economic and security relationships, as well as by immediate and severe challenges to its domestic stability and to the very survival of the Hashimite monarchy. Jordan's harsh methods in dealing particularly with the PLO challenge had significant negative repercussions for its regional alignment status. For the most part, Jordan was shunned by other Arab states. Interestingly, Saudi economic relations with the Hashimite Kingdom continued as before, despite almost obligatory criticisms of King Hussein's suppression of the PLO. This quiet continuity, below the surface of diplomatic censure, was noted with some satisfaction by then Prime Minister Ahmad al-Lawzi. Regardless of their official rhetoric, he argued, many of the countries within the Arab world were sympathetic to the Jordanian position in 1970.[15] In essence, no Arab allies were available between 1970 and 1973, as Jordan existed in a virtual pariah status. This period of relative isolation was only brought to an end through war.

The empirical analysis of Jordanian policy and inter-Arab alignments therefore picks up the narrative at this point, extending the analysis across almost forty years of inter-Arab relations and Jordanian foreign policy. Specifically, the empirical analysis is based on a close reading of a series of key case studies, each of which represents a major alignment decision in this time frame. The cases listed and described below run the entire gamut of alignment possibilities, from loose entente, to customs union, to alliance. In each case I have structured and focused the comparative analysis to examine the same three sets of factors: *external security, domestic politics,* and *political economy.* This focus allows us to see the relative influence of these different spheres and hence allows us to better draw conclusions regarding such approaches to alliances and alignments as the balance of threats, budget security, and regime security. As the cases will make clear, neither of the former perspectives can alone account for the range of alignment decisions. Indeed, despite their differences, both the balance of threats and budget security approaches tend to be too uni-causal in orientation, as each is rooted in one of the above spheres only. The regime security approach, in contrast, allows us to better see and understand the multi-causal realities of inter-Arab politics, precisely because it accounts for all three spheres (with the regime as the center of all three), and it is therefore able to capture such key dynamics as regime maneuvering between internal and external security dilemmas.

The Case Studies: Jordanian Policy and Arab Alignments, 1970–2008

I will briefly describe here the specific cases that are each explored in more detail in the chapters that follow.

The 1973 October War Coalition

The October War Coalition or "Trilateral alliance" of Egypt, Syria, and Saudi Arabia was the major Arab alliance of the time, but it pointedly excluded Jordan. Yet when the tide of the 1973 war turned against the Arab states, Anwar Sadat prevailed upon the Jordanians to open a third front against Israel. Jordan never did so, but the kingdom did send a small detachment of troops to help Syria on the Golan Heights. Chapter 5 examines the several alliance decisions imbedded in these events: why was Jordan excluded from the most important alliance of the day? And why did it refuse to open up an eastern front during the war, yet send troops to aid Syria? And what, ultimately, was the price that Jordan paid for this both-participant-and-bystander policy?

Alliance with Syria

For a time, Jordan remained isolated within Arab politics. Yet, to the surprise of many, the second half of the decade was marked by the warming of Jordanian-Syrian relations. The resultant Jordanian-Syrian alignment began as a loose entente in 1975, and soon progressed to a full alliance involving not only military cooperation but also substantial economic integration, before ultimately collapsing in 1979 in an atmosphere of deep hostility and near war between the two countries. Chapter 6 analyzes why Jordan aligned toward Syria and why the alignment so heavily emphasized economic integration.

Alliance with Iraq

In 1978–1979, as the Jordanian-Syrian alliance collapsed, Jordan realigned toward Iraq (in a move that seemed just as surprising as its early alignment with Syria). The alignment with Iraq took on renewed urgency once the Iran-Iraq war began in 1980. For the eight years that followed, Iraq was locked in war with Iran (with Jordan backing Iraq, and Syria allying with Iran). The war turned out to be a boon to the Jordanian economy, and may have inspired Jordanian policymakers to expand beyond the bilateral alignment. Chapter 7 investigates why Jordan realigned from Syria to Iraq, and why this alliance proved so long lived.

The Arab Cooperation Council

By the end of the 1980s, the Jordanian alignment with Iraq had lasted far longer than its brief attachment to Syria, culminating in the creation of a new (and Jordanian-initiated) bloc in regional politics—the Arab Cooperation Council (ACC)—as Jordan attempted to create a multilateral political, economic, and security bloc within Arab politics. The ACC included not only Iraq and Jordan, but also Egypt and Yemen, and it achieved real political cooperation and economic integration, before it came crashing down in the fires of the 1990–1991 Gulf War. Chapter 8 examines the Jordanian role in the rise and fall of the ACC, explaining why the Hashimite regime decided to form this multilateral bloc in Arab politics.

The First U.S.-Iraq War

In the 1990 Gulf crisis, Jordan was one of very few regional states *not* to realign. The Iraqi invasion of Kuwait and the resultant regional and global crisis triggered a major regional realignment, yet Jordan's alignment policy was particularly striking for defying conventional predictions and maintaining its previous alignment with Iraq, thereby jeopardizing its relations with Egypt, Saudi Arabia, and the United States. Chapter 9 examines Jordanian policy as it attempted to navigate through this web of alliances and alignments, and explains why the kingdom risked its Western and Gulf alliances in order to maintain alignment with Iraq.

Peace with Israel

Chapter 10 moves beyond strictly inter-Arab alliances, to examine Jordan's decision to make peace with Israel. Having weathered the 1991 war, the Hashimite regime quickly used this rare moment in its domestic and regional politics, by turning to the peace process in order to recoup its economic and political losses. Once the PLO reached its historic 1993 Accord with Israel, the Jordanian government gambled on a complete international realignment toward Israel, the U.S., and the European Union. In a sense, the regime expended much of its domestic political capital, in an effort to shore up the Hashimite monarchy in a post-Cold War, post-Gulf War, and eventually post-King Hussein world. Chapter 10 explains not only why Jordan finally decided to formalize peace with Israel, but also why it chose to do so at that particular time.

Ending the Cold War with Syria

In 1999 King Hussein of Jordan died after a prolonged battle with cancer, but not before abruptly changing the royal line of succession from his long-serving brother, Prince Hasan, to his eldest son, now King Abdullah II. Initially at least, Abdullah inherited from his father a very stable set of global and regional alliance relationships. Yet he also inherited a decades-long Cold War with Syria (interrupted only by the 1975–1979 Jordanian-Syrian alignment). The Abdullah regime surprised many by bringing that Cold War to an end and even attempting to create a new Jordanian-Syrian alignment. While the alignment never fully materialized, and regional crises even led to renewed Jordanian-Syrian tensions, these paled in comparison to the earlier Cold War between the two states. Chapter 11 provides an analysis of the shift in Jordanian policy from the Hussein to the Abdullah regimes, and explains how and why the new regime attempted to end years of Jordanian-Syrian tensions and even create a new Jordanian-Syrian alignment.

The Second U.S.-Iraq War

Ultimately, the brief post-succession period of stability for Jordan was quickly shattered by the terrorist attacks of September 11, 2001, on the United States and the subsequent U.S. invasions of Afghanistan and Iraq. Chapter 12 examines Jordan's responses to these events, its attempts to retain existing alliances, and most importantly its complex reactions to the second war between a global ally, the United States, and a local alignment partner, Iraq.

Finally, in Chapter 13, I discuss the main conclusions we can draw from this analysis of regime security, shifting Arab alliances, and Jordanian foreign policy.

PART II

Arab Alliances and Jordanian Foreign Policy under King Hussein

Jordan and the October War Coalition

Despite surviving the 1970–1971 civil war, Jordanian policy makers were left with little breathing room, as the region plunged once again into war in 1973. The seeds for the 1973 war had been sown in the June 1967 conflict, just six years earlier, when Israeli land and air forces had inflicted a devastating defeat on the Egyptian, Syrian, and Jordanian armed forces. For each of the three Arab combatants, the disastrous results of 1967 had included the occupation of territory they had previously controlled. Egypt lost the Gaza Strip (and far more importantly for the Egyptians, the Sinai peninsula), while Syria lost the Golan Heights and Jordan lost not only East Jerusalem but also the entire West Bank. In addition to their regional strategic concerns vis-à-vis Israel, all three Arab regimes saw their domestic legitimacy and security linked, at least to some extent, to the retrieval of these territories.

For Jordan in particular, the loss of territory to Israel had also been accompanied by a massive influx of Palestinian refugees, as well as PLO guerilla fighters. The Jordanian economy was thus reeling from the loss of its most agriculturally fertile and economically productive territory, made worse by the additional socio-economic strain on the system by the sudden surge in population and demands on resources.

These strains provided the underpinnings for the PLO-Hashimite conflict of 1970–1971. But the effects of territorial loss were felt elsewhere too, particularly in Egypt and Syria where new leaders—Anwar al-Sadat and Hafiz al-Asad—felt domestic and regional pressures to reverse the results of 1967 and thereby solidify the basis for their rule. These various pressures and changes would prove central elements to the first alignment case in question: the formation of the Trilateral Alliance and the launching of the October 1973 war, also known as the Yom Kippur War and the Ramadan War, since it took place during these Jewish and Muslim holidays. This chapter examines Jordan's response to the 1973 war and Jordan's specific decisions regarding the Arab alliance against Israel, an alliance in which the kingdom neither went to war nor remained entirely neutral.

In 1971 the governments of Egypt, Syria, and Saudi Arabia began the process of establishing the Trilateral Alliance. The alliance was intended to marshal Arab military and economic strength against the state of Israel in an effort to change the results of the Six Day War of 1967, which had been an unmitigated disaster for the Arabs. The alliance became a war fighting coalition in October 1973, following the failure of diplomatic attempts to remove Israeli forces from Arab territories occupied since 1967. The alliance was never formally concluded, underscoring the informality typical of even the most central and powerful inter-Arab alignments.

Standing in sharp contrast to the Trilateral Alliance are its two immediate predecessors: the Federation of Arab Republics (comprising Egypt, Libya, and Syria) and the "merger" between Egypt and Libya. In both cases these "alignments" were accompanied by much rhetorical fanfare, but amounted to little beyond the paper they were written on. To some extent, both align-ments—while essentially meaningless—were intended by Sadat to placate the regime of Mu'ammar al-Qadhafi in Libya at a very public level, while at a more private and even secret level a far more substantial alignment was being concluded between Egypt, Syria, and Saudi Arabia. Like Jordan, Libya was left out of the Trilateral Alliance and of the planning for the October War.

The alliance had been constructed through repeated and highly secretive contacts at the highest government levels, including the personal diplomacy of the three heads of state: President Sadat of Egypt, President Asad of Syria, and King Faisal Ibn 'Abd al-Aziz of Saudi Arabia. King Hussein and the Jordanian government, however, were included in none of these meetings, until a very late summit in Cairo on September 10, 1973. And even then it was agreed that Jordan would not enter the war unless the Egyptian and Syrian offensives were successful.

As the key planner of the October War, Sadat's main intention was actu-ally rather limited. If an outright military victory could not be achieved, he intended at the very least to break the diplomatic deadlock by changing the territorial and strategic status quo, thereby forcing negotiation through military fiat. While both Syria and Egypt had agreed to pursue only lim-ited military objectives, their respective interpretations of these objectives seemed to vary. Unlike the regime in Damascus, Sadat seemed to have no real intention or expectation of pursuing a military victory, but instead hoped to create a military stalemate, salvaging Arab pride dashed in 1967 and forcing negotiations for the return of Arab territories. The Egyptian regime was, of course, particularly concerned with the retrieval of the Si-nai. Sadat also hoped that careful maneuvering would enable him and his regime to realign from the Soviet Union toward the United States, allowing Egypt to tap into the U.S. pipeline of arms and aid, and hopefully to stimulate Western investment in Egypt.[1]

It quickly became clear that Sadat's limited objectives were not shared entirely by his allies, leading to considerable consternation and misunderstanding between Cairo, Damascus, and Riyadh. The lack of communication was even more profound for those states that had been excluded from the planning, particularly Jordan.[2]

Jordan and the October War Coalition

Like Egypt and Syria—and unlike Saudi Arabia—Jordan had also lost territory in the 1967 Six Day War. Indeed, it had lost far more than any other Arab state, by losing not only the Holy city of Jerusalem but also all of the West Bank. Yet Jordan was not a party to the Trilateral Alliance, nor was it included in the highly secretive planning that led to the early victories in the October War. But soon after the war began, and particularly as the tide began to turn against the Arabs, Sadat called on Jordan to enter the war and open up a third front against Israel. The Hashimite regime was therefore faced with a crisis decision: to join the alliance and therefore the Arab war effort, or to remain aloof, avoiding the hostilities and their concomitant risks of further territorial losses. Another at least theoretical (if not plausible) alignment choice would have been to aid the Israelis against the Trilateral Alliance. Finally, there also remained the possibility of in some way combining these seemingly stark alternatives.

In Walt's framework, states have only two possible policy choices: balancing or bandwagoning.[3] Jordan could either balance against Israel, or it could bandwagon with it. Because of the narrowness of this theoretical framework, Walt is led to interpret the Jordanian position as actually bandwagoning with Israel.[4] In the event, however, Jordanian troops were sent to bolster the Syrians on the Golan, whereas no assistance of any kind was lent to Israel. At the same time the Jordanian effort was indeed limited, involving the dispatch of a single armored division to Syria, followed by a second division later, which arrived just before the hostilities ceased. While the Jordanian contribution to the Arab war effort was minimal, it nonetheless remains clear which side of the conflict the Hashimite regime supported, which seems to belie the notion that Jordan "bandwagoned" with Israel. Bandwagoning with Israel would require either support for the Israeli war effort or lack of support for the Trilateral Alliance, and perhaps some expectation that Jordan would in some way have been able to enjoy the fruits of an Israeli victory. None of this, however, was the case.

Walt's misinterpretation may be the result of attempting to force the empirical evidence into one of only two activities—balancing or bandwagoning—which allow no room for limited policy gestures, mixed policies (such as supporting both sides), or outright neutrality. As Jordanian policy makers knew in October 1973, the options available to them included more than the two extremes of balancing or bandwagoning.[5] In addition, the assumption that all alignment behavior must be either an act of balancing or bandwagoning skews interpretations only toward external threats, since that is what a state balances against or bandwagons with. It allows no room for alignments influenced by economic considerations or domestic security concerns. Such a limited framework can thus lead an analyst to force empirical evidence into one of only two available boxes, where it may not actually belong.

The Jordanian decision in 1973 is a case in point, showing that even in the midst of war, when one would expect external threats to be most clearly determinant, other factors can also enter the policy matrix and affect the outcome. As the analysis below makes clear, for the Jordanian policy makers in 1973, both the regime's regional and domestic security were key factors in the decision.[6] The Jordanian government pursued a policy that it deemed to be both cautious and prudent but that predictably satisfied none of its neighbors. Jordan elected to join the Arab allies in their war against Israel, but without opening up a Jordanian-Israeli front. The sections below examine the various factors affecting this half-hearted alignment decision.

External Security

The Jordanian decision, which seemed to foreshadow its later fence-straddling in the 1990 Persian Gulf Crisis, must be seen in its temporal political context. Timing, in short, was a critical factor. In October 1973 the Hashimite regime was still rebuilding its military and consolidating its own domestic position after the series of domestic and regional challenges to its survival. The few years immediately prior to the 1973 war had witnessed the greatest Arab military defeat by Israel; the loss of territory with profound political, economic, and religious significance; and a bloody internal war in Jordan between King Hussein's regime and the PLO. This series of events provided the immediate backdrop for the Jordanian decision regarding the 1973 war.[7] Indeed, it was precisely because of the monarchy's recent destruction of the PLO position in Jordan, and the presumed questionable commitment of the

Hashimite regime to the Arab cause, that the states forming the Trilateral Alliance had seen fit to exclude Jordan from participating.

Presidents Sadat and Asad had learned the value of strategic surprise in the Arab losses in 1967, and they were determined to utilize it as a weapon in their favor in 1973. Sadat and Asad seemed to have viewed regimes like that of King Hussein or even Colonel Qadhafi as dubious allies at best, and therefore deemed them too risky to include in the sensitive plans. But as events unfolded, and the initial military gains across the Suez and the Golan were reversed, a Jordanian front became critical to Sadat's goal of, at the very least, avoiding another humiliating Arab defeat. But according to one of Jordan's top generals at the time, war was not an option for Jordan, still recovering from the debacle of the 1967 war and the disastrous 1970–1971 civil war:

> We lacked air defense, and sufficient numbers of troops. And in addition to that, they (Egypt and Syria) did not choose to inform Jordan in the first place (about the planned attack). And they then tried to drag Jordan in, with inevitable catastrophic effects. I asked Asad, why do you *now* ask us? Asad argued that there were political advantages to be reaped. But I responded that there will be no Jordan left to reap the advantages. If Syria liberates the Golan, Egypt liberates the Sinai, then you've got a point . . . We convinced them, that if Jordan joined the battle, it would become the main target of the Israelis. We were dragged into the 1967 war and we lost the West Bank. We couldn't afford to lose the East Bank . . . Asad seemed to understand our position, but he still disagreed. But what they were facing in the Golan and Sinai still left the vast majority of Israeli forces facing Jordan . . . Anyway, we did compromise. We did send units to the Golan. But this did not involve direct confrontation with Israel through our lines.

Similarly, Jordan's prime minister during the war, Ahmad al-Lawzi, also emphasized the regime's security fears in making its alliance decision. But even twenty years after the event, he also remained convinced that Jordan had no other choice:

> Naturally, the October War affected our (Syrian and inter-Arab) relations because we did not participate at the beginning. We sent forces to Syria, of course, along with the Moroccans and Iraqis there. But we did not participate in the planning of the war. Because of the feelings of Egypt and Syria we did not open up a new front. So we participated

to the greatest extent possible while still preserving the security of Jordan.[8]

Ironically, Jordan's specific military contribution, the 40th Armored Brigade, had fought against the Syrian army during the 1970 invasion of Jordan. Merely three years later, it found itself fighting alongside the Syrians in defense of the Golan Heights.[9]

Despite the fact that Jordan had not yet even entered into the Arab alliance and war-fighting coalition when the war began, it was torn between the two horns of the security dilemma within alliance politics: entrapment and abandonment.[10] As discussed in chapter 2, entrapment occurs when a state is dragged unwillingly into a conflict it intended to avoid, while abandonment occurs when conflict breaks out, and one's allies are not there to provide support. Given Jordan's recent domestic and regional security crises, its military weakness, and particularly its anxiety over Israeli air superiority, Jordan's policy makers especially feared entrapment by their potential Arab allies into a conflict they felt they could not possibly win.[11]

A Jordanian front in particular would certainly have taken Israeli military resources away from the Egyptian and Syrian fronts, aiding the Arab war effort. But this would also have meant a full frontal assault on Jordan—no longer buffered by the strategic depth of the West Bank. The Israelis would easily have been able to travel the open highway from the Jordan river to Amman in a matter of hours. Entrapment into a hopeless military situation was a central factor in Jordanian calculations, since this time it was believed that further military and territorial losses would mean the end not only of the Hashimite monarchy but possibly also of Jordan as an independent state.[12]

From a military-security standpoint, the regime did not like what it saw. First, the Jordanian armed forces were still rebuilding from the 1967 and 1970 conflicts, as well as making the transition from British to American supplied arms and materiel. Jordan's military commanders questioned whether the armed forces were really sufficiently prepared to enter the fighting, since they had, after all, received almost as little warning as had Israel. Secondly, Jordan's political and military leadership had recent and direct experience with the capabilities of the Egyptian and Syrian armies in 1967 and, in the later case, 1970 as well. Their performance, to say the least, was not impressive. These points were stressed in particular by King Hussein's envoy to Presidents Sadat and Asad, Lt. General 'Amr Khamash. Khamash, along with General Habis al-Majali, had been in charge of the reconstruction of the Jordanian military after 1967. In the 1973 war, General Khamash noted, Jordanian commanders had assessed the Israeli order of battle. They concluded that Israel had held its elite units in reserve—deployed neither in the Golan nor in the Sinai. These units, in the view of Jordan's top military commanders, would have been unleashed against the Jordanians if they had opened the third front. "We have the longest lines against Israel," General Khamash stated, and "if Jordan [had] joined the battle, it would [have] become the main target of the Israelis."[13]

In short, Jordanian policy makers had little faith in Arab military capabilities and serious doubts about the preparedness of their own forces, leading to extreme reluctance to engage Israel directly. The consensus among policy makers and military analysts was that the opening of a Jordanian front could only end in disaster for Jordan and for the Hashimite monarchy.

Domestic Politics

While Jordanian policy makers worried over the dangers of entrapment into a losing war by alliance with Egypt and Syria, they also feared that failing to support the Arab effort would be read by their Arab allies as abandonment of them—even if Jordan had technically been left out of the Trilateral Alliance. Interestingly, the notion of abandonment that is part of the alliance security dilemma affected the Jordanian policy makers in an unusual way, for they did not *themselves* fear abandonment. Rather, they feared the consequences of the perception of themselves as being *guilty* of abandonment. This fear was particularly pressing in regard not to external threats per se, but more directly to the regime's domestic security situation.

To be seen as guilty of abandoning the Arab cause in the middle of a war with Israel would be read as nothing short of treasonous. Such rhetorical charges were not new to the Hashimites, but neither were they to be encouraged or taken lightly. In this regard, the security threats that might accompany such accusations would not come only from the "radical" Arab states, but also from among Jordan's own population.

In addition, Jordanian policy makers feared that failure to assist the members of the Trilateral Alliance might also lead to abandonment in the reverse direction—that is, that the Arab participants in the war might abandon Jordan in the post-war period. This, in turn, might have even more malevolent effects in the near future, such as active support by other Arab states for domestic unrest in the kingdom and even the overthrow of the Hashimite regime, just after it had fended off its domestic challengers and was still in the process of consolidating its position. The civil war of 1970–1971 remained fresh in the minds of Jordanian policy makers, and it was not a scenario which they were willing to risk repeating.

Jordanian Prime Minister Ahmad al-Lawzi and his cabinet were particularly cognizant of the potential linkage between regional hostilities and renewed domestic conflict in Jordan.[14] Al-Lawzi had taken over the premiership only two years earlier, after his predecessor—Wasfi al-Tal—was gunned down in Cairo by Palestinians believed to be supported by Syria. In addition, some Jordanian elites believed that only Egyptian connivance could explain the apparent failure of security measures for the Jordanian Prime Minister. Prime Minister Ahmad al-Lawzi himself emphasized two key factors influencing Jordanian foreign policy at this time, and both factors were rooted in domestic security concerns. "There are two points," he noted, "first the conflict with the *fedayeen* (Palestinian guerilla fighters) and second, the assassination of Wasfi al-Tal; these affected our external relations."[15] Having only recently re-entered the mainstream of inter-Arab affairs, Al-Lawzi and other Jordanian elites had no intention of providing a pretext for renewed domestic and regional hostility toward the Hashimite regime.

While the 1970 conflict had left the regime with hostility toward the PLO as an organization, it also left lingering fears within the regime regarding the Palestinian population within Jordan. Although the fedayeen guerilla fighters had been expelled, and hence a large and armed domestic threat seemed to have been eliminated, the fact remained that as much as 60 percent of the kingdom's population was Palestinian, and the regime had won few friends in that community with its actions against the PLO.[16] The extent of popular feeling provided simply another in a long list of constraints on the regime's maneuverability. In this context, the option of staying aloof from the alliance's war effort was really no option at all. Even if it were the safer option regarding external threats, it carried with it enormous risks in terms of domestic regime security. It was not, in short, a risk that the regime could afford to take.

Thus in addition to the external and regional security considerations discussed above, the option of avoiding the Arab cause entirely, with all its military risks, also carried with it potentially high domestic costs in terms of the legitimacy and security of the Hashimite regime. Public opinion was unlikely to forgive what would surely be construed as Jordanian abandonment—and hence betrayal—of the Arabs. While a perceived anti-Arab policy would only have deepened the regime's domestic legitimacy crisis, perhaps contributing to renewed domestic security threats, a policy of even minimal assistance to the Arab cause might actually recoup some of the regime's Arab status in the aftermath of the events of 1970. In short, a cautious policy might make the best of an otherwise bad situation.

The key, it seemed, was to finesse the policy options in order to avoid both entrapment and abandonment. The result was the policy that Jordan did indeed pursue: of limited involvement designed to avoid entrapment into a more direct war with Israel, while also skirting charges within the Arab camp and Jordanian society that the regime had abandoned its Arab neighbors.[17] While somewhat awkward, this policy was intended to avoid the post-war wrath of the states in the Trilateral Alliance as well as that of Jordan's domestic populace. It seemed, in short, to be the best option among a number of bad alternatives, which would minimize domestic and regional risks and costs while preserving not only the security of the regime, but also the remaining territorial integrity of the nation.

The attempt to avoid Arab hostility following the war was not entirely successful. In speeches at the 1974 Rabat Summit of the Arab League, Sadat and others lashed out at Jordan's limited role in the war effort. Jordan had become, in fact, a convenient scapegoat for the performance of the Egyptian armies in particular. 'Amr Khamash, who accompanied King Hussein as one of his main national security advisors at the conference, claimed that he confronted Sadat directly following the Egyptian president's speech. He demanded that Sadat repeat the anti-Jordanian charges while looking him directly in the eye. Sadat refused to either look at or speak to the general for the remainder of the conference.[18]

Political Economy

After the regional imbroglio of the 1967 war, and the domestic upheaval of September 1970, the next major crisis to confront the Hashimite regime was economic. Jordan paid a heavy price in inter-Arab relations, including key economic linkages, for crushing the Palestinian movement. Wealthy oil-producing states, such as Kuwait and Libya, ceased sending financial subsidies to Jordan.[19] As noted earlier, however, Saudi aid was not interrupted, and this was interpreted by some Jordanian policy makers as tacit approval of their policies toward the Palestinians. At the same time, the near-fatal crisis for the Hashimite regime had reinvigorated its supporters from outside the region, as Great Britain and the United States each increased their aid to bolster the Jordanian position and to allow King Hussein's regime to fulfill its budgetary commitments.

As the regime attempted to recover from these domestic and regional threats to its security, the powers within the Arab world left Jordan isolated in virtual pariah status until the country's support was needed in the heat of crisis. The hostility of the Arab regimes toward King Hussein and his government lingered and on occasion was vented publicly.[20] This hostility struck a chord within the regime itself, and feelings ran high within the newly re-consolidated domestic coalition. The Jordanian regime was regionally isolated and decidedly on the defensive. Key elements within the regime were led to take advantage of a bad situation by focusing entirely on domestic political consolidation and economic development, rather than on inter-Arab or Arab-Israeli affairs.

The economic price to be paid for inter-Arab isolation—a type of abandonment—added another dimension to the regime's view of the alliance security dilemma it faced. As discussed above, the regime worried about the high costs of military entrapment on the one hand, while on the other the regime feared that staying completely out of the Arab war effort would carry with it the risk of continued abandonment in inter-Arab relations. But this fear also had a strong economic component to it. A purely diplomatic pariah status was something which the regime did not welcome, but nonetheless could survive. The economic costs of abandonment, however, were not to be taken so lightly. More specifically, abandonment in this sense would probably involve the suspension of financial aid from the Arab Gulf states. In particular, abandonment by wealthy Saudi Arabia—the main financial power within the Trilateral Alliance—would carry with it a substantial economic price, which would directly affect Jordan's domestic economy and hence the regime's stability. And these economic linkages both to Saudi Arabia and to other Gulf states were critical underpinnings of the regime's domestic as well as regional security.[21]

In 1973 Jordan was feeling particularly constrained economically, as its 112.65 million Jordanian dinar (JD) expenditures had long since outstripped its 46.18 million JD of domestic revenue. As a result, the shortfall was made up through external loans and grants, leaving the regime with a -23.10 million JD deficit. In short, Jordan was not in a position to afford even the slightest loss of external economic support, nor could it afford the domestic economic costs of full participation in yet another war.

In deliberating over their alignment options, therefore, Jordanian policy makers had to take into consideration the short- and long-term economic ramifications for the kingdom of these various policy alternatives. Most important among these economic considerations were Jordan's aid linkages to the Arab Gulf states, as well as the country's increasing reliance on access to Gulf labor markets as sources of labor remittances. In terms of its dependence on external aid, however, Jordan also relied on Western aid donors. With the United States supporting Israel, and with Saudi Arabia actively engaged in the Arab effort through the use of the Arab "oil weapon," the difficulty was in producing a policy that would avoid a cut-off in aid from *either source*. In effect, Jordan produced a policy that satisfied neither major financial patron, but which managed to "satisfice" both of them.

Conclusions

The general conclusion that emerges from this episode is that Jordan's alignment decision in October 1973 cannot be separated from the Hashimite regime's extreme sense of insecurity and vulnerability, particularly given the timing of the crisis. The regime's concern for maintaining its own stability and survival were central factors leading to its middling policy decision, as it attempted to find a compromise policy position that would avoid both regional and domestic threats, in effect balancing between internal and external security dilemmas. The timing of the alliance's assault on Israel found the Hashimite regime regionally isolated and domestically precarious, as it attempted to reconsolidate itself following regional war in 1967 and a bloody civil war in 1970–1971. In short, the determinants of the regime's alignment decision are found not only in external security constraints, but also in the domestic political sphere and the regime's economic dependency. Jordan's alliance decision may therefore be seen as "over-determined" in the sense that all three spheres—external security, domestic politics, and political economy—pushed the regime in the same direction.

The main external factors affecting the decision were the threat of confronting Israeli military superiority head-on and the reciprocal dangers of Arab hostility if Jordan were not to act at all. Part of the alliance decision was therefore based on the idea of avoiding entrapment. The threat of direct conflict with Israel, and the conviction on the part of Jordanian elites that this could only be a military disaster for Jordan, meant that joining the alliance whole-heartedly was not regarded as a serious option. But similarly, staying completely out of the fray and refusing to back the alliance was also seen as nonviable. Such a move would be read in the broader, both national and regional Arab public sphere as abandonment of the Arab cause. Thus the security fear here was actually largely internal, as Jordanian policymakers feared domestic instability (especially given the kingdom's large Palestinian population) and even domestic destabilization by more radical Arab states in the postwar period. Having only recently survived a major domestic challenge, they were unwilling to risk another.

Economically, the regime was influenced by its pronounced economic dependence. Jordanian policy makers were determined to preserve and even expand Jordan's financial aid links to Saudi Arabia, a key member of the alliance. In addition, they hoped to take the opportunity of even limited participation in the war to rejoin the Arab community and end the costly period of isolation. By returning to the status of a "frontline state" in the conflict with Israel, Jordan hoped to reap substantial economic rewards from the wealthier Arab countries. On the other hand, by not directly engaging Israel, the chances of disrupting aid to Jordan from Israel's main external ally—the United States—were also minimized.

Thus, after fending off major regional and domestic challenges to its survival, Hashimite Jordan had become involved in yet another Arab-Israeli war. The setbacks continued even after the war, however, as the Arab states attempted to pick up the pieces. Israel, Egypt, and Syria were all intimately engaged with the United States in attempting to iron out disengagement agreements and to foster a new round of peace diplomacy in the region. Because of its limited involvement, however, and particularly due to the absence of a Jordanian-Israeli front, Jordan was left out of most of the post-war negotiations.

While the Hashimite regime felt that it was being snubbed once again, a final blow to its regional and international standing came at the 1974 Arab League Summit called to assess the post-war Arab situation. By unanimous vote, the Arab states including Jordan agreed to declare the PLO, and hence not the Hashimite monarchy, to be the "sole legitimate representative of the Palestinian people."[22] Jordan's acquiescence emerged only after vigorous Jordanian lobbying efforts against the resolution. When it became clear that even Egypt intended to support the resolution—a revelation that generated considerable anger from the already frustrated Jordanians—the Hashimite regime felt compelled to go along with the tide. They could not, in the end, afford to be seen as the only country defying the general will of the Arab nation, and thus they swallowed what they believed to be a bitter pill. But immediately after the summit and for the following several years, the Hashimites worked to deflate the status of the PLO and to restore their own influence in regional affairs.

To Jordanian policy makers, the Rabat resolution undercut their standing and negotiating clout in both Arab-Israeli and inter-Arab affairs. Once again, the regime opted to turn inward, as it had earlier attempted to do until the 1973 war interrupted its period of ostracism. Emphasis was placed on domestic political and economic development and the longer-term consolidation of the Hashimite state. For this it still needed allies, but the new approach would be based squarely on material interests and linkages at the level of "low politics," and not on the more tumultuous and unfavorable arena of high politics.

This desire for a more meaningful and profitable alignment strategy led Jordan to invest its energies in specific bilateral relationships, rather than alignments linked to broad regional conflicts. What resulted was an ever-deepening political and economic alignment with a partner that would have seemed highly unlikely a mere four years earlier: Syria.

The Jordanian Alliance with Syria

In the aftermath of the October War, Jordan sought to capitalize on its (albeit limited) participation in the conflict as a means to re-enter the mainstream of Arab regional politics. One of the countries most receptive to Jordan's attempt at inter-Arab reconciliation was Syria. Given the frequent bouts of hostility emanating from Damascus, which the Hashimite regime had come to regard as virtually routine, this reception seemed rather surprising. Yet Jordan's period of inter-Arab isolation, from 1970 to 1973, had very quickly shifted in the post-war period to a steadily warming relationship with Syria.[1] This chapter examines why Jordan shifted toward alliance and even economic integration with Syria, despite the two states' long history of mutual antagonism.

The long periods of Jordanian-Syrian hostility had been rooted in the politics of the Arab Cold War of the 1950s and 1960s. The Arab Cold War, which featured an inter-Arab struggle for power and influence, was an ideological conflict pitting conservative, pro-Western monarchies (such as Saudi Arabia, Kuwait, and Jordan) against more radical, revolutionary republics (such as Egypt, Iraq, Libya, and Syria). The military officers-turned-presidents in these latter states were themselves often the result of various military coups d'etat that had toppled earlier conservative, pro-Western monarchies. But even within that broad regional dynamic, Jordan and Syria remained in many respects a classic study in opposites, as well as in rivalry.[2]

Jordan's King Abdullah I had founded the kingdom with British support, while his grandson King Hussein had led the development of the modern Jordanian state, maintaining close ties to the United Kingdom and the United States. Hussein's Jordan became the classic conservative monarchy with a foreign policy that was virulently anti-communist, moderate in its policies toward Israel, and an ally of Western powers. Syria, in contrast, remained fiercely anti-colonial and became virtually the archetype of the revolutionary republic, led by various colonels and generals following a succession of coups d'etat, until the 1970 coup brought Hafiz al-Asad to power. Asad changed the country's image as a coup factory, establishing his own

Ba'thist authoritarian regime and ruling until his death in 2000. While Jordan allied itself closely with the United States, Syria allied with the Soviet Union—and both countries relied heavily on the military and economic support of their superpower patrons.

At both the global and regional levels, both countries had constructed identities that stood in contrast to one another.[3] The Hashimite Kingdom was, of course, decidedly royalist, moderate in its foreign policy, cautious, and conservative. Syria was anti-monarchist, more militant in its foreign policy, revolutionary, and radical. These socially constructed images are held even today by many participants and observers of Middle East politics. But these images remain constructs from as early as the 1950s, and are today only partly accurate, and partly national stereotype. Still, for most of their modern histories, the two countries were often pitted against one another in various ways. And in terms of bilateral relations, both during the Nasir era and indeed long after the Arab Cold War, Jordan and Syria more often than not maintained a cold war of their own; and that is precisely why the Jordanian-Syrian alignment was so surprising.

The alignment began with a flurry of meetings and diplomatic exchanges, which resulted first in a series of economic agreements and later evolved to include cooperation in security affairs as well. In March 1975 Jordanian Prime Minister Zayd al-Rifa'i first broached the subject of closer Jordanian-Syrian relations in a visit to Damascus, where he met with President Asad. The very fact that Rifa'i had been appointed Prime Minister at this time, given his known Syrian connections and pro-Syrian views, made clear the Hashimite regime's determination to develop stronger bilateral ties. The March 1975 meeting in Damascus produced a favorable and substantive response to Jordan's overtures as both countries agreed to establish a joint committee to help coordinate the strengthening of their relationship.[4]

The Prime Minister's successful trip to Damascus was quickly followed by an official state visit by King Hussein to the Syrian capital in April 1975. Once again, substantial progress was made, and the development of a Jordanian-Syrian alignment was well under way as the two heads of state signed a bilateral trade agreement. The momentum accelerated with a reciprocal visit by President Asad to Amman—his first trip there—in June 1975. This time the level of ties was elevated by the creation of a Joint Higher Committee, which moved beyond the economic issues covered by the earlier committee to include political and diplomatic coordination as well.[5]

In short, the new alignment spanned the range of low and high politics issues, and to a large extent was consciously constructed in Prime Minister

Rifaʻiʼs own words "from the bottom up."[6] The Jordanians in particular were eager to build a solid basis for the alignment, in order to create substantive bilateral linkages—and thereby firm roots—across a range of issue areas from trade and manufacturing to communications and education. These goals did indeed succeed for a time. Political unity, security cooperation, and even economic integration were all fast becoming a reality for Jordanian-Syrian relations in the mid- and late 1970s. By the end of the decade, however, these achievements would give way to mutual suspicion, mistrust, and hostility.[7] This chapter examines the specific factors that led both to the rise and to the eventual fall of the Jordanian-Syrian alliance.

External Security

The main external and regional changes affecting the development of the new alignment were the results of the October 1973 War. While not a clear victory for the Arab forces, neither was the warʼs outcome the decisive defeat that the 1967 war had been. This outcome in itself helped to explode the myth of Israeli invincibility and restored some level of Arab pride. For the regimes involved in the war, the outcome also meant that, having demonstrated their willingness to use force, they now had greater room for maneuver in pursuing a diplomatic offensive toward peace. This gain was particularly important to state-society relations for these regimes, which were now less vulnerable to charges of weakness or timidity in their dealings with Israel.

For Egypt, Syria, and Jordan, the central elements of a peaceful settlement with Israel concerned not only the rights of the Palestinians but also more immediately the return of their own territories occupied since 1967. While Egypt and Syria were still technically allied with one another, their relationship had soured in the immediate aftermath of the war, with the Asad regime believing that Sadat had essentially abandoned Syria during the war itself. Furthermore, Asad found Sadat an unreliable ally, mistrusted his motives, and suspected him of planning a separate peace with Israel.[8]

Thus the regional relationships and external pressures had changed from maneuvering aimed at establishing a successful war fighting coalition to jockeying for success in post-war diplomacy and peace negotiations. As the distance grew between the Egyptian and Syrian positions, so did the rift between Egypt and Jordan. As noted in the previous chapter, this rift had been triggered in particular by Sadatʼs anger at Jordan over its failure to open up a third front against Israel. The Jordanian regime, in contrast, felt that it had fulfilled its obligations exactly as it had promised before the war. Sadat, the Jordanians charged, had changed his mind in the midst of the war, only when the tide of battle had turned against him, and had simply wanted a Jordanian offensive to allow him a better chance at maintaining his own military position in Sinai. While Sadat publicly and bitterly denounced Jordan after the war, policymakers within the Hashimite regime argued that Sadat's high-sounding intentions were not really for the good of the broader Arab cause, but rather were characterized by a willingness to fight to the last *Jordanian* in order to liberate Egyptian territory.[9] In effect consciously marketing to both their own societies and the broader Arab world, each regime attempted to present its wartime behavior as the more responsible Arab position.

The external dynamics shaping post-war regional politics consequently involved a cycle of charges of abandonment. The Syrian government vented its anger at Egypt, while the Egyptians denounced Jordan, and the Jordanians argued that they were being made a scapegoat for Egyptian failures. In Saudi Arabia, meanwhile, King Faysal reminded all three countries of the risks Saudi Arabia had taken by unleashing the oil embargo in support of a less than stellar performance by its Arab military allies. As these exchanges continued, however, it became clear to the regimes in both Damascus and Amman that they had in common a similar type of conflict with the Sadat regime in Cairo.

These changes within the regional system may have led in part to the opening between Jordan and Syria, and while Jordan's role in the defense of the Golan Heights was minor, it was nonetheless appreciated in Damascus. The wartime act of solidarity thus became a useful symbol of cooperation between the two regimes, and may have eased the process of rapprochement between them by providing a historical bridge between the unfortunate 1970 episode of armed conflict (during the Jordanian civil war) and the 1975–1979 development of a full-fledged alliance.

While these external and strategic considerations may have had some influence on policymakers, there is little evidence that they were decisive or even central concerns. The rapprochement between Jordan and Syria did amount to a united front in the diplomatic arena of the Arab-Israeli conflict and peace process, especially vis-à-vis Israel and Egypt, but the overwhelming majority of the discussions, negotiations, and agreements that led to the alignment were economic in nature.

Still, the Syrian-Jordanian alignment, while initially concerned mainly with economic and political cooperation, did evolve to include external security and defense issues. Syrian military planners began to adjust their strategic plans to include defense of the Irbid Heights, in northwest Jordan, as a link to the Golan Heights and as a possible way to outflank Israeli forces in a future conflict.[10] Cooperation regarding the defense of northern Jordan against any Israeli attempt to invade Syria around (rather than through) the Golan Heights was to include the use of Jordanian ground troops with Syrian air support. Coordination along these lines developed to include joint military maneuvers and exercises.[11]

In more active policy terms, Jordan signaled its willingness to support Syria in its intervention in Lebanon and its increasing political conflict with Iraq.[12] Within a month of Prime Minister Rifa'i's first meeting in Damascus, intended to lay the foundation for the new alignment, Lebanon had erupted into a civil war that would last more than fifteen years. In 1976, Syrian military forces intervened in the conflict in order to prevent a victory by the coalition of leftist Lebanese factions and the PLO over the Maronite Christian forces that dominated the government. While essentially a civil conflict, the Lebanese civil war involved the PLO from the outset, and soon saw intervention from Israel as well as Syria and numerous other states including Iran, France, and the United States.

This is not the place to go into the details of that complex conflict. Suffice it to say, however, that Lebanon's civil affairs were not viewed as purely a domestic Lebanese matter in either Damascus or Amman. Rather, the mutual fear of a too-independent PLO emerging victorious in Lebanon, and the dread of Israeli intervention leading to another Arab-Israeli war, found both Syria and Jordan strategically in the same corner. Despite their Pan-Arab rhetoric, both regimes took a markedly conservative stance against any revision of the status quo, or at least any revision which they themselves could not be certain of controlling.[13]

Neither Jordan nor Syria found its stand to be popular in the broader Arab world, but their political instincts in this case helped lead to the coalescence of the already-growing alignment between them. Thus the Lebanese crisis was not itself an external cause leading to the initial alignment, but it did help to reinforce it, particularly when King Hussein immediately made clear his support for Syrian intervention.[14] Outside Lebanon, reactions to Syrian intervention were mixed, but some governments were quick to make clear their hostility to the Syrian ploy, which some viewed as a brazen attempt at consolidating Syrian control over Lebanon. The Israelis viewed the Syrian action as a significant security threat, eventually leading to skirmishes and aerial combat after Israel launched its 1982 invasion of

Lebanon. In the Arab world, opponents of the Syrian policy included Egypt, Iraq, and Libya. The regional and strategic ramifications of the Lebanese conflict quickly elevated it beyond a domestic Lebanese affair to the status of a major and prolonged regional crisis—a crisis in which Syria needed external allies more than ever.

Finally, a second crisis in regional affairs contributed still further to Jordanian-Syrian solidarity: the growing hostility between the regimes in Damascus and Baghdad.[15] The Lebanese crisis, in fact, helped to trigger a renewed political conflict between Syria and Iraq. As Iraqi statements became more belligerent toward Syria, Jordanian forces were redeployed to Jordan's eastern border with Iraq, and the Hashimite regime made clear that it would support Syria against any Iraqi invasion. While the actual threat of such an invasion had been slight at best, the Jordanian action nonetheless rendered it virtually impossible.[16]

Jordanian policy had remained fairly hostile toward Iraq not only at this time, but ever since the overthrow and brutal execution of the members of the Hashimite royal family of Iraq in 1958. While Jordanian-Syrian relations were renowned for their dramatic ups and downs during the 1958 to 1975 period, Jordanian-Iraqi relations had remained at a low point throughout. Given the long chill in Jordanian-Iraqi relations, it is ironic that, only three years after this saber-rattling border incident, the two countries would begin laying the foundation for a new and long-lasting alignment in inter-Arab politics.[17]

Domestic Politics

One of the most prominent domestic factors affecting the development of the Jordanian-Syrian alignment was the presence within Jordan of a core constituency, led by the Prime Minister, which saw closer alignment with Syria as a necessary measure to ensure more lasting stability and security for Jordan. Yet, particularly at the start of the rapprochement, there remained many elites within the Hashimite regime who were highly skeptical regarding Syrian intentions. And certainly the 1970 Syrian invasion of Jordan remained vivid in the memories of all Jordanian policymakers.

Pro-Syrian factions, however, stressed that the present regime in Damascus was different from the more hostile ones that had preceded it, and that President Asad in particular had refused to support the earlier Jadid regime's invasion of Jordan.[18] While Jordanian elites were at first split in their views of the external strategic incentives and disincentives to alignment with Syria, the issue that led to the development of an increasingly strong pro-alignment constituency, among both public and private sector elites, concerned the economic opportunities to be gained through closer alignment.

The most influential player amongst the pro-Syrian elites in the Jordanian regime was Prime Minister Zayd al-Rifaʻi. As a member of a key regime family, Rifaʻi had close ties to Syria and was long noted for his pro-Syrian sympathies and his personal and familial connections to Damascus.[19] As was suggested above, the fact that the king chose Rifaʻi to head the Jordanian government was in itself a strong signal of the monarchy's desire for warmer relations with Syria. Indeed, for Rifaʻi, whom many came to regard as the architect of the Jordanian-Syrian alignment, the *natural* state of Jordanian relations was unity with Syria. It was the absence of this unity that was the aberration, not the reverse:

> On any priority list [in inter-Arab relations], Syria would have to be at the top. This is due to a host of factors, including the shared historical heritage of the two states. Damascus is closer to Amman than Aqaba. And close ties exist regardless of the diplomatic climate at any given time. There are close trade, education, and family links . . . Close relations with Syria are the natural state of affairs, not just normal friendly relations as with other Arab states.[20]

Rifaʻi was not alone in this view, and his tenure in office provided the opportunity for other pro-Syrian elites (particularly from northern Jordan) to participate actively in the many committees and joint projects set up in order to further the progress of the alignment. Thus a key domestic change within Jordan involved the ascendancy of factions within the Hashimite ruling coalition, made up of government and business elites drawn to the economic opportunities that greater integration with Syria appeared to offer.

These views and this growing pro-Syrian constituency were cultivated and encouraged by Rifaʻi, and they helped give the alignment its character: explicitly building cooperation and alignment between the two countries, first by creating agreements in areas of low politics, particularly trade and manufacturing linkages, and later by moving upward to the high politics of joint defense policies and coordinated foreign policy. While Syrian elites were in general more concerned with high-level political coordination, Jordanian elites were more reluctant and cautious—fearing domination by their northern alignment partner—and seemed far more concerned with the business opportunities which the alignment made possible.

What is particularly striking about this period is how much it stands in contrast to the previous eight years, when Jordan had survived two regional wars and a civil war. In short, the internal and external security dilemmas facing the kingdom were, at least comparatively speaking, much more moderate than they had been in 1967, 1970, or 1973. Yet by allying so strongly with Syria, the Hashimites did manage to gain the additional benefit of neutralizing any threat of domestic subversion from Syria, in effect silencing their most strident ideological critic in this post-war rebuilding period. The alliance also allowed the Hashimites to pursue greater economic prosperity. Both the rebuilding effort and the pursuit of prosperity were designed to enhance the regime's domestic security.

Political Economy

As the above discussion of domestic politics suggests, economic incentives also affected the Jordanian-Syrian rapprochement and the eventual development of an alliance. Jordanian elites in the private sector had long had links to Syria, given the overland transport route from Jordan's port on the Red Sea, Aqaba, to Damascus and across Syria toward Turkey and Europe. In addition, the close proximity of Damascus and Amman in particular led to numerous business linkages between the two capitals, despite the periods of hostility that had characterized their political relations. Not surprisingly, any hint of warming relations between Jordan and Syria found immediate and active support from among many private business elites.

By serving on the joint committees and subcommittees set up to foster greater Jordanian-Syrian cooperation, these elites pressed for agreements between the two states aimed at lowering economic barriers between them and thereby facilitating cooperation in profit-making ventures. As noted in the introduction to this chapter, numerous economic agreements were reached between Jordan and Syria as the alignment began to take shape. These included agreements to remove all tariff barriers between the two states, to coordinate customs charges and restrictions, and to cooperate on tourism. In addition, several joint economic projects were established, including companies involved in food production and textile manufacturing as well as land and sea transportation.[21]

In addition to the motives of private business elites, however, there were also strong economic incentives for closer alignment with Syria from the perspective of public sector revenue. One of these revenue motivations behind the alignment involved the desire to coordinate with Syria as a key front line state in appealing for aid to the wealthier Gulf states. Both Jordan and Syria had been promised considerable Arab aid at the 1974 Rabat Summit of the Arab League. It was hoped that, by cooperating in the form of a "united front," Jordan and Syria together would be able to pressure the Gulf states to follow through with their financial pledges.[22]

Another consideration in this economic vein concerned the desire to prevent, in the future, the economic costs that had often characterized the assorted Jordanian-Syrian rifts of the past. In short, Jordanian officials wanted the economic dimensions of the Jordanian-Syrian alignment developed not only for short-term profitability, but also to create longer-term profitability and more solid relations through a foundation of strong and irrevocable economic ties. Previously, at times of extreme crisis in their bilateral relations, Syria had frequently closed off its border, with immediate economic repercussions for Jordan. The most recent border closure had occurred during the events of 1970. The border closures had invariably carried with them economic costs, due to the reliance of much Jordanian trade and transport on Syrian routes northward to Turkey and Europe.

Close economic integration was therefore intended not only to create a firmer basis for political coordination in the alignment, but also to provide strategic insurance against any future deterioration of political relations by preventing the possibility of any more costly border closures.[23] By solidifying the economic basis of the alignment, or its "low politics" foundation, the Jordanians hoped that the economic dimensions of the bilateral relationship would be insulated from future disagreements over "high politics" issues. And conversely, they hoped that the solid and mutually beneficial economic basis of the alignment would serve to temper any disagreements in the realm of high politics.

In sum, unlike the temporary wartime pacts that had emerged between Jordan and Syria in 1948 and in 1967, the alignment of the late 1970s had a more solid basis in economic motivations and in successful economic cooperation. According to Jordan's Prime Minister Rifa'i,

> All previous (inter-Arab) mergers, however, were on the basis of mergers from the top down. We wanted to build both up. Top and bottom. On the basis of what we called "complementarity." This began with joint economic and agricultural projects. Then proceeded by unifying curricula in schools. And then moved on to political coordination, regarding the movement of peoples, policy coordination, and internal security cooperation.[24]

Strategic Triangle or "Three's a Crowd?" The Collapse of the Jordanian-Syrian Alliance

Given the early successes in consolidating the Jordanian-Syrian alliance, an alliance whose many economic foundations were specifically designed to make it long lasting, it is perhaps ironic that it unraveled so quickly. But the security factors that led to its undoing had more to do with Syrian-Iraqi relations than with anything else. Iraq had in the late 1970s begun an intensive lobbying effort to lure Jordan into its orbit, in the immediate aftermath of a failed Syrian-Iraqi rapprochement. The issues in the growing Jordanian-Iraqi alignment are examined in detail in the next chapter; however, suffice it to say that the warming of Jordanian-Iraqi relations was viewed with hostility from Damascus, and came in a context of severe domestic and regional insecurity for the Asad regime.

Syria had become mired in the bloody war in Lebanon, was faced with major bouts of domestic unrest and even urban terrorism from a resurgent militant Islamist movement, and had just experienced the rapid rise and fall of its own brief flirtation with Iraq.[25] Aware of Syrian misgivings regarding the warming Jordanian-Iraqi relations, Jordan's new prime minister, 'Abd al-Hamid Sharaf, had taken pains to stress to Syrian officials that the new alignment did not in any way constitute an anti-Syrian bloc.[26] His colleagues in Damascus, however, did not share his optimistic views of the new alignment.

Similarly, when Syria and Iraq had engaged in negotiations to create a new alignment and even union, the Jordanian regime had been not at all enthusiastic, particularly if that union had any future desire to absorb Jordan as well. Such a "union" would potentially have rendered the Hashimite regime itself unnecessary, and even a looser form of integration would still have marked Jordan as by far the weakest partner. While not happy with the idea of a full-fledged Iraqi-Syrian union, Jordanian policymakers had nonetheless hoped to increase their links to Iraq while also preserving their alignment with Syria. When Iraqi-Syrian relations plummeted back to their more familiar hostility, however, it became clear that Jordan would soon be faced with a choice: either Syria or Iraq, but not both. Lamenting this general pattern in inter-Arab relations, one of King Hussein's military advisors noted that

> We try always for balance with all our Arab neighbors, but sometimes they have differences. And if we have good relations with Iraq, Syria gets upset. If we have good relations with Syria, the Iraqis get upset.

If we have good relations with both, the Saudis get jittery. We try for balance, but never of a military nature.[27]

The Arab League Summit held in Amman on November 25, 1980, made abundantly clear that the once close Jordanian-Syrian alignment was indeed over. While laying bare the depth of the Jordanian-Syrian rift, the summit also underscored the broader political divisions within the Arab world. Syria not only refused to attend the meeting, but also organized a boycott which came to include Algeria, Lebanon, Libya, the PLO, and South Yemen. Arab positions regarding the outbreak of war between Iran and Iraq marked the line of demarcation in this inter-Arab polarization and fed into an atmosphere of recriminations and accusations between the Arab regimes. This new conflict in the Persian Gulf had come on the heels of the earlier inter-Arab rift over Egypt's separate peace with Israel. King Hussein's intentions in particular, as host of the 1980 summit, were focused on rallying an Arab world divided over Sadat's treaty with Israel, in order to provide a united front against revolutionary Iran. The Syrian-led boycott of the summit, however, only served to underscore the disunity of Arab ranks.

Making the Jordanian position clear, King Hussein was unreserved in his criticisms during a speech at the summit. He roundly condemned Syria and Libya in particular for supporting Iran in its war against Iraq. Iraq had invaded Iran earlier that year, while Iran was still experiencing the early fallout of its revolution toppling the shah. For the Syrians, however, the disunity was rooted in Baghdad, not Damascus. According to one Syrian political analyst,

> Asad saw through the causes of that (Iran-Iraq) war. Syria was in desperate need of an ally. It was still in a state of war with Israel, but Egypt was suddenly neutralized. How to counterbalance Israel? People were all talking about strengthening the Eastern front, and so rapprochement began with Iraq in 1978 and 1979. Asad saw Islamic Iran, compared to the shah's pro-Israeli Iran, as very positive. He saw the revolution as a very positive development . . . and here Iraq starts a war . . . the wrong war. The real war was on the Western front.[28]

In contrast to the Syrian position, the Hashimite regime had in fact played an extremely active role throughout the Arab League summit as the key lobbyist rallying pan-Arab support for the Iraqi war effort.[29]

Given the level of hostility that existed between Damascus and Baghdad, the Asad regime viewed the Hashimite actions as nothing less than a betrayal. And as noted above, this challenge from its former ally came at a particularly vulnerable time, as the regime in Damascus attempted to meet not only regional challenges to its security, but also even more severe domestic threats from Islamist militancy throughout Syria. In interviews years later, one of Jordan's top officials suggested that the Syrians were actually correct in claiming a Jordanian link to domestic unrest in Syria starting in the later 1970s and carrying well into the 1980s:

> Ironically, internal security was the reason we drifted apart. The government was supporting the Muslim Brotherhood against the regime in Syria. They [the Syrians] were right [when they accused Jordan of supporting their enemies] but the king did not know. The prime minister at the time had close relations with the Muslim Brotherhood and was trying to create a constituency for himself.[30]

It is also worth noting, however, that two of Jordan's prime ministers at this time, Mudar Badran and Ahmad Ubaydat, both dismissed this argument as baseless.[31]

The Asad regime, however, responded to the king's comments at the Arab League summit with more than words. Immediately after the meeting had ended, 247,000 Syrian troops and more than 800 tanks were deployed along the Jordanian border. Jordan responded with 57,000 troops of its own, setting the stage for a major confrontation.[32] Despite its feeling that it was being besieged on both domestic and regional fronts, the Asad regime was still capable of demonstrating to its southern neighbor and former ally the dangers of invoking its power and its wrath. According to one of President Hafiz al-Asad's political advisors, the Iraq situation was the death blow to the Jordanian-Syrian alignment. "In the summer . . . the Syrian-Iraqi crisis—the most important one—broke out," he said, "Jordan acted first as intermediary, then sided whole-heartedly with Iraq. And this made Syria exercise her military strength vis-à-vis Jordan in both covert and overt ways."[33] Active mediation by Saudi Arabia was instrumental in defusing the military confrontation and pulling the two countries back from the brink of war. The high level of political hostility, however, would remain between the two countries with implications not only for regional security, but also for the domestic security of both regimes, as each attempted to subvert the other in the 1980s.

Long-held stereotypical views reemerged as Syrian rhetoric returned to its characterization of Jordan (and particularly of King Hussein) as a fundamentally unreliable ally, and one that amounted to little more than a Western puppet state masquerading as a member of the Arab camp. For many Jordanians, meanwhile, images resurfaced of Syria as a wolf only occasionally garbed in sheep's clothing, poised to dominate or subvert the kingdom.

Conclusions

Unlike Jordan's earlier affiliation with the Trilateral Alliance, the development of the Jordanian-Syrian alignment appears to have been influenced far less by external security concerns. To the contrary, there is little evidence, even though the alignment developed to include military cooperation, that external threats were a primary concern. Externally, there were indeed regional changes affecting the alignment as it progressed—particularly Jordan and Syria's mutual rift with Egypt over the direction of post-war Arab diplomacy. While regional changes did, therefore, help reinforce the Jordanian-Syrian alignment, they did not appear to trigger it, nor can these changes be said to have involved any increase in external security threats to Jordan.

In contrast, the economic incentives for this alignment, and the development of an increasingly large and influential pro-Syrian coalition within Jordanian domestic politics, were very influential factors. First, alignment with Syria included a host of economic agreements intended to raise the level of bilateral trade, allow for the establishment of joint manufacturing ventures, and enhance cooperation in the transportation and tourism industries. Each economic linkage carried with it a profit motive for private business elites as well as the Jordanian state, and each was intended by the regime as one more piece of insurance against the costly border closures that had rocked the Jordanian economy in the past. Finally, an additional economic factor influencing the Jordanian-Syrian alignment was the desire to present, in effect, joint petitions to the wealthy Gulf states to ensure that financial pledges made in 1974 would be honored. Yet it is essential to recognize that every economic factor noted here was explicitly intended to shore up the domestic regime security of both Jordan and Syria. For the Jordanians in particular, all the emphasis on economic linkages was also intended as a means to dissuade Syrian meddling in Jordanian domestic politics, as Damascus had so often proved a thorn in the side of Jordan's domestic regime security in the past.

After years of hostility, the two states had abandoned their Cold War in favor of coordination in trade, investment, tourism, joint ventures, and collective lobbying for aid from the oil-wealthy Gulf states. And unlike the many unsuccessful acts of "unification" that had emerged as a part of inter-Arab relations in the 1950s and 1960s, the less-heralded Jordanian-Syrian alignment of 1975–1979 had involved far greater economic integration, political cooperation, and security coordination. It was, in short, a much more substantial alliance than its more ideologically charged predecessors from the Nasir era. Yet, despite the strength of this alliance, Jordan and Syria both fell victim to the Ba'th versus Ba'th rivalry that plagued relations between Damascus and Baghdad. When forced to choose between its current alliance with Syria and its growing alignment with Iraq, Jordan chose the latter.

The Jordanian Alliance with Iraq

This chapter examines why Jordan realigned toward Iraq, and why this alignment would last throughout the 1980s. The emergence of the new alignment was quite striking given the history of Iraqi-Jordanian relations, which had tended to oscillate between coldness and outright hostility, especially from 1958 to 1978. Prior to 1958 Iraq, like Jordan, was also a Hashimite Kingdom. In fact, both countries were originally artificial creations of European imperialism out of the ashes of the Ottoman Empire. Both were British Mandates before achieving independence under their respective Hashimite regimes. But the Hashimite Kingdom of Iraq, ruled by King Hussein's cousin, Faisal II, was destroyed in a bloody military coup in 1958.[1]

In the years following the Iraqi revolution, the various regimes that governed the new Republic of Iraq tended to view the Jordanian monarchy with deep suspicion. Indeed, the feeling was even more intense on the Jordanian side. Unlike his less fortunate kin in Iraq, King Hussein had thwarted a coup attempt against his own regime in 1957; following the murder of his cousin King Faisal in 1958, the Jordanian monarch naturally regarded the successive Iraqi republican governments with fear and loathing.[2] Yet King Hussein had no intention of allowing revolutionary Iraq to subvert his domestic position, and his regime maintained a cool distance in its relations with Baghdad.

Within domestic politics, meanwhile, the Hashimite regime also took the opportunity in 1957–1958 to wrest political control from the parliament, concentrate power in the royal palace, and generally consolidate its domestic position.[3] That earlier episode remains a case in point of the deliberalization that can result from the clash of internal and external security dilemmas.

More than twenty years after the Iraqi revolution, the regimes in Amman and Baghdad began not only to establish increasingly cordial relations, but also—to the surprise of those aware of the history—to develop closer and closer ties.[4] This alignment shift was, in short, a radical departure from recent historical trends. Iraq and Jordan had not been allied with one another since the short-lived Arab Federation, an alliance of the two Hashimite Kingdoms, which had emerged largely in response to domestic security fears and threats of internal subversion sponsored by Nasirist and other nationalist forces. The Iraqi-Jordanian Federation lasted only from February 14, 1958, to July 14, 1958—the date of the coup in Baghdad.[5] Twenty years later, Jordan once again allied with Iraq.

External Security

The new Jordanian-Iraqi alignment emerged in the context of major changes in the politics of the regional system, particularly between 1977 and 1980. This brief but tumultuous transitional period to the 1980s began with Egyptian-Israeli peace accords (widely regarded as Egyptian defection from the Arab camp) and ended with the eruption of a new regional war. This time, however, the war was not between the State of Israel and its Arab adversaries, but between Iraq and Iran, resulting in significant destabilization of the Persian Gulf region. Indeed, the Middle East had been shaken by a bewildering sequence of major shocks: the Egyptian-Israeli peace process, from 1977 to 1979; the 1979 revolution and overthrow of the shah in Iran; the 1979 Soviet invasion of Afghanistan; and, finally, the 1980 Iraqi invasion of Iran, triggering an eight-year war of attrition between the two dominant powers in the Persian Gulf. In short, the transition from the 1970s to the 1980s was a period of extreme turbulence and regional crises.

The first signs of a full-scale regional realignment, however, began to emerge in the wake of the Camp David Accords in 1978, and became very clear following the signing of the Egyptian-Israeli Peace Treaty in 1979. Ironically, then, it was not the crises that entailed the outbreak of *war*, but rather the crisis involving the emergence of *peace* that was perceived as the greatest threat to many Arab regimes. The unilateralism which characterized the approach of Egyptian President Anwar al-Sadat toward the Arab-Israeli peace process was widely regarded in the Arab world as treasonous and at the very least dangerous.

Sadat had surprised allies and critics alike by a series of dramatic moves, starting with his sudden announcement in 1977 that he would go to Jerusalem. In an unprecedented move, Sadat did indeed make the journey to Jerusalem and, in a speech before the Israeli Knesset, announced his intention to make peace. A year later, in 1978, Sadat along with Israeli Prime Minister Menachim Begin and United States President Jimmy Carter signed the Camp David Accords. By 1979, these accords had led to the first Arab-Israeli peace treaty, the treaty between Egypt and Israel. Sadat's peace initiatives had sent shock waves throughout the Arab world, leading to widespread condemnation of Egypt, and triggering a major regional realignment, the scope of which would not be seen again until the 1990 Iraqi invasion of Kuwait.

The Jordanian response to the Sadat initiative was characteristically cautious. It became clear early in the Egyptian-Israeli peace process that the main non-regional actor, the United States, hoped that Jordan too would follow Sadat's lead and enter the negotiations. Decision makers in Washington seemed to misjudge entirely the depth of the domestic constraints on the Hashimite regime's maneuverability. These domestic aspects of the Jordanian alignment will be discussed in the next section, but it remains to be seen whether external threats helped propel Jordan from its alignment with Syria to a new alignment with Iraq.

The external stimulus of the "peace crisis" may well have led Jordanian decision makers to reevaluate their alignment commitments. But this likelihood does not explain Jordan's specific choice to realign, nor the kingdom's specific choice of partners. Jordan's shift from Syria to Iraq cannot be accurately read as an act of balancing or bandwagoning against an increased Israeli threat, although Jordanian decision makers did fear that Israel was emerging as a greater threat at that time.[6] It may seem perplexing that an Israeli peace treaty might be read as heightening rather than relaxing external security threats to the kingdom. But the Peace Treaty effectively neutralized Egypt as a military and political power among the "frontline" Arab states in the continuing conflict against Israel, leaving them more vulnerable than before. This was especially significant since Egypt was the most populous Arab country, with the largest army, and strategically located to the southwest of Israel. This forced the Israeli Defense Forces always to spread themselves thin in order to deal with at least a two-front war should a conflict arise. The sudden removal of Egypt from the military equation correspondingly elevated Israel's power status relative to any remaining constellation of Arab forces.

Worse still, Jordanian policymakers believed, the disappearance of an Egyptian-Israeli front left the Israelis with the ability to redeploy their forces on the Jordanian border and on the Golan Heights. The Jordanians feared that the absence of an Egyptian deterrent would free a hawkish Likud-led Israeli government to indulge in adventurist or expansionist policies. It must be remembered that many Israeli officials in the Likud government spoke of a "Greater Israel," which some considered to include historically all of Jordan.[7] Others continued to speak of a "Jordan Option" in which the Hashimite Kingdom would vanish to become instead the Palestinian state.[8]

A balance-of-threats approach would lead us to believe that the remaining frontline states would be driven into each other's arms in order to counter the enhanced status of Israel and the reduced collective prowess of the Arab frontline states. While Iraq, like Syria, had a large and powerful army, it was not on or near what would be the frontlines of any future Arab-Israeli war; but Syria was. Yet Jordan still gravitated steadily away from Syria, just as the regional balance of threats should have been driving the two back together to confront a heightened Israeli threat.

Something else was clearly a more important consideration for the Jordanian policymakers: the economic support that Iraq could give to Jordan, to an extent that Syria could not hope to match.[9] That consideration was so important to Jordan, and seen as so critical to Hashimite security, that the regime was willing to sacrifice even a crucial frontline ally in the Arab-Israeli military balance, in the interests of shoring up the longer-term economic underpinnings of its domestic security and stability.

Yet this starker choice—shifting entirely from Syria to Iraq—would be made only later; originally, the Jordanians hoped to achieve a positive sum increase in their security by developing alignments with *both* Syria and Iraq. But when forced to choose between these two, Jordan chose the latter. It is important to note here, however, that the strictness of this choice—and, indeed, the need to choose at all between these alternative partners—was not a Jordanian idea. It was, rather, pushed on Jordan by the state of the Iraqi-Syrian relationship itself which, as noted in the previous chapter, was known for its mutual belligerency. But the relations between the two Ba'thist states had degenerated even more than usual following the failed attempt at union in 1978 and Iraqi charges of Syrian subversion.[10]

Jordan did not want to lose the access it had gained to Syrian markets, did not desire to lose a needed frontline ally in either war or peace negotiations with Israel, and did not want to risk renewed domestic insecurity by triggering Syrian meddling in Jordanian internal politics. Yet a series of factors reinforced Jordan's steady drift toward alignment with Iraq. First, Iraq itself actively courted the Hashimite regime, attempting to lure it into its highly lucrative orbit. Second, Syria and Jordan, in response to the various regional crises, had begun to differ in their foreign policy outlooks. Syria pushed for a hard-line stance against the Egyptian peace initiative, while Jordan opted for a more moderate and less confrontational approach, hoping to lure Egypt back to the Arab fold.[11]

Two alternative Arab blocs had emerged to counter Sadat's unilateral peace initiative: (1) the hard-line "Front for Steadfastness and Confrontation" (*Jabha al-Samud wa al-Tasadi*), formed in December 1977 and led by Syria; and (2) the slightly more moderate "Rejection Front" (*Jabha al Rafd*), led by Iraq, which actually formed earlier in October 1974, but came to represent an alternative to Syrian-led opposition to Sadat in the later 1970s. While these amounted more to policy declarations than substantive alignments, Jordan attempted to lean toward the latter grouping while refraining from declaring itself a full part of the bloc. Finally, in 1980, only one year after the Egyptian-Israeli Peace Treaty, the Iran-Iraq war began, and Jordan immediately backed Iraq while Syria departed from Arab ranks and actively supported Iran. While the Jordan-Syria alignment was over by the onset of the 1980s, bilateral relations continued to worsen as the decade wore on. The Syrians in particular felt increasingly isolated in inter-Arab relations in the 1980s. As one of President Asad's advisors noted,

> Jordan was one of the first to renew relations with Egypt. The Jordanian-Egyptian rapprochement reflected badly on the relationship of Jordan and Syria. One of the worst points was in 1984, when the Palestine National Council meeting was held in Amman. The whole Sunni constellation was against Syria—King Hussein, Arafat, Saddam Hussein, and Mubarak. And they were all more moderate vis-à-vis Israel and the West. So 1984 was the main year Syria felt besieged by its neighbors.[12]

In sum, the external crises—from Camp David to the Iranian Revolution to the Iran-Iraq war—did affect the security considerations of all Middle Eastern states, but their effects on Jordan were such that they only reinforced a decision that had already been made. They were not, therefore, causal in themselves. Once the Iran-Iraq war began, however, Jordan backed Iraq unequivocally, and that backing turned out to be the final straw for Jordan's earlier alignment with Syria. Having lost that alignment partner, however, the Jordanians put great efforts into making sure that their decision to ally whole-heartedly with Iraq would work. Jordan became a key strategic asset to Iraq during its long war with Iran. Those eight years of war served to reinforce the Jordanian-Iraqi alignment, which ironically would have significant effects on the Hashimite regime's ability to maneuver in a later Gulf crisis, as we shall see in chapter 9.

Jordanian support for Iraq was critical throughout the long war with Iran, but primarily in logistical terms, and not in active military support. Jordan did not send its regular army troops to fight beside its ally, although the regime did organize and send a largely symbolic volunteer force—the 2,000-man Yarmuk Brigade—to Iraq.[13] This volunteer force, however, was the entire extent of Jordanian direct military support to Iraq during eight years of war. It is also important to note that the Yarmuk Brigade did not have combat duties.[14] Rather, its role was largely one of symbolic support, which allowed the Hashimite regime to demonstrate its alignment with Iraq while avoiding any commitment to send units of Jordan's regular armed forces to the Persian Gulf.

Jordan's main—and indeed, vital—role in the Iraqi war effort, was not military but economic. With Iranian naval forces threatening Gulf shipping, and given Iraq's limited access to the Gulf in the first place, both the exporting of oil and the importing of needed supplies and materiel were made problematic at best. This difficulty was compounded by Syria's decision to ally with Iran against Iraq, supporting the former's war effort, and most importantly, shutting off the overland oil pipeline from Iraq to the Syrian coast.

The cutoff of the Syrian pipeline and the harassment of shipping lanes in the Gulf both served the same two purposes. First, the Iranian and Syrian actions made the export of Iraqi oil difficult, thereby cutting back on oil revenues just as they were desperately needed to fund the war effort. Second, the limits on Iraq's petrodollars in turn affected its ability to pay for goods and supplies, while the harried sea lanes cut back on the flow of these goods in any case. It is in this context that Jordan's economic role became critical to the national security of Iraq, and to the regime security of the Ba'thist state in particular.[15]

Jordan became Iraq's main supply corridor for goods and materiel as well as its main outlet for oil exports. In addition, the kingdom played a key diplomatic role between Iraq and the other Arab states.[16] It was largely Jordanian efforts that had led to Arab League unity against Iran, for example. In more material terms, Jordan's role included rallying not only enthusiasm but also real financial support from key countries, such as the Arab Gulf monarchies. In this sense, Jordan was serving in the same capacity for Iraq as Iraq was for Jordan. Both were actively rallying the oil states to make good on their commitments to Jordan and Iraq, justified as frontline states in two different Arab conflicts: Jordan with Israel, and Iraq with Iran. Jordan's loyalty to Iraq throughout the war was rewarded in many ways, not least of which were the shipments of free oil which the kingdom came to depend on. In late 1980 and early 1981, however, the Iraqi regime also made clear its appreciation by giving a gift to the Jordanian military in the form of more than fifty U.S. M-60 tanks that had been captured from Iran in the early phases of the war.[17]

Iraq did have some military and strategic significance for Jordan as well. Yet these factors appeared to be fortuitous additional benefits and not the driving force behind the decisive shift from Syria to Iraq. Although Jordanian elites used the term "strategic depth" in describing the value of Iraq for Jordan's regional position, Iraq was nonetheless not the only country capable of giving Jordan this asset.[18] Syria not only was an additional candidate for that role, but already had a close alignment with Jordan. Syria might more logically help Jordan vis-à-vis Israel, while Iraq might be a greater asset vis-à-vis Iran. Indeed, Iraq formed an enormous and formidable buffer zone against revolutionary Iran. As one of Jordan's prime ministers put it, "the Iranian revolution was for export, and Iraq was the gateway to the Arab world."[19] Similarly, former Foreign Minister Marwan al-Qasim argued that the Iran-Iraq war amounted to "continued bleeding of two major threats to the region," but that Iran constituted a far more dangerous threat to domestic stability than Iraq. "It was a matter of conviction that by supporting Iraq you were in fact supporting yourself."[20]

Jordanian policymakers made clear, however, that Iran was not considered a direct military threat to Jordan itself. Rather, they viewed Iran as a larger abstract threat to Arab unity, and far more importantly as a direct threat to Jordan's main regional sources of aid and its main external labor markets—both in the Arab Gulf states. The threat that Iran represented to the Hashimite regime, therefore, did not include fears of military attack on Jordan; rather, the kingdom feared Iran's power to damage its aid and labor lifelines in the Gulf on the one hand, and its potential ramifications for Jordanian domestic stability on the other. It is to this domestic side of the regime security equation that we must now turn.

Domestic Politics

Given the tumultuous nature of regional politics in the late 1970s and early 1980s, the Hashimite regime was naturally concerned for its own domestic stability. The first jolt to stability had come as a result of the Egyptian-Israeli peace negotiations. In this context, it must be remembered that Palestinians constituted anywhere from 50 to 60 percent of the overall population of Jordan. For that reason, any issue touching on a final settlement of the Arab-Israeli conflict was of vital interest and importance to the Jordanian populace and regime. And the public response to the Sadat initiative was predictably uneasy and mistrustful.

These feelings appeared fully justified as the Egyptian-Israeli process deepened, with scant reference to the Palestinians themselves, and no thought at all of PLO participation. While the Hashimite regime may not have objected to PLO exclusion per se, it did prefer to speak itself for the Palestinians. But the regime also had to take note of the hostility toward Sadat and his "Egyptianism" (as opposed to Pan-Arabism) from the majority of the population in Jordan. Jordanian public opinion, in short, was a matter of domestic regime security as this "peace crisis" deepened. The depth of anger only increased with the official signing in 1979 of the Egyptian-Israeli Treaty, further constraining the regime's options. Despite the volatility of Jordan's domestic political scene, the United States, betraying a failure to grasp the connection between Jordanian domestic politics and foreign policy, pushed King Hussein to follow in Sadat's footsteps and join in the peace process with Israel. As Valerie Yorke has noted:

> The Carter Administration thus made a serious error of judgement in trying to persuade King Hussein to join the Camp David process and endorse the 1979 Egypt-Israel Peace Treaty. The sustained attempt to do so reflected American political insensitivity concerning the Hashemites' domestic security concerns and Jordan's finely-balanced position in the Arab world. Washington appeared to have little realistic understanding of how the Hashemites' internal political game limited the kind of policy the king could safely pursue on the Palestinian issue.[21]

For many within Jordan itself, however, the U.S. initiative toward the Hashimites did not come as a surprise. For King Hussein's regime had long been viewed with suspicion by many in its own Palestinian population, not to mention from other more radical Arab states. Jordanian nationalists tend to object strongly to such regional portrayals of Jordan's role, but the image persists in Arab politics nonetheless. The roots of this suspicion were deep, based mainly on Jordan's controversial role in the Arab effort to restore Palestinian rights. The bloody 1970 suppression of the PLO in Jordan was not yet a decade old, nor was Jordan's limited commitment to the 1973 October War. Furthermore it was widely believed that King Hussein remained bitter about the Arab League resolutions that had followed that war, particularly the 1974 Rabat Summit resolution declaring the PLO, not the Hashimite regime, to be the "sole, legitimate representative of the Palestinian people." Despite verbal acquiescence to the resolution, King Hussein had thereafter exerted much of his political energy in an effort to nullify the outcome from Rabat, or at minimum to restore a key Jordanian role in resolving the Palestinian question.

Both Syria and the PLO had dedicated themselves to preventing any kind of unilateralism in the Arab-Israeli conflict and peace process; both seemed to view President Sadat and King Hussein as the most likely candidates for just such a "defection"; and both of these key regional players exerted considerable influence on Jordanian domestic politics. Syria, as we have seen, was Jordan's closest Arab ally in the late 1970s, with strong ties to key Jordanian political and business elites; while the PLO was recognized by much of Jordan's Palestinian majority as their true representative. Therefore, when Sadat did make his move, focusing global attention on Egypt and Israel, the focus within Jordan itself was on the Hashimite regime. The question was a simple one: would the Hashimites follow suit, and would this mean abandoning the Palestinians?

This domestic attention and pressure was so significant, in fact, that it constrained Jordanian alliance options by eliminating Egypt as a potential alignment partner. Until Sadat's surprise initiative, both Jordan and Saudi Arabia had been considering establishing closer ties with Egypt. Before the peace treaty, both the Hashimite and Saudi regimes had come to view Sadat as a pragmatic leader and one they could, in effect, do business with. This does not suggest that there was any personal love between these leaderships, but simply that a coalescence of interests in a less conflictual approach to the Arab-Israeli dilemma had developed in Amman, Cairo, and Riyadh. In addition, a symbiotic set of relationships in the regional political economy had emerged, in which Jordanian and Egyptian labor flowed to oil-rich (but labor-poor) Saudi Arabia, while labor remittances and Saudi aid flowed back in the other direction. But Sadat's unilateral moves erased from the realm of possibility what might otherwise have developed into a strong two or three-way alignment.

With any thoughts of an Egyptian alignment dashed, the Jordanian regime concentrated on following the lead of other Arab states as they responded to the crisis, to ensure that Jordan would not be isolated or left behind, as Egypt soon would be. In addition, the regime pressed forward in its efforts to establish a more long-term solution to its internal and external security dilemmas.

In an examination of the Jordanian domestic scene, particularly in 1979, what becomes apparent is that the population and the regime were out of sync. While the regime had been considering closer ties to Egypt, the peace treaty in that year only confirmed much of the Jordan population's most dire expectations and suspicions of Sadat. But the state-society relationship was even more askew over the other major regional crisis: the Iranian Revolution. The response of King Hussein's regime was immediate and outright hostility to the new Iranian government, while the popular reaction was quite positive.[22] Indeed, several Jordanian towns, including Salt, just outside the capital, were scenes of pro-Khomeini demonstrations—promptly put down by Jordanian government forces.[23]

For most Jordanians, the toppling of the shah, widely viewed as a pro-Zionist Western puppet, was to be welcomed. This was particularly true of the Islamist movement within Jordan, which applauded the toppling of an authoritarian monarch by a popular Islamic revolution. But that same issue was the source of dread for King Hussein and his regime; the Iranian revolution had, after all, overthrown a conservative and strongly pro-U.S. monarchy. For all the differences between the two situations, the fact remained that the spectacle of the Iranian revolution had struck close to home for many regime elites in Jordan. And for that reason, they viewed revolutionary Iran as a serious threat to the *domestic*—not external—security of the Hashimite regime.

Jordan's geographic distance allowed the kingdom to be far more sanguine than, for example, the Arab Gulf monarchies were about the unlikelihood of any direct Iranian attack. But Jordan's fear remained just as real as, if more indirect than, that of other Arab nations. Jordan's fear was of internal subversion and heightened Islamist militancy within the kingdom. Certainly, throughout the region, there was much concern regarding the future of the Arab monarchies: from Morocco to Jordan to the Gulf. If the shah of Iran—with the best-equipped army and the most sophisticated internal security apparatus in the Islamic Middle East—could be overthrown by a coalition led by Islamists, then the days of these considerably weaker monarchies might well be numbered. While in retrospect such an expectation might appear unduly alarmist, it does convey the tenor of the time, and it was the perception rather than the reality that informed Jordanian policy. Jordan's fear, in turn, helps explain the intense level of Hashimite support for Saddam's Iraq after the latter invaded Iran in 1980.

Still, two points require clarification here. First, while the external events had divergent impacts on state and society in Jordan, in turn constraining state policy, neither the Egyptian nor the Iranian crises caused Jordan's alignment shift to Iraq. As noted in the previous section, the timing of Jordan's drift toward Iraq preceded both the Egyptian-Israeli Peace Treaty and the Iranian Revolution. Indeed, the drift had begun in 1978, mainly over economic issues. The second point, however, is that the domestic responses to these events were nonetheless noted with concern by the regime, which attempted to accommodate public opinion on the Sadat question, but which nonetheless felt compelled to run opposite the public on the Iranian issue.

In short, the regime saw Iran as a threat in two ways: as an example for successful domestic revolt, and as a danger to Jordan's key sources of economic aid and labor markets in the Gulf. This perceived threat led Jordan to rapidly increase the pace of its alignment with Iraq and its break with Syria. In doing so, particularly in its virulent opposition to Khomeini's regime in Iran, the Hashimites were running headlong against popular opinion. The domestic risk, however, was deemed manageable compared to the far greater risk of allowing Iran's avowed intent—to export revolution—to go unchecked. This pro-Iraqi and anti-Iranian initiative was led directly by King Hussein himself. Looking back on that time, Prime Ministers Zayd al-Rifa'i (1973–1976, 1985–1989) and Mudar Badran (1976–1979, 1980–1984, 1989–1991) both stressed the accuracy of the king's longer-term vision in contrast to what they saw as a public failure to appreciate the threatening nature of the Khomeini regime.[24]

When the war broke out in the Gulf, King Hussein's official condemnations of Iran and declaration of unequivocal support for Iraq were met with some surprise and consternation in the Jordanian street. But the regime quickly embarked on a campaign to sell this unpopular alignment move to the Jordanian public. In a form of ideological marketing, and perhaps in an attempt to preempt both Arab nationalist and Islamist critics of the regime, both Arabism and Islam reemerged in regime arguments supporting the war effort; in effect, the war was presented as being between a Sunni and Arab state against a Shia and Persian one. Eventually, public opinion did come around, although perhaps not in response to regime arguments. The material aspects of this shift may be just as important as the ideational ones, as ties to Iraq increased over time, as business opportunities linked to Iraq boomed, and as a seemingly endless set of Iraqi grants for specific Jordanian groups and associations (including the Jordan Press Federation) helped sway more and more of Jordanian public opinion to the alliance with Saddam Hussein's Iraq.[25]

Political Economy

In the late 1970s, even as the alignment with Syria was in full swing, Jordan had established more cordial, if not warm, relations with the regime in Baghdad. The relationship at this point, in the middle 1970s, fit the diplomatic cliche of "businesslike" interaction. Jordanian agricultural goods were being shipped to Iraq at moderate levels, which would later increase dramatically once the Iran-Iraq war began. More importantly for Jordan's domestic affairs, however, were a series of investment initiatives in which Iraq sent aid earmarked specifically for developing the port facilities at Aqaba as well as other aspects of Jordanian infrastructure, such as the road system, particularly the roads from Aqaba to Baghdad.[26]

While this development would turn out to be critical to Iraq's war effort in the 1980s, the original initiative from Baghdad seems to have been concerned primarily with Iraq's vulnerability to Syrian economic sabotage, should the frequent Iraq-Syrian quarrels result in border closures, shutting off Iraq's access to Mediterranean ports. Following the initial businesslike contacts between Jordan and Iraq, the Iraqi regime came to view a warming of Iraqi-Jordanian relations initially as at least prudent, and only later as critical to both Jordanian and Iraqi regime security. Jordan's value to Iraq, in short, came simply from its geography and certainly not from its military or economic strength. But vital economic lanes to Iraq from other neighbors were—even at the best of times—questionable, given Iraq's longstanding problems with Syria, Iran, and even Turkey, not to mention Iraq's recurring rifts with the Gulf states, and particularly Kuwait. Tying Jordan ever closer to the Iraqi economy would give Iraq at least one reliable ally, and one certain source of imports and outlet for key exports such as petroleum.

While Iraq had a series of strategic economic motives for the alignment, Jordan stood to benefit as well. Generous Iraqi aid to the kingdom had begun with Iraq's first overtures to the Hashimite regime, and continued to reinforce the predilection to turn toward Baghdad. This aid came not only from Iraq itself, but also from Saudi Arabia, which was also aligning more and more closely to Iraq at the same time Jordan was. In this sense, the alignment with Iraq carried direct benefits in terms of increased trade, aid, and access to Iraqi labor markets. In terms of trade, for example, by 1984 Iraq had become Jordan's largest import and export partner in the Arab world. In that year, Jordan exported U.S. $174.9 million worth of goods to Iraq, while imports were valued at U.S. $15.6 million. Although exports were relatively steady for the remainder of the decade, the import figures jumped to U.S. $190.4 million in 1985 and continued to increase each year thereafter. In short, the volume of trade increased dramatically as the alignment deepened, but Jordan's trade balance with Iraq gradually came to tip heavily in favor of Baghdad.[27]

Just as importantly, the alignment with Iraq gave Jordan greater access to the latter's Saudi ally as well, and here the flows of aid and labor in particular were even more critical to the Jordanian economy.[28] Once the war in the Persian Gulf began, Jordan had only more reasons to back the regime in Baghdad. Iraq had by then become Jordan's aid lifeline, its main source of oil, and eventually its largest regional trading partner. The economic benefits of alignment with Iraq also included a boon to Jordan's port of Aqaba as well as its overland transportation sector, as the kingdom became Iraq's main economic link to the outside world during the war with Iran. Finally, and less directly, the increasingly close alignment with the dominant Arab state in the Persian Gulf gave additional weight to Jordan's frequent requests for more aid from the oil-producing Arab Gulf states.

In return for Jordanian loyalty, Saddam Hussein's regime endorsed and pressed for Jordan's requests, giving these loan and grant applications the swagger power of a military giant, in a way that Jordan itself could never have achieved alone. Jordan's virtual aid bonanza had begun with the 1978 Arab League summit in Baghdad, amounting to $1 billion from Iraq and Saudi Arabia, dwarfing Jordan's then-current aid from all other sources.[29] These increasing economic linkages to Iraq and the Gulf states also helped add urgency to Jordan's fears regarding Iranian intentions in the Gulf. Interestingly, the increasing warmth of Jordanian-Iraqi relations from 1978 on, and the correspondingly increased level of tension between Jordan and Syria, while resulting in a political crisis and costing Jordan its Syrian alignment, nonetheless entailed relatively low economic costs. Indeed, even at the height of the tensions and angry diplomatic exchanges between the Jordan and Syria, trade relations continued and even industrial contracts, made before the collapse of the alignment, continued to be honored.[30]

Conclusions

Jordan's alignment shift from Syria to Iraq followed several steps. First, the initial impetus for the new alignment came not from Jordan, but from Iraq, as Saddam Hussein's regime actively courted the Hashimite Kingdom into its own orbit. At first the Jordanian regime attempted to gain the benefits of alignment with Iraq without alienating Syria at all. Given the deep hostility between the regimes in Damascus and Baghdad, however, for Jordan to maintain alignments with both Syria and Iraq soon proved impossible. The second step, then, came when Jordan was forced by its own feuding allies to choose which side it was on. In the end, it was the economic considerations that caused Jordan to side decisively with Iraq. And these economic benefits, as noted above, included not only increased aid, trade, and other sectoral linkages to Iraq itself, but also the lure of tapping into Gulf coffers for even more aid by joining into a larger alignment which was increasingly directed from Baghdad.

Iraq had started the realignment process when it launched the initiative urging the Arab states to meet the financial needs of the frontline Arab regimes, in response to the Camp David peace process. Iraq then added to this initiative more specifically during the 1978 summit, pushing the other oil states into supporting its efforts. As host of the conference, Saddam Hussein made ample use of his role to rally the Arab states, much to the financial gain of Jordan. These financial incentives were well worth the risk of damaging Jordan's relationship with Syria. Iraq offered larger markets for Jordanian goods, a massive increase in aid, and extensive oil resources—all of which Syria could not hope to match. Budget security, therefore, was a very important factor in the shift in alignment from Syria to Iraq. Yet this factor does not explain the depth of the alignment. Why did financial benefits amount to an actual alignment, and not just a warming of economic relations? Here the answer lies more squarely in the security dilemmas confronting the regime.

The third and final step in the realignment process occurred as the regional security situation changed dramatically, due to the Iranian revolution and later the outbreak of the Iran-Iraq war. It was then that the Jordanian regime chose to deepen its Iraqi relationship still further. The Jordanian alignment with Iraq was rooted partially in economic considerations, to be sure, but it was also and primarily the result of the regime's concerns for its own domestic stability and security.

The alignment shift did not, therefore, represent simply a balance-of-threats type of response to external stimuli. As this chapter has noted, the emergence of the revolutionary and belligerent regime in Tehran was viewed with trepidation by most Arab regimes, including monarchies like Jordan. But the Jordanian decision to stand firmly behind Iraq was not rooted in a concern for balancing against Iran as an external military threat. The Jordanians saw Iran as a potentially direct threat to their Arab Gulf *allies* (including Iraq and the Gulf monarchies), but not to Jordan directly. Rather, the Hashimite regime saw Iran as much more of an *internal* threat, specifically fearing Iran's revolutionary Islamist influence and its potential subversive actions against the regime's domestic security.

The perceived Iranian threat to Iraq and the Gulf states, in turn, threatened the two key pillars of the Jordanian economy: its aid sources from the Arab oil economies and its access to the labor markets in these same oil-producing countries. And finally, the regime was concerned with heading off domestic unrest, both from Palestinian agitation regarding a peace process that had left them out, and from Islamist militancy inspired by or even actively aided by Khomeini's Iran. For the Hashimite regime, the answer to both these potential sources of domestic instability lay in the same place: rapid improvement of the kingdom's domestic security and economic position in an effort to defuse radicalism and shore up the regime. The alignment with Iraq carried with it the means to provide an immediate stimulus to the economy, as well as prospects for a pattern of more permanent and consistent economic benefits.

The Hashimites were also allying themselves with a regime that styled itself (however dubiously) as leader of Pan-Arab nationalism. Working so closely with that regime in its war effort against Iran enhanced the Hashimite regime's otherwise shaky legitimacy. In an era that had seen the fall of two far more powerful, moderate, and pro-U.S. leaders—the Shah of Iran and President Anwar Sadat of Egypt—the Hashimites were understandably concerned with shoring up domestic regime legitimacy through enhanced Arab nationalist credentials, and hence these concerns underscore the normative dimension to regime security itself.

Jordan's concerns for the political and economic underpinnings of domestic regime security were so important, in fact, that the regime would later attempt not only to maintain its bilateral alignment with Iraq, but also to move beyond it by creating a multilateral alliance bloc in the form of the Arab Cooperation Council.

Jordan and the Arab Cooperation Council

On February 16, 1989, the heads of state of Egypt, Iraq, Jordan, and North Yemen met in Baghdad to announce the formation of the Arab Cooperation Council (Majlis al-Ta'awun al-'Arabi).[1] This chapter examines the Jordanian role in creating this new multilateral alignment and explains why the Hashimite regime seemed so intent on creating an alignment bloc for political and economic integration, rather than a more traditional military alliance.

The formation of the ACC reflected, in part, a broader trend in Arab regional politics, as its creation was followed the very next day by the formation of the Arab Maghrib Union (AMU), which included Algeria, Libya, Mauritania, Morocco, and Tunisia. Both the ACC and AMU had been preceded much earlier by the creation of the Gulf Cooperation Council (GCC) in 1981. The GCC included Bahrain, Kuwait, Oman, Qatar, Saudi Arabia, and the United Arab Emirates. In contrast to the ACC, both the GCC and AMU were more geographically centralized organizations, representing distinct sub-regions of the Arab world. Taken together, the presence of these three alignments within Arab politics meant that fifteen Arab states held membership in major economic and political blocs beyond the Arab League itself.

Perhaps just as important, however, was the list of countries left out of these blocs. That list included some of the most politically restive areas of the Middle East and North Africa, such as Sudan and Lebanon. But most glaring in its absence was one major regional power: Syria. As one of Jordan's former prime ministers noted:

> The ACC was our idea. Given the emergence of the GCC and the Maghrib Union, only the very heartland of the Arab world was left unorganized. We decided to settle this gap first, then move on to coordination between the three councils . . . As far as membership is concerned, the GCC had excluded Yemen, and the North African countries had excluded Egypt from the Maghrib Union.[2]

From the Jordanian regime's perspective, however, the absence of Syria was a hindrance to the long-term cooperation and success of the ACC, and this problem would eventually have to be redressed. Given the longstanding hostility between Iraq and Syria, however, the Jordanians were well aware that adding Syria to the alliance would be a difficult and lengthy task.[3] One of Jordan's former prime ministers made clear the dilemmas:

> Syria was in none of these groupings [the GCC, AMU, or ACC]. But we didn't forget Syria. They accepted to join the council in principal. But there were differences in procedures between Iraq and Syria. Syria wanted to join the council, then normalize relations with Iraq; while Iraq wanted to normalize relations with Syria, and then let it join the council. But in the end, there was not enough time. Other events intervened. First the events of April 1989 [the International Monetary Fund riots in Jordan] and then the Gulf war. This changed everything.[4]

The formation of these regional blocs caused a great deal of speculation regarding the future of inter-Arab politics. There was considerable optimism and hope placed in the three alignments, which seemed to many observers to mark the beginning of a new era in Arab politics, an era dominated by practical steps toward economic integration and political cooperation, rather than by the ideological conflicts that had long characterized inter-Arab power struggles.[5] The 1990 Iraqi invasion of Kuwait, however, would shatter many optimistic predictions and throw the entire Arab world into greater disorder. But before events in the Gulf brought the ACC to a standstill, real progress was made toward political cooperation and economic integration.[6]

The statutes and bylaws of the ACC declared that the main goal of the alignment was "the achievement of the highest degree of cooperation, coordination, integration and solidarity among the member states."[7] The ACC Charter stressed the economic dimensions of inter-Arab cooperation, in contrast to the ideological-political bases of earlier pan-Arab attempts at more formal unification. Even more conspicuously absent from the Charter was any mention of military ties amongst the member states.[8] As the following analysis reveals, however, the ACC did later move in the direction of greater security coordination.

Nonetheless, at first all emphasis was placed on economic cooperation. All four member states came into the ACC highly indebted, and all were still suffering from the decline in global oil prices. While this most directly affected Iraq as a major oil-producing country, it also strongly affected the other three states, whose economies had become tied to the regional economy of oil. As at least semi-rentier states, Egypt, Jordan, and North Yemen had become closely tied to and dependent on Gulf labor markets and hence on remittances from the Gulf. Each had felt the sting of the contracting regional oil economy.

Thus one purpose of the ACC was to facilitate labor flows between member states, particularly sending Jordanian and Egyptian labor to Iraq to assist in the reconstruction that followed the eight-year war with Iran. In June 1989, at the first ACC summit meeting, the four states agreed to abolish entry visa requirements between them, vastly facilitating the free flow of labor. Each member state further agreed to give hiring priority to ACC nationals over all other laborers.[9] Beyond concerns with labor flows, the ACC was also to serve as a common market to increase inter-Arab trade. Finally, an additional financial goal of the ACC was for all four states as a bloc to approach donor countries and institutions in renegotiating outstanding debts.[10]

Even though the ties of the ACC states were strengthened on the basis of mutual economic interest, it soon became clear that the member states differed considerably in their visions of the ACC's political role. But, at least initially, all four states shared in the general cooperation goals of the Jordanian policymakers who were among the prime movers behind the formation of the new regional alignment.[11]

External Security

Although the ACC member states emphasized at every opportunity the economic dimensions of their alignment, there were also broader political and strategic concerns at work. The ACC emerged in a context of major systemic changes, particularly at the regional level. The Iran-Iraq war had just been brought to a close, leading to considerable anxiety in the Gulf regarding future Iraqi intentions. And Iraq had, after all, been left out of the Gulf alignment when the Gulf Cooperation Council formed in 1981. The cessation of hostilities in the Persian Gulf marked a major strategic change in the regional system, and Iraq had throughout the war counted on the support of each of the other states that would soon comprise the ACC: Egypt, Jordan, and North Yemen. Each had supported the Iraqi war effort in various ways, but by far the most extensive support had come from Jordan.[12] As noted in the previous chapter, Jordan's port at Aqaba and its overland transport routes had provided Iraq with its only major economic lifeline during eight years of war. In a sense, the creation of the ACC simply institutionalized these bilateral linkages, transforming them into a multilateral alignment bloc.

For the Hashimite regime, however, the major regional changes that took place in the 1980s involved not only Gulf security, but also Jordan's role in the Arab-Israeli conflict. In 1988, King Hussein renounced Jordan's claims to the West Bank, thereby radically changing the strategic situation in the conflict and placing much of the burden of conflict resolution on the Israeli government and the PLO. With the renunciation of West Bank ties, however, Jordan's strategic role and position seemed suddenly unclear. Jordanian policymakers saw in the ACC a means to retain relevance and influence in regional politics beyond simply the longstanding tyranny of the shadow of the Arab-Israeli conflict.[13]

On the one hand, the ACC enhanced Jordan's diplomatic and military position vis-à-vis Israel, by bringing together in the same alignment Egypt (the only state to have signed a peace treaty with Israel) and Iraq (the state that Israel now viewed as one of its most serious military threats). Jordan was assured of having key allies, regardless of which contingency emerged in regional politics—either deepening of the peace process or further war. In essence, Jordan was in the pivotal position of bridging the gap between these two extremes, and therefore in a position to help extend the peace process to include even Iraq. In the event of increased tensions and hostility, Jordan would be backed up by a major military power. One of the most common terms used by Jordanian policymakers at this time, referring to the utility of their alignment with Iraq, was "strategic depth." That depth bolstered not only Jordan's external security vis-à-vis Israel, but also more tangentially the security of the Arab Gulf states (and hence Jordan's critical sources of aid) against threats from Iran.[14]

The strengthening of ties to Iraq and Egypt also enhanced Jordan's strategic position in relation to Syria. Here the regime took great pains not to isolate the Asad regime or to provoke it; at the same time, the new alignment ensured a more comfortable position between Jordan and its northern neighbor. Either Syria would join the ACC at a later date, nullifying any Jordanian-Syrian tensions, or it would be held in check by Jordan's powerful Arab allies, even if hostility were to reemerge between Amman and Damascus.[15]

Thus, even without formal defense agreements initially, the ACC was a formidable bloc among other states in the region, a bloc that could act as a powerful deterrent against potential attackers. Yet the presence of both Iraq and Egypt in the same regional alignment created considerable uncertainty and security fears in neighboring states. Marshalling together the military might of both Egypt and Iraq was reassuring indeed for Jordan's Hashimite regime, but it was worrisome for the Israeli government and for the ruling regimes in Kuwait, Saudi Arabia, and Syria.[16] The ACC represented a profound imbalance of regional military might within the Arab world.

In the view of Jordan's former Prime Minister Zayd al-Rifa'i, the ACC added an unwanted layer of tension to Saudi-Jordanian relations, which only worsened later with the onset of the 1990–1991 Gulf crisis. In March 1989, shortly after the ACC was founded, Saudi King Fahd made a high-profile visit to both Cairo and Baghdad, seeking reassurances regarding the security implications of the new alliance. Saudi anxiety was deep enough that King Fahd even signed a non-aggression pact with Iraq before leaving Baghdad.[17]

Largely to reassure other Arab states, particularly Saudi Arabia, the ACC states repeatedly stressed the economic dimensions of their alignment and denied any political or military intentions. But during the June 1989 meeting of their Supreme Council (made up of the four heads of state) in Alexandria, Egypt, the ACC countries called for greater coordination of their foreign policies, agreed not to use force amongst themselves, and further committed themselves to the establishment of a joint defense pact.[18]

These developments may have only added to the security anxieties of Kuwait, Saudi Arabia, and Syria, reinforcing their earliest suspicions regarding ACC intentions. All three countries had reason to fear any resurgence of Iraqi power in the wake of the recent Iran-Iraq war. In their attempts to calm these fears, the ACC states stressed that—unlike the other two Arab regional organizations, the Gulf Cooperation Council (GCC) and the Arab Maghrib Union (AMU)—the ACC was not limited in its membership to a geographical subregion, but was instead open to all Arab states that wished to apply for membership. Comparing the openness of the ACC with the exclusivity of the GCC, one Jordanian policymaker dismissed the Gulf organization as "exclusively an oil-producing countries country club."[19]

For the Jordanians, however, the key question was the role that Syria would play. To avoid Syrian hostility, the Hashimite regime kept the Syrians apprised of all developments and made clear to them that the new axis was not actually intended to oppose any state. King Hussein, in an effort to extend the membership of the ACC, further made use of his personal diplomacy in an attempt to reconcile Iraq and Syria. As early as 1986, before the ACC had come to fruition, the Jordanians arranged a secret meeting between Syrian President Hafiz al-Asad and Iraqi President Saddam Hussein at an air base in southern Jordan.[20] The attempt at mediation and inter-Arab reconciliation was unsuccessful.

Although Jordan's various efforts failed, they did not go unappreciated in Damascus. The Ba'thist regime made clear that, while it would not itself become an ACC member, it would not oppose the grouping. Syrian officials, however, still regarded the assorted subregional organizations—the ACC, GCC, and AMU—all, by subdividing the Arab world, as counterproductive to real Arab unity. From the Syrians' perspective, in short, the three alignments were working backwards. In addition, the Syrians made clear that they did not expect the ACC to last long.[21]

Although the Jordanians, as ACC members, felt themselves to be in a more comfortable external security position, security considerations were not the sole causes of the alignment. Rather, Jordanian policymakers viewed the military strength of their Egyptian and Iraqi allies as an additional asset to a largely economically oriented alignment. The strategic depth gained by the political-economic alignment was, in short, an added bonus.[22] Indeed, the Hashimite regime was deeply concerned with its decaying economic position and with rising domestic insecurity. Thus, while the creation of the ACC caused non-member states to reexamine their strategic positions and to assess the security implications of the new alignment, external security concerns do not appear to have been the primary motivation for the alignment, even on the part of the militarily weak Jordanians, much less of the Egyptians or Iraqis. It is necessary, therefore, to look elsewhere for the main motivations behind the ACC.

Domestic Politics

The decision to pursue the formation of the ACC came in a context of profound domestic change in Jordan. Like many other states in the region, Jordan's domestic political and economic scene had been deeply affected by the decline in the regional economy. For many years, the Jordanian regime had been able to ride the wave of the oil boom, growing increasingly reliant on external sources of aid to meet its budgetary needs, but by the mid-1980s that boom had long since ended. As aid and worker remittances declined and the domestic economy contracted, the Jordanian regime was forced into an extremely unfavorable economic position.

In addition to Jordan's declining regional economic fortunes, the Hashimite regime also felt the pressures of change in the global East-West struggle.

With the Cold War drawing to a close, the Western powers became less interested in Jordan as a geostrategic asset, and hence their external aid and support for Jordan also declined. This exacerbated the country's already difficult economic situation. The increasingly severe economic constraints soon affected the domestic stability and security of the Hashimite regime, leading to rioting and political violence in April 1989, in response to an austerity program sponsored by the International Monetary Fund (IMF).[23]

The April riots, sometimes referred to within Jordan as an *intifada* (uprising), reflected far more than economic unrest.[24] The IMF program had merely provided the spark for an explosion of much deeper dissatisfaction with the regime. While the Hashimites had been aware of their increasingly precarious economic position, they had sorely underestimated the political depth of their legitimacy crisis vis-à-vis their own society. It is perhaps ironic that this unequivocal signal to the regime occurred within months of the founding of the ACC. Most importantly, the April riots were not really reflective of the usual Palestinian versus Transjordanian—or West Banker versus East Banker—rift within Jordanian society, but rather were instigated largely from within the East Banker community itself. Indeed, the unrest originated in Ma'an, in the south of Jordan, a community that the regime took for granted as a bedrock constituency for the House of Hashim.

The domestic unrest served as a wake-up call for the regime, prompting the government to accelerate its already initiated program of political reform.[25] The Hashimites had attempted as early as 1984 to adjust domestically to more difficult circumstances through a program of limited political liberalization, intended to broaden the bases of the regime's domestic support coalition and to co-opt broad segments of Jordanian society.[26] But except for the recall of parliament in 1984 (for the first time since 1967), little else had been accomplished, despite considerable rhetoric. With the political upheaval in 1989, however, the regime rapidly increased its project of renegotiating a kind of social contract with its populace. Given the depth of public anger, this project required significant concessions. The cabinet was reshuffled and the extremely unpopular prime minister, Zayd al-Rifa'i, was sacked. New elections were announced and held in the same year. Additional measures would eventually be taken to loosen government oversight of the media, lift marshal law, and legalize political parties.[27] After earlier stalling tactics and disappointments, the political liberalization process finally appeared to be at a real takeoff point.[28]

What is significant about these events is the depth of the regime's domestic insecurity as the Hashimites worked to bring the ACC to fruition. In effect, the regime was pursuing both domestic and foreign policies designed to re-achieve long-term stability for Jordan and—most importantly—the long-term survival of the Hashimite regime. A major domestic program was required to reestablish sufficient domestic legitimacy, while external alignments were needed to shore up the regime through increased aid and market access. In this difficult domestic context, the ACC can be seen as the external vestige of a broader adjustment program to ensure the long-term viability and survivability of the Hashimite regime.

Thus the regime's decision to opt for an alignment that would aggressively pursue genuine economic integration must be seen in this context of severe insecurity in domestic politics. While the regime saw internal political liberalization as a necessary measure when the regime's domestic insecurity seemed dangerously precarious, the external side of this broader adjustment strategy—the ACC itself—was the foreign policy side of the regime's agenda. While the April riots reinforced the regime's desire to achieve meaningful cooperation in the new alignment, they also forced a set of reform policies on the domestic front. In this sense, the regime was attempting to balance between and in effect mollify its internal and external security dilemmas. In any case, the regime felt that the success or failure of either front lay in more stable external economic and political relationships.[29] These were the keys to long-term regime security.

The domestic liberalization process, however, also served to open the system to greater political activity on the part of elites who were highly enthusiastic about the potential of the ACC. The liberalization effort, in fact, helped create new policy coalitions and also opened the way for them to have more influence on the political process than ever before. This enhanced the political role of the commercial bourgeoisie in particular, which found some of its interests in sync with those of the Hashimite monarchy. One aspect of this policy convergence was the push for market access to increase Jordan's export profits. Already heavily engaged in Iraqi markets, Jordan's export sectors wanted to increase their access to Egyptian markets, and also to have an institutional and organizational structure to ensure that increased access would continue and could therefore be relied on.[30]

Since the private sector was largely dominated by Palestinians, favorable regime policies toward increased market access functioned as payoffs to co-opt this key segment of Jordanian society at a particularly difficult time economically and politically. The export industries that benefitted the most from Jordan's increased trade and investment relations with Iraq, and later with Egypt and North Yemen, included agriculture, cement, fertilizers, and pharmaceuticals.[31] By working with these elite segments within the Jordanian political economy—including ethnic Transjordanians dominant in the public sector export industries—the regime met their demands for increased inter-Arab trade.

This trade came at a critical time, not only because of change in the global and regional economy, but also in the wake of the regime's renunciation of ties to the West Bank, which forced Jordan's majority Palestinian population to reassess its loyalties. The trade and investment potential that the ACC embodied may have helped to bridge the Palestinian-Jordanian divide at an otherwise awkward time, with favorable results for the regime's domestic security and stability. Inter-Arab trade amounted, therefore, to much more than budget security alone. The state was not so much filling its own coffers as it was allowing key domestic constituencies to fill theirs.

One of the Jordanian political economy sectors that most strongly pursued the formation of the ACC and the strengthening of existing ties with Iraq was the construction industry. Compared to its counterparts in Egypt and Iraq, this sector was relatively small. But the elites involved in this industry, in both the public and private sector, saw in the post-war reconstruction of Iraq the potential for windfall profits. Just as the overland transportation sector and the port of Aqaba had benefitted from the Gulf War by acting as Iraq's main supply lines, the construction industry believed that it was poised to reap the financial benefits of peace.

In sum, the Hashimite regime's effort to bring together the ACC was deeply influenced by domestic insecurity and the resultant need to adjust to severe domestic challenges and changing economic conditions. Key domestic variables included not only the regime's concerns for its own security and survival, but also the opening of the political system and the emergence of pro-ACC constituencies.

Political Economy

The founders of the ACC went to great lengths to stress the economic dimensions of the alignment, downplaying any security implications and underscoring the benefits of joint economic action. While domestic politics played an important role in the formation of the ACC, there were also broader economic trends that influenced the particular form of the new Arab alignment, as well as that of the Arab Maghrib Union in Northwest Africa. Both organizations were influenced by the earlier formation of the Gulf Cooperation Council. Some analysts have suggested that the similarity in the names of the GCC and the ACC underscores the influence of the former on the latter.[32]

Perhaps of more importance, however, was the larger systemic economic change found in the looming 1992 date for full European integration. Like other areas of the world, the Arab states of the ACC were influenced by the shifts in the global economy in the direction of larger trading blocs. And they were particularly concerned with the economic implications of European integration for their own extensive European trade links.[33]

In terms of its inter-Arab dimensions, economic coordination within the ACC was to include free movement of labor and capital among member states, as well as increasing communication and transportation linkages between them.[34] Economic integration was also to include joint projects in manufacturing and agricultural production. In addition to agreements on cooperation in industry, agriculture, transportation, communications, and labor flows, the ACC states also agreed to greater coordination in social affairs, including education, health, and cultural exchange. The agreements of the ACC made clear that the four-country grouping was seen as simply the beginning of a larger alignment dedicated to "comprehensive Arab economic integration."[35]

Jordan's push for the establishment of the ACC came in a dismal economic context. With the drop in the regional economy, the resultant painful decline in Arab aid to Jordan had helped create a payment crisis for the regime, which became clear in February 1989—just as the ACC was founded—and led to extreme instability for the Jordanian dinar.[36] The precipitous decline in oil prices, Arab aid, and remittances from Jordanian labor had revealed a deep and dangerous debt situation for the kingdom. Summing up the extent of Jordan's debt crisis in 1989, one economic analysis noted that "debt servicing has emerged as the millstone around Jordan's neck."[37]

One of the most blatant signs of Jordan's increasing difficulty was the decision by the government to have Jordan's Central Bank cease all loan repayments to individual country lenders (two-thirds of the national debt) beginning in January 1989. This policy was only announced, however, in March of 1989, when the government also made clear that it had very reluctantly turned to the International Monetary Fund and the World Bank to request a rescheduling of its debt repayments.[38]

As noted earlier in this chapter, in the discussion of domestic politics, the IMF-sponsored austerity program triggered a violent public response. The riots of April 1989 shocked not only the Hashimite regime, but also the Arab Gulf states, many of whom quickly responded by rushing emergency transfers of aid and even oil shipments to the kingdom in an attempt at shoring up the monarchy and reestablishing stability in Jordan. While the Jordanian authorities welcomed these critical grants of economic support, there was nonetheless bitterness at both the elite and popular level that severe domestic upheaval had been needed before such aid began to arrive. The official government line on the disturbances, for example, included scathing attacks on these same Gulf states for failing to fulfill their pledges of aid which had been made at the 1978 Baghdad summit.[39] In short, the regime was quick to place the blame on policies outside its own control, rather than focus on economic mismanagement or political bungling in the country's domestic affairs. Public hostility, however, was more far-reaching in its accusations, and even delegations of East Bank or Transjordanian elites, the traditional basis for Hashimite rule, carried petitions to the king, demanding political reform. Public concern and scorn was directed in particular at government nepotism and corruption.

While much of this hostility was directed at government ministers, and particularly at the soon-to-be-sacked Prime Minister Zayd al-Rifa'i, the general disillusionment with the ruling elite continued toward the governments that followed. After the 1989 elections, for example, the caretaker government of Zayd Ibn Shakir was replaced by that of a very familiar prime minister, Mudar Badran, who then came under verbal attack for his earlier political service. Badran, a longtime loyalist and confidante of the king, had previously served as prime minister for most of the period from 1976 to 1984. In the emerging climate of political liberalization and greater openness of the media, inter-elite squabbles also came to the fore. A surprised Badran actually had to fight to win a vote of confidence in the parliament in order to begin his new administration, fending off attacks by other powerful elites regarding the ethics of his own previous public service.[40]

Despite the political fallout that continued in Jordan in the years following the April 1989 uprising, the immediate effects of the quick money transfers from sympathetic Arab regimes in the Gulf, coupled with the IMF agreement, did ease Jordan's balance of payments difficulties. But at the same time, the political uprising had also underscored not only the need for a new and firmer domestic basis for the regime's rule, but also the need for more durable arrangements for Jordan's external economic relations. This need added extra importance to the formation of the ACC, as it provided the regime with an institutional structure for economic integration with its allies—integration which, it was hoped, would boost the Jordanian economy as a whole.

Thus the main reason the Jordanians were careful to reassure the Gulf states about the ACC's intentions had little to do with the alignment's military and security implications. Rather, the Jordanians wanted to make sure that while they were reaping the economic benefits of their membership in the ACC, they were not sacrificing the kingdom's critical aid and labor linkages to the GCC states.

In sum, the Hashimite regime's overriding concern with its own security and long-term maintenance was focused not only on re-establishing a stable domestic political foundation for its rule, but also on the regime's dependence on external economic allies. The external economic linkages of Jordan's alignment strategy were consequently a vital part of the Hashimite regime's domestic security. The regime attempted to mold the ACC specifically to meet Jordan's economic needs, which were, in turn, seen as the critical underpinnings of the regime's long term survival.

Conclusions

The short-lived Arab Cooperation Council found itself essentially defunct following Iraq's 1990 invasion of Kuwait. In the resulting 1990–1991 Gulf crisis, the two most powerful ACC states—Egypt and Iraq—abruptly lined up on opposite sides. Both Jordan and Yemen, meanwhile, made awkward but sincere attempts at mediation; their attempts cost the two states dearly in their relations with the GCC states. But even before the crisis marked the end of the ACC, the member states had run into difficulties in moving beyond political and economic coordination, toward more extensive security cooperation.

Ultimately, the problems here turned on fundamentally different visions of the political role of the ACC. For the Jordanians, the ACC was a political-economic bloc that would start with the four countries and later extend to a far broader regional alignment. Yemen appeared to share this general view. But the real problem lay with the two more powerful members, as Iraq made consistent attempts to politicize the ACC and bring it in line with Iraqi foreign policy, particularly as a force against Syria. Egypt strongly resisted these attempts and tried to avoid closer political or security ties while stressing the purely economic aspect of the alignment.[41]

In some respects Egypt had accomplished its main goal for the ACC, once the country—largely through ACC pressure—was readmitted to the Arab League. For Iraq, in contrast, the political and economic linkages within the alignment were only the beginning of a broader political agenda. These ulterior motives led to conflict within the alignment and to considerable resentment on the part of the Jordanians. While the Jordanians believed in the greater potential of the ACC, they felt that their two larger partners may have been pursuing cynical political strategies from the start.

Reflecting on what went wrong with the ACC, one Jordanian official remarked that, while Jordan and Yemen worked well together, "the other two were of course trying to dominate the show." Another official concluded with more bitterness that "the ACC was a disaster. We wanted a forum for economic and political cooperation, the Egyptians wanted purely an economic forum, and the Iraqis just wanted to take advantage of us."[42]

With the Iraqi invasion of Kuwait, much of this debate became moot. The ACC never officially collapsed, yet neither did it revive. In sharp contrast to the fanfare and the ceremony that had marked the inauguration of the new alignment in 1989, the ACC in essence simply faded away as its charter expired in 1991 and continuing hostility between key members prevented its renewal.

In terms of the theoretical conclusions that can be drawn from this case study of Jordan and the Arab Cooperation Council, a full explanation of Jordan's alignment decisions can be found through a regime-security perspective. External security concerns and the regional balance of threats were not major variables leading Jordanian decision-makers to form the ACC. Economic factors, on the other hand, appeared to be a more important motivation for this alignment.

Yet the regime was also highly motivated by domestic regime insecurity, in which its defensive response—the political liberalization process—began transforming Jordanian domestic politics. This process, in turn, allowed constituencies within Jordanian society (particularly in the public and private business sectors) to attempt to mold the ACC in directions favorable to themselves, and in particular to their material well-being. The regime saw this alignment, then, as a way to assuage many constituencies within Jordanian domestic politics, thereby easing the internal security dilemma that had erupted in such force in the 1989 riots.

The domestic imperative was so great, in fact, that the external alignment was not itself sufficient to shore up the regime economically and politically. Rather, the domestic side to the regime's strategy of adjusting to dramatically changing conditions was now expected, by the Jordanian public, to finally move beyond cosmetic reform to include a more genuine process of liberalization and democratization. This domestic reform process would further serve to increase the role that domestic politics would play in the next case of Jordanian alliance decisions and foreign policy: the kingdom's response to the 1990–1991 Gulf crisis.

Jordan and the First U.S.-Iraq War

With the onset of the Persian Gulf Crisis of 1990–1991, Jordan's main Arab alliance, the Arab Cooperation Council, became instantly deadlocked as its two most powerful members—Iraq and Egypt—shifted overnight from alignment partners to military adversaries. Notwithstanding the numerous Hashimite attempts at defusing the crisis, the ACC proved an empty shell in the face of its own members' hostility to one another. And after the crisis, when the smoke had cleared from Operation "Desert Storm," few noticed that the deadline for renewal of the ACC charter had come and gone.

The ACC was, for all intents and purposes, dead; yet the Jordanian architects of that regional bloc had a profound decision to make in their alignment relationships for the immediate future. Which set of Arab and non-Arab allies would Jordan support as the threat of war loomed closer and closer? To the surprise and chagrin of its Western allies, Jordan's historically conservative and pro-Western regime did not follow conventional expectations and support the U.S.-led coalition against Iraq. To the contrary, the Hashimites were charged (falsely) with aiding and abetting the aggressive regime of Saddam Hussein. With the entire region undergoing a massive realignment, Jordan was one of the few countries that did *not* realign. Rather, it maintained its alignment with Iraq while simultaneously attempting to appease all sides of the crisis. This chapter examines the Jordanian response to the Gulf crisis, and particularly examines Jordan's alignment decision, which confounded most contemporary observers and analysts, seeming to defy all predictions.

Between Iraq and a Hard Place? Jordan's Dilemma

While it has become conventional to date the onset of the Persian Gulf Crisis to the Iraqi invasion of Kuwait on August 2, 1990, in reality the regional crisis had been underway for several months, only coming to a head with the invasion. Indeed, the invasion itself signalled the end of the earlier crisis—that between Iraq and Kuwait—and marked the beginning of a new crisis well beyond the Gulf region alone.[1]

The earlier, more localized, crisis had emerged in the wake of Iraq's eight-year war with Iran. In the period between the cessation of hostilities in 1988 and the invasion of Kuwait in 1990, the Iraqi regime had concentrated on rebuilding its war-torn country and had also actively asserted its regional leadership and status, largely in an effort to gain much-needed aid from the Gulf states to finance post-war reconstruction. Iraq had steadily increased its demands for aid and also for concessions in oil pricing policies within OPEC, culminating in a series of diatribes by Iraqi officials against both Kuwait and the United Arab Emirates.

The Iraqi-Kuwaiti crisis escalated with the deployment of additional Iraqi troops to the Kuwaiti border in mid-July 1990. While some observers may have believed the crisis to have been quickly defused following the show of force, all such perceptions were quickly dashed by the sudden invasion of Kuwait on August 2.[2] The surprise invasion, in turn, triggered a new crisis, far more global in scope than the Iraqi-Kuwaiti dispute itself.

Within 24 hours, Iraq infantry and armored units had crushed Kuwaiti opposition and consolidated control over the small country. Although the crisis began as the most severe of inter-Arab conflicts, Kuwait's geo-strategic importance to the major industrial powers of the world ensured that it quickly became a global concern. The international political confrontation that followed the invasion was succeeded, in turn, by a major regional war as an international coalition of forces, led by the United States, inflicted a devastating defeat on the Iraqis between January and March 1991. The defeat of Saddam Hussein's armed forces resulted in Iraqi withdrawal from Kuwait and hence in the political liberation of that Gulf emirate.

Within hours of the news of the initial invasion, the Jordanian position began to form, and was repeated consistently in the months that followed, right up to the outbreak of the war in January 1991. King Hussein immediately attempted to take on the role of mediator in the crisis and began a lengthy set of shuttle diplomacy missions to various capitals. The Jordanian government attempted to forge a role for itself as a neutral mediator between the Iraqi and Kuwaiti regimes, and in a broader sense, between Iraq and the rest of the Arab world.

As the crisis become increasingly global in scope, the Jordanian effort at avoiding war expanded accordingly. In the first four weeks following the invasion, the king had shuttled to the capitals of Middle Eastern countries including Algeria, Libya, Mauritania, Morocco, Sudan, Tunisia, and Yemen, as well as those of European states including France, Italy, Germany, Spain, and the United Kingdom. The king had further maintained frequent contact with Husni Mubarak of Egypt, King Fahd of Saudi Arabia, and Saddam Hussein of Iraq, and had met with United States President George Bush at Kennebunkport, Maine. In short, the Gulf Crisis was clearly deemed urgent enough to the Hashimite regime's own security that personal diplomacy at the highest possible level was exercised in what would ultimately be a failed effort to avert war.

In all these visits by the king, and by Jordanian government officials to other countries, the Jordanian position was reiterated. Jordan rejected the admissibility of the acquisition of territory through conquest, but it also rejected foreign intervention. The only lasting solution to the crisis, King Hussein asserted, had to be within "an Arab framework only."[3] Critics of the Jordanian position tended to see this as simply waffling or an awkward attempt at fence-straddling at best. As tensions mounted, however, the predominant view, particularly in the Western capitals, was that Jordan had allied itself with Saddam Hussein and against its longstanding friends in the West, as well as against pro-Western regimes in the Arab world, such as those in Egypt and Saudi Arabia. A more accurate view, however, might see Jordan's position—for good or ill—as the very definition of a balanced, middle-of-the-road stance.

Regardless of how one chooses to see the Jordanian stand, the context of the decision-making process remains the same. Jordan's decisions were taken in the context of extreme vulnerability, both domestically and region ally, in which no choice was without heavy costs. Jordan called for Iraqi withdrawal, continued to recognize the al-Sabah government of Kuwait, and rejected the Iraqi claim to have annexed Kuwait. While many individual Jordanians signed up as volunteers to defend Iraq, the Jordanian armed forces were strictly neutral and did not fight alongside the Iraqi army. Contrary to Western and Gulf views of the Jordanian stance, Jordanian policymakers saw themselves as having picked neither side in the looming conflict. Just as importantly, they saw themselves as among the very few (along with their colleagues in Yemen) who were attempting to find a diplomatic and peaceful solution to the crisis. Marwan al-Qasim, Jordan's Foreign Minister during the Gulf crisis, emphasized Jordan's efforts at conflict resolution:

Why were we ostracized during this period? Immediately when King Hussein heard of the invasion that morning, in a call from King Fahd, he (Hussein) felt that it could blow up beyond the region. Our policy was one of containment from 5 a.m. that morning onward. We tried to set up an ACC summit meeting in Saudi Arabia, to come up with a solution, which would include an Iraqi withdrawal.[4]

Perhaps one reason for the differing interpretations of Jordan's Gulf War alignment position is the failure to differentiate between official Jordanian government policy and the popular mood of the Jordanian people. Indeed, Jordanian street demonstrations in favor of Saddam and against the West were broadcast repeatedly throughout the world. While these media broadcasts accurately conveyed the mood of many Jordanians during the Gulf crisis, they were too often seen as synonymous with Jordan's official stance. Jordanian Foreign Minister Qasim emphasized "the difference between the emotional response of the people, in the streets and so on, and the posture outlined by the king." Suggesting that some of the misperception was willful, he continued, "but in the West, Jordan's position was seen as that of the street. Some misunderstood. Some understood but had an interest in a misperception of Jordan's policy."[5] In reality, there was a critical difference between the popular and official positions, as the considerable enthusiasm on the part of the public contrasted markedly with the Jordanian government's anxiousness to avoid a regional confrontation.

Adnan Abu 'Awdah, King Hussein's national security advisor during the crisis, also noted the disconnect between state and society, and the failure of many outside Jordan to appreciate the domestic pressures on the regime:

Jordan did not realign. Jordan in fact refused to go to a certain camp. Refused the division. Jordan did not accept the invasion of Kuwait and certainly did not accept its annexation. But Jordan differed from the Arab states that allied with Saudi Arabia over one important point: that the solution to this problem should be, should take place within the Arab League . . . what made things more difficult and complicated was the way the Jordanian people reacted. The Jordanian people reacted by being on the side of Iraq. So the American media did not find difficulty portraying Jordan as being on the Iraqi side.[6]

Indeed, many members of the international media were in fact covering the crisis and war from Jordan, not Iraq, and may therefore have been more likely to amplify this general representation of Jordan. As Abu 'Awdah added, "Amman was the nearest station to Baghdad. And they (the journalists) came here, and it was a fact that the people were sympathizing with Iraq, and so Jordan was taken to be on the other side."[7]

In their quest to avert a new regional war, Jordanian officials engaged in a concerted effort at mediating and defusing the crisis. An initial component of this strategy was to thwart any official condemnation of Iraq by the League of Arab States, particularly before a mini-summit could be convened in Jiddah, Saudi Arabia, which was to include a direct meeting between Iraqi and Kuwaiti officials. Saddam Hussein's promises to King Hussein of withdrawal from Kuwait were predicated on preventing an Arab League Resolution against Iraq. In this context, Jordanian Foreign Minister Marwan al-Qasim was dispatched to the meeting of Arab foreign ministers in Cairo to argue against such a resolution. "If the resolution proposed (condemning Iraq) is adopted," Qasim argued, "then there will not be a summit, and this will encourage foreign and hostile forces and will pave the way for foreign involvement."[8] Such involvement, he suggested, would be beyond the scope of the Arab states to contain.

Yet the resolution passed, with abstentions only by Jordan, Algeria, and Yemen, while Sudan, the PLO, and Mauritania expressed reservations. Arab League Resolution 195 condemned Iraqi aggression, rejected annexation, called for Iraqi troops to withdraw, and authorized Arab forces to defend Saudi Arabia and other Gulf states.[9] The battle over the resolution deepened the antagonisms between Arab states and also increased the conviction, held by many Jordanian policymakers, that key Arab states such as Egypt and Saudi Arabia were under severe pressure from the United States. The U.S. government also tried, unsuccessfully, to influence Jordan to support the coalition. Yet Jordanian policy makers operated under an additional series of constraints, all of which pointed to maintaining the same policy— rejecting the invasion while continuing to work against foreign military involvement and war. In addition to obvious fears of a confrontation with Israel if the war spread beyond the Gulf, Jordanian policy makers worked in the context of strong domestic and economic pressures as well.

External Security

Jordanian policy makers believed that their options were constrained by their vulnerable geographical position and their social, political, and economic links with the various participants in the ever-widening crisis, particularly their links with fellow Arab states. Despite Jordan's being linked within the same alliance as Iraq, the latter's invasion of Kuwait seems to have come as a surprise to Jordan as well as to Egypt and Yemen.[10] But Iraq and Egypt, at least, were unequivocal in their changed alignment positions. Friends had become enemies overnight, and soon Egyptian troops would be facing their Iraqi counterparts across the deserts of Kuwait. For Jordan, however, no such clarity of position was believed to be prudent or feasible. Indeed, every policy option seemed to lead to the destruction of Jordan's carefully constructed system of allies. The Jordanian government consequently hurled itself in between the Arab antagonists—between Iraq, Egypt, Kuwait, and Saudi Arabia—in an effort to head off the inter-Arab confrontation entirely.

The Hashimite regime's first goal was "containment."[11] The crisis was not to be permitted to go beyond that of the "Arab family."[12] King Hussein and his government ministers warned the other Arab states of the dangers of internationalizing the crisis: it could only mean foreign intervention, thereby escalating the crisis and perhaps creating a broader conflict with the potential to engulf the entire region. The depth of feeling beneath these dire predictions should not be underestimated. Indeed, the mood of the king and Jordanian government officials was often nothing short of apocalyptic. If the crisis could not be handled within the Arab camp, the prescription was certain to involve war; and many Jordanians believed that such a war would inevitably bring in Israel, making Jordan a battleground in an Israeli-Iraqi confrontation.

It should be remembered that the Gulf crisis had followed quickly on the heels of Iraqi threats of chemical weapons attacks on Israel—threats made only months before the invasion of Kuwait. While these threats were certainly received with alarm in Israel, they were a source of mixed emotions for most Jordanian officials. On the one hand, they welcomed a powerful Arab leader who would give "strategic depth" to the kingdom in its dealings with Israel. On the other hand, they worried about such reckless threats on the part of their ally. They feared, therefore, a key feature of the alliance security dilemma: being dragged into an unnecessary war by one's own ally.

Not only were Jordanian officials convinced that their own military forces were no match for the Israelis, but they were also deeply aware that they—and not Iraq—shared the longest border with Israel. It was Jordan that would bear the brunt of any Israeli offensive, not Iraq. Thus Iraqi belligerency, while popular with the Jordanian public, was also the source of considerable uneasiness for regime officials. Some were skeptical whether Saddam Hussein would ever follow through with his threats. Others, however, noted that after its verbal attacks on Kuwait the Iraqi regime had demonstrated clearly that it would back up its threats with extreme force.[13]

As a result, some Jordanian officials were unsure which threat to fear more: their enemy to the West, Israel, or their "ally" to the East, Iraq. Saddam Hussein had, after all, lied to his ACC allies about his passive intentions vis-à-vis Kuwait, and he had demonstrated fully his willingness to invade one Arab country; why shouldn't his allies worry about the future directions of his aggression? Even for those policymakers who held no such reservations about their Iraqi alignment partner, there remained the threat of an Iraqi-Israeli confrontation. Once the crisis in the Gulf began, the issue of which country might start such a conflict became largely a moot point. Regardless of whether Israel or Iraq fired the first shots, the Jordanians were well aware it was Jordan that would suffer the most.[14]

Yet if the crisis could be contained, and international confrontation avoided, an Iraqi withdrawal could perhaps be achieved. While some might argue that an Iraqi retreat was never likely, the fact remains that many Jordanian top officials believed Iraqi withdrawal to be a real possibility, so long as Arab and Western states allowed Jordan enough time to mediate and took no provocative action against Iraq. What is important in assessing Jordanian policy is not Iraqi intentions, but rather the perceptions held by Jordan's policymakers of those intentions. Jordan's Foreign Minister Qasim noted Jordan's weakness vis-à-vis its neighbors, and hence the inherent difficulty of taking what in effect was a principled stand. "Our borders make us more vulnerable even than Kuwait . . . we couldn't condone a coercive act of one state against another," he stated, but noted further that Jordan had to avoid turning its allies into enemies in the heat of the crisis.[15]

It seems clear that Jordanian officials believed in their own abilities, and especially the good offices of the king, in persuading Saddam Hussein to withdraw his armies from Kuwait, averting a regional war. The Jordanians were to be uniformly disappointed in these efforts, although, in the aftermath of the war, there was widespread disagreement among Jordanian officials regarding who was more at fault—the U.S.-led coalition or the Iraqi regime.[16]

Clearly, the Jordanians felt threatened from multiple directions. Yet, if we were to analyze the Jordanian alignment stance based only on Walt's Neorealist framework, we would have to focus only on external security stimuli and choose to label the Jordanian position as either balancing or bandwagoning.[17] No other policy options seem to be available. And once again, a domestically and regionally insecure regime such as Jordan demonstrates the inadequacy of a limited and stark set of options. That the Jordanians were able to finesse seemingly limited political situations, developing more nuanced and middling policies designed specifically to avoid such stark outcomes as those posited in the Walt framework, is one of the reasons King Hussein and Jordan itself were regularly described as "survivors" in Middle East politics.[18]

It is a mistake, therefore, to characterize the Jordanian position as a simple case of either balancing or bandwagoning. Jordan during the Gulf crisis demonstrated once again the fine art of fence-straddling. By attempting to alienate no one, however, the Hashimite regime may well have succeeded instead in alienating almost everyone, at least for a time. Jordan rejected the invasion while also rejecting Western military intervention. It continued to recognize the al-Sabah government of Kuwait while also refusing to abandon Iraq entirely. And perhaps most importantly, it sent none of its armed forces to assist either the U.S.-led coalition or Saddam Hussein's army, while also remaining noticeably lax in its enforcement of the embargo against Iraq. In sum, Jordan was even more middling in its tightrope walk through the Gulf crisis than it had been back in 1973, during another regional crisis and the resulting Arab-Israeli war.

Although the external security threats to Jordan could be seen as abundant and coming from several possible directions, they were neither new, nor were they determinate in Jordan's ultimate alignment decision. Although the regime clearly was concerned with the dangers that regional war would present to Jordan and to the regime itself, it was at least as concerned with a security threat from another direction, regardless of which way regional events unfolded: the threat from *within*. In making the decisions regarding Jordan's external alignment stance, the regime weighed carefully its domestic situation, particularly in light of the popular outpouring of enthusiasm for Saddam Hussein.

In retrospect the stability and durability of the Hashimite monarchy at that time is readily apparent, but Jordanian elites themselves were under no such illusions at the height of the crisis. King Hussein in particular chose to run largely with the public, rather than against them. In short, the key to understanding Jordan's Gulf crisis alignment stance lies not in external balancing or bandwagoning, but in the regime's domestic relations with its own society.

Domestic Politics

The Jordanian alignment decision during the Gulf crisis must be understood in the context of profound change in the domestic politics of the kingdom. As noted in the previous chapter, Jordan in 1989 began a process of political liberalization that opened up its political landscape, creating and energizing a domestic public sphere debate across a host of issues, including foreign policy. It would be an overstatement to describe Jordan's reform initiatives as full-scale democratization; rather, the process is better termed liberalization, in the sense of opening up the political system to more (but not unlimited) participation. For Jordan's experiment still maintained clear limits on the level of popular participation in politics and policy. No notion of democratization extended to the monarchy itself, for example, but the act of opening the legislative end of the system to pluralism and elections did provide for a more active and vibrant parliament than Jordan had seen since the 1950s. Before turning to domestic influences on the Gulf crisis alignment decision, I will examine briefly this process itself, and then its effects on decision making.

The regime argued that the liberalization process had begun as early as 1984, with the recall of parliament for the first time since 1967. Yet little occurred to deepen the process until the April 1989 IMF riots triggered an accelerated response on the part of the regime.[19] The riots were the crisis that provoked the real takeoff of the Jordanian democratization process. The Hashimite regime began the effort to renegotiate the social contract with its populace, aimed at achieving a new basis for political legitimacy, and ultimately a new basis for its own survival.[20] The process, in short, emerged not simply from the graciousness of the government, but from the Hashimites' sense of political vulnerability, which had steadily increased during the 1980s through a series of economic and political setbacks. According to 'Abd al-Latif 'Arabiyyat, leader of Jordan's Muslim Brotherhood and then-speaker of parliament, the riots served as a wakeup call for the government and the monarchy, and made clear the depth of domestic discontent and popular demands for real reform.[21]

In November 1989, despite the continuing ban on political parties, Jordan held its first parliamentary elections since April 1967. These elections were restricted, allowing only one organized opposition group to participate: the Muslim Brotherhood (al-Ikhwan al-Muslimun). Secular and leftist opposition existed as well, but these forces were not permitted legal status and thus suffered from an inability to organize as overtly and effectively as the Brotherhood. The result was a parliament mixed between supporters of the Hashimite monarchy and a strong and vocal opposition represented by the Ikhwan and independent Islamists.[22]

In addition to the emergence of competitive elections, the Jordanian liberalization process involved loosening restrictions on the press and reducing government oversight of the media in general. On the whole, Jordanians responded with cautious optimism to the liberalization initiative. This series of reforms, enacted over the span of several years, opened the Jordanian political system more than at any time in the past, including its brief experience with legal political parties and vibrant parliamentary life in the 1950s.

Yet the first real foreign policy test of this newly-opened system would come barely a year after the process began. Thus the Iraqi invasion of Kuwait in August 1990 triggered a regional and global crisis that Jordan had to face during a period of dramatic domestic change. The National Charter (*Mithaq al-Watani*) had not yet been concluded, for example, and so the Hashimites had yet to achieve that critical piece of political legitimization for themselves, while a parliament dominated by the Muslim Brotherhood became vocal and active in its first foreign policy crisis.[23]

Both the parliament and the Jordanian public made their voices heard during the crisis, taking positions that tended to be far more clear and unequivocal than those of the Hashimite monarchy itself. With the coincidental timing of the liberalization effort and the Gulf crisis, many political elements in Jordan had only recently found their voices; but they made ample use of them in street demonstrations, on the floor of the parliament, and in newly established newspapers and magazines. These elements spanned the political spectrum, from the religious right (including the Muslim Brotherhood within parliament) to the secular left (including a newly active contingent of pro-Iraqi members of the Jordanian Ba'th Party). It must also be remembered that the already-existing Jordanian-Iraqi alignment had real effects for many Jordanians, who, after ten years of establishing an increasingly close bilateral relationship, now felt that it was their regime's duty to stand as a firm ally to Iraq. Jordanian policymakers were well aware of the internal pressures, and saw these in turn as linked to Jordan's extensive economic links to Iraq:

> There was the internal constraint. We had the internal constraint because most of the people were highly emotional and we had to take that into account in our position . . . I think the economic relationship was the major factor in shaping people's attitude because we have to remember that when the Gulf crisis took place, it was preceded by an eight-year war between Iraq and Iran, during which the economic

situation in Jordan became stronger due to the fact that we were almost the only inlet for Iraqi imports. Our economy flourished because
of that, so the people felt that they owed the Iraqis something.[24]

The Jordanian domestic front was indeed intensely politicized, to a point
that some policymakers viewed as near hysteria. The majority of the Jordanian population supported Saddam Hussein and saw the conflict in terms
of an Arab nationalist leader standing up to the West. Spontaneous demonstrations erupted across Jordan in favor of Saddam and against Western
intervention. For some Jordanian policymakers, the intensity of domestic
politicization during the crisis operated as a powerful constraint on decision making, possibly preventing any major shift from the initial Jordanian
stand. It was the street demonstrations in particular that caught the attention not only of the foreign press, but also of Jordanian policymakers. The
Jordanian public had clearly taken the "political opening" to heart, and their
pro-Iraqi views were made amply clear to a decision-making elite unused
to such vocal and visual demonstrations of public opinion. All of Jordan's
policy decisions, therefore, were taken with domestic political ramifications
in mind.

King Hussein's much quoted speech in February 1991, at the height of the
bombings of Baghdad, must be seen in this context. It was, in short, aimed at
a domestic audience. The outrage against the West at that point had hit fever
pitch, and the regime fell into similar levels of rhetoric, describing the war
as a battle waged not only against Iraq, but against all Arabs and Muslims.

But while the government attempted to present itself as a public opinion leader, the reverse seemed closer to the truth, as the regime confronted
unrest in the streets and a highly vocal lower house of parliament, led by
representatives of the Muslim Brotherhood and its emerging political party
wing, the Islamic Action Front (*Jabha al-'Amal al-Islami*). The public and
parliament, in short, seemed to be running far out in front of the king and
the cabinet, and the latter attempted to keep pace, mixing occasional fiery
rhetoric with constant pleas for restraint and reconciliation, as the regime
attempted to appease both domestic and external audiences.

What this suggests is that the Hashimite regime was not at all autono-
mous vis-à-vis public pressures. Indeed, the crisis, and Jordanian policy,
cannot be understood without reference to the timing of the events. The
opening of the political system had satisfied some demands for broader participation, but it had also led to further demands as the population started

to taste real political activity. The newly elected parliament actively sought a role for itself. The parliamentarians elected in 1989 were not even one year into their terms when the crisis first broke. Many did not hesitate to utilize the Gulf crisis as a grand opportunity to redefine the relationship between the parliament and the palace. To some extent these efforts paid off. Never before had the Jordanian parliament been so active and vocal, and never before were its members so regularly consulted by the palace, as occurred during the crisis.[25]

As Marc Lynch has pointed out in his study of public sphere politics, the vibrancy of debates in the Jordanian public sphere stood in relative isolation from that of the broader Arab public sphere. The leading Arab states had, in fact, joined the U.S. coalition and accepted international intervention, in contrast to Jordan's insistence that the crisis be solved by the Arabs themselves. They appeared, in fact, to be threatened by the Jordanian approach, and therefore attempted to undermine and even misrepresent the Jordanian position. This, in turn, placed Jordan in an unaccustomed position in the great debates of inter-Arab politics:

> Because of the divergence between the Jordanian frame and the "official" Arab position, Jordan found itself largely excluded from the Arabist public sphere. This exclusion meant that the Arabism of Jordanian behavior would primarily be determined in the Jordanian public sphere. Jordanian policy was framed in Arabist terms, despite its exclusion from the Arab consensus. For perhaps the first time in Jordanian history, the Hashemite isolation from the Arab consensus was viewed by Jordanian—and Palestinian—publics as the result of the superior Arabism of the Jordanian position. This provided great normative value for the regime, while largely insulating it from Arab criticism: for once it was the Syrian and the Gulf positions which were seen by public opinion to be corrupt, inauthentic, and anti-Arabist.[26]

Despite the severe economic costs and the dangers of regional war, Jordanians across the political spectrum were proud of their regime's stance. Maintaining that stance, then, meant maintaining domestic stability.

In short, the coincidental timing of the Jordanian liberalization process and the outbreak of the Gulf crisis constrained Jordanian policy makers by limiting their alternatives, to the point that abandoning Iraq—and hence running against an already-inflamed public opinion and an active parliament—was not a serious consideration. To the contrary, for the first time in a long time, the regime and the public were not running on a collision course. The Muslim Brotherhood leader, Dr. Arabiyyat, even described the parliament and monarchy as in "harmonization" with one another during the crisis.[27] But the costs of Jordan's stance were also clear. Jordan suffered severe economic hardship as a result of its position, as the U.S. and the Arab Gulf monarchies cut off all aid to Jordan. Contrary to exclusively economic models of alliance politics, Jordan's alignment decision therefore triggered a profound level of budget *insecurity*.

The domestic effects of the alignment stance, however, are perhaps even more striking. For, despite the economic damage suffered during the long months of the crisis, and despite the massive drop in foreign aid to Jordan, King Hussein was never so popular domestically, and his population never so united, as during the Gulf crisis. Even the traditional rift between East Banker and Palestinian communities had been bridged to a greater extent than ever before. Despite the fact that Jordan's situation was rarely so dire regionally and internationally, the king had greatly increased his domestic political legitimacy.

The net effect of the political liberalization process, coupled with the depth of domestic sympathy for Iraq during the Gulf crisis, was that the nature of the alignment dilemma facing Jordan had forced the regime into an entirely defensive and reactive posture. The question was not whether it was possible to support Iraq and stand in the face of traditional Western allies. Rather, the questions facing the regime were the reverse: was it possible for the regime to abandon Iraq? Could the regime afford too close an association with an anti-Iraqi coalition? In regard to both questions, the answer that regime elites read from their own populace was a resounding "no."

In sum, severe concern for its own domestic survival (and some level of genuine conviction) drove the regime to make its highly controversial stand during the Gulf crisis—a stand it believed to be even handed, but which it also knew would be interpreted as pro-Iraqi and anti-coalition. The regime would have to pay for the external ramifications of that perception, but it also reaped domestic profits from the same perception held by its own people. Despite the heavy damage to Jordan's external relations, including to some of its oldest extra-regional alliances, the benefits included the preservation and even improvement of domestic support for the regime during a critical crisis period, and hence may have provided for the survival of the Hashimite regime itself.

Political Economy

Despite King Hussein's domestic popularity during the Gulf crisis, the fact remains that Jordan suffered severe economic repercussions for its stance. Aid from the United States, Kuwait, and Saudi Arabia was abruptly halted. Exports to and from most Arab countries also declined rapidly. The port of Aqaba was eventually all but shut off to commercial traffic, leading to a sharp decline in port revenues as well as in goods entering the country. Given the state of tension in the region, Jordan's much-needed tourism income effectively evaporated. And finally, as a result of the anger of the Arab Gulf states at Jordan's policy choice, several hundred thousand Jordanians and Palestinians were expelled first from Saudi Arabia and later from liberated Kuwait. In addition to eliminating Jordan's critical source of labor remittances from the oil states, these repercussions also added a severe strain on housing and services in the kingdom, as half a million laborers and their families abruptly arrived back home.

Given the economic and social disasters that followed Jordan's policy choice, the question remains whether any economic factors pushed the kingdom in the direction of maintaining its Iraqi alignment. One of the keys to understanding the economic underpinnings of Jordan's Gulf policy lies in its ties to the Iraqi economy and particularly in its trade relations. That bilateral trade relationship had continued to develop from 1979 onward, when Jordan had shifted its main Arab alignment from Syria to Iraq. By the time of the Gulf crisis, Jordanian-Iraqi economic ties had become so deep that some regarded the relationship as a "de facto federation."[28] These ties had increased throughout the 1980s to the point that by 1989, Iraq was the main source of Jordanian imports (17.3 percent) as well as the main destination of Jordanian exports (23.2 percent).[29]

In addition, most of Jordan's oil supply came from Iraq, an arrangement that had developed in return for Jordan's support of the Iraqi war effort against Iran. Further, these oil shipments came at no charge to Jordan, but rather were deducted from Iraq's large wartime debt to the kingdom. Jordan's dependence on Iraqi oil had become so great, in fact, that it no longer imported oil from most other Arab Gulf states, relying on Iraq for anywhere from 70 to 100 percent of its oil imports, depending on the particular year. Given this level of economic ties to Iraq, and indeed this level of dependency, the Jordanian government felt that Western intervention against Iraq could only result in economic and political disaster for the region and certainly for Jordan's largest trading partner and its almost exclusive source or petroleum.[30]

Thus, despite its dependence on aid from the West and Arab Gulf states, the kingdom also depended on its linkages to the Iraqi economy. In the end, the regime opted to risk losing its main aid sources, banking on its own political importance to any Arab-Israeli peace settlement in the region, and believing that its geo-strategic significance would mean that any break with the West would be temporary only. Also, the regime felt that if it finessed its position, it might be able to avoid any aid disruptions altogether—hence its fence-straddling position, and its attempt to act as good-faith mediator in the crisis.[31]

In the final analysis, the economic risks of staying with the Iraqi alignment (while assiduously avoiding any military commitment to Iraq) were not believed to be great enough to warrant de-alignment from a longstanding ally. And perhaps most importantly, even those Jordanian decision makers who wanted to put distance between Jordan and Iraq realized that the depth of economic ties made de-alignment virtually impossible. In retrospect, the economic effects that followed from Jordan's decision not to de-align were significant, but not as severe as some had originally feared. Nonetheless, the damage was felt in Jordan, even long before the war broke out.[32]

While initially angered at Jordan's failure to join the anti-Iraqi coalition, Western states were even more vexed with Jordan's apparent reluctance to enforce UN-sponsored sanctions against Iraq. Jordan, in this context, was seen as one of three key countries in ensuring the success of the trade embargo on Saddam Hussein's regime. Unlike Iraq's other two transit routes for imports and exports—Turkey and Saudi Arabia—Jordan did not comply immediately with UN directives. Rather, Jordan stalled at first by requesting detailed clarifications regarding trade and transport restrictions, meanwhile allowing the flow of goods to continue largely unabated.

One reason for this reluctance was the immediate economic costs to the kingdom of enforcing the embargo, for to do so threatened three critical components of the Jordanian economy: revenues from the port of Aqaba, revenues from the export and re-export of goods to Iraq, and access to oil imports coming from Iraq. On the one hand, the regime was wary of shutting off supplies to Iraq, given the volatile political mood within Jordan itself. On the other hand, Jordan's reluctance to fully implement the embargo on goods to Iraq was widely interpreted as being based solely on Jordanian sympathy for the Iraqi regime. But in fact, fear may have played a far larger role than love. Indeed, Jordanian policy makers feared retaliation from Baghdad if they were to shut off Iraq entirely. Jordan had long since established itself as the key economic lifeline to Iraq, especially during its eight long years of war with Iran.[33] The Hashimite regime therefore approached compliance with UN sanctions slowly and with caution, in contrast to the immediate closure of Iraq's borders by Turkey and Saudi Arabia.

Gradually, however, the regime complied more and more with UN guidelines, although some supplies (particularly medical and other humanitarian goods) continued to slip through. Ultimately, the regime was relieved of the responsibility for what Iraq would surely have considered economic treachery by a trusted ally. Due to the Western naval presence in the Red Sea, fewer and fewer ships docked at the port of Aqaba. Trade through Aqaba accordingly dropped off steadily until it became little more than a trickle to the port city, with even less traffic continuing on to Iraq itself.[34]

This development saved the Jordanian regime from the difficult decision of whether or not to comply entirely with the United Nations, and helped ease decision makers' fears regarding wartime or post-war Iraqi hostility. Over the course of a more than ten-year alignment, Jordan and Iraq had become so closely linked, economically, that Jordan could not unilaterally leave the alignment without severe damage to its own economy.

But even here, the real worry was about the effects of such a move on the regime's own *domestic* political stability. The Hashimite regime was careful to give Saddam Hussein no excuse for anger at Jordan, and no opportunity to turn pro-Iraqi public opinion against the Jordanian regime itself. As Jordanian officials were well aware, alignment links to Western aid benefactors and even to Gulf labor markets might be reestablished later, but Jordan would have to continue to live beside Iraq, no matter how the crisis turned out. And as Baram has noted, "in the king's view the safest courses of action were to drift with domestic public sentiment and avoid Iraq's wrath."[35] Similarly, Brand has argued that "a Gulf policy even remotely pro-coalition might well have led to severe instability, if not the end of the monarchy."[36]

These concerns for domestic stability and regime survival were so strong that they were allowed to outweigh the heavy economic and political costs that could result from Jordan's risking its ties to all of its traditional allies outside the region—particularly the United States and the United Kingdom—as well as regional economic benefactors such as Saudi Arabia. In the years following the Gulf war, this gamble appeared to have paid off.

Conclusions

For the Hashimite regime, the regional realignment triggered by the Gulf crisis represented only a lose-lose situation. All policy choices appeared to carry negative consequences for Jordan and were differentiated only by degree. External balancing considerations were indeterminate at best, and the regime's chief external security concern was not with a general image of the regional balance, but rather with the specific issue of avoiding a regional war.

Furthermore, if the regime had joined the U.S.-led coalition, in effect "balancing" against Iraq, it would have triggered its internal security dilemma to such an extent that the monarchy might not have survived. Meanwhile, the Hashimite regime's fears of regional war were informed not only by Jordan's military weakness, but also by the intricate linkages between the Jordanian and Iraqi economies—linkages that had been built for more than a decade. Jordan's extensive oil dependency and import/export dependency on Iraqi markets limited the regime's ability to de-align from Iraq and gave the Hashimite regime a stake in preventing damage to its chief economic partner. Yet maintaining the alignment also carried severe economic costs. The budget security approach to this crisis, therefore, yields no clear alliance expectations, as the regime had deep economic ties to both sides in the looming confrontation. The economics of budget security pulled the regime in opposite directions. The difference, however, was that domestic politics pointed the regime in one direction only.

The Hashimite regime was hemmed in by its own public's deep sympathies for Iraq, a situation dramatically accentuated by the recently begun political liberalization process in the kingdom. The regime's own much-heralded program of democratization had opened up a series of channels for the populace to make its views abundantly clear through the press, the parliament, and street demonstrations. While liberalization did not provide for a broadening of the circle of foreign policy decision makers, it did greatly amplify the indirect but ultimately determinate domestic security constraints on that decision-making elite.

This analysis has demonstrated that the impact of liberalization on the making of Jordanian foreign policy has indeed been significant; so significant, in fact, that Jordan's stance during the 1990–1991 Gulf crisis cannot be understood outside the context of the political liberalization process. The opening of the political system, coupled with the intensity of popular feeling during the crisis, left the Hashimite regime with few alternatives. For King Hussein and his regime, the Gulf crisis presented such a dire situation that deft political maneuvering was required, regionally and especially domestically, if Jordan would even survive as a state—and, most importantly, as a Hashimite state.

Beyond Arab Alliances?

Jordan's Peace with Israel

As the smoke cleared from the 1991 Gulf war, the U.S. administration of President George Bush Sr. turned its attention to reviving the Arab-Israeli peace process.[1] As the peace process began, Jordan remained essentially isolated in inter-Arab and even global politics. Iraq lay largely in ruins, facing yet another post-war reconstruction, but this time coupled with a debilitating economic sanctions regime. Jordan had survived the regional crisis and war, but remained ostracized in inter-Arab politics, especially by the most influential Arab countries: Egypt, Syria, and the Arab Gulf monarchies. When these regional powers gathered together in Damascus to launch a new Arab alignment to be known as the "Damascus Declaration," no one thought about including the Jordanians.[2] Similarly, major powers such as the U.S. and United Kingdom pointedly ignored their once-favored Arab ally.

It was in this context of severe isolation, yet renewed domestic regime legitimacy and security, that the regime decided to make a fairly radical move, one that the monarchy had long desired but had never felt secure enough to accomplish: making peace with Israel. On October 26, 1994, King Hussein of Jordan and Prime Minister Yitzhak Rabin of Israel signed a peace treaty marking an official end to the state of war that had existed between their two countries for more than forty years.

This chapter examines Jordan's decision to make peace with Israel after so many years of either warfare or tacit cooperation.[3] While this rapprochement is clearly not an *Arab* alignment, it is a major milestone in Jordanian policy, Arab politics, and Hashimite regime security. Just as importantly, this rapprochement is part of Jordanian and regional alignment politics. I will examine Jordan's peace with Israel, therefore, in the context of alignment and foreign policy decision making.

Throughout the history of the Arab-Israeli conflict, Jordan held the dubious distinction of being politically, militarily, and economically the weakest of the Arab "front line" states in the long conflict with Israel. Of all the Arab states, Jordan shared the longest border with Israel and consequently had the most difficult front to defend. And over the years of conflict, within Jordan's borders, the kingdom absorbed so many Palestinian refugees that the Hashimite monarchy ruled over a population more than half of which was Palestinian. These facts alone reinforced the kingdom's chronic sense of domestic and international insecurity and helped lead Jordan's traditionally cautious monarchs toward moderate policies in their dealings with the Jewish state. Indeed, although Jordan went to war against Israel in 1948 and 1967, and although the Hashimite regime offered a limited commitment to the war of 1973, the regime generally maintained an understanding with Israel's various prime ministers—an understanding that was long rumored to include frequent face to face meetings between King Hussein and Israeli leaders—for decades before the peace treaty was signed. This relationship can be traced back further still, to the early contacts between King Abdullah I and Zionist leaders before the foundation of the State of Israel.[4]

Those sympathetic toward the Hashimite monarchy tended to view the kingdom's approach to Jordanian-Israeli relations over the years as representing moderation; critics, in contrast, have tended to see this as collusion.[5] But in either characterization, central questions remain: given the longstanding tacit understanding between Jordan and Israel, despite instances of war, why did the kingdom decide to sign a peace treaty in 1994? Why not earlier? Why sign a treaty at all? When the kingdom did finally decide to sign a full peace treaty, why did the Jordanian negotiators appear to rush headlong into the arrangement, following the initial breakthroughs barely a year earlier? Was Jordan in effect de-aligning from inter-Arab alliance politics altogether, and re-aligning with its longtime adversary, Israel?

The answers to these questions require an analysis that examines more than simply the whims of King Hussein. Most writing about Jordanian policy tends to focus on the personality and proclivities of the Hashimite monarch, with King Hussein serving more or less as a proxy for Jordan as a state and society.[6] While it would be impossible to ignore the role of the king in any study of Jordanian policy, this analysis examines Jordanian decision making in its broader context, taking into account the complexity of state-society relations within the kingdom. The king's role can then be seen in a more empirically accurate light, in which the monarch and his regime maneuver between political factions and coalitions on the domestic front, while attempting to balance domestic political and economic concerns against regional and other external security factors.

External Security

Jordan's external vulnerability toward both Israel and its Arab neighbors has always been a key element in the kingdom's approach to the peace process. After Egyptian President Anwar al-Sadat's trip to Jerusalem in 1977, there was considerable speculation and even expectation that King Hussein would soon follow in Sadat's footsteps. These expectations increased with the signing of the Camp David Accords in 1978 and the Egyptian-Israeli Peace Treaty in 1979. Yet, despite its moderate and pro-Western king, Jordan did not join in the Egyptian-Israeli peace process. Indeed, the expectation that Jordan would do so reflected a lack of understanding, on the part of the American administration and others, of the fine line that the Hashimite regime had to tread in order to preserve its security in both domestic and inter-Arab regional affairs. Most Arab states, as well as Jordan's own Palestinian population, reacted with hostility to what they viewed as Egypt's separate peace with Israel.

Yet, if Sadat's treaty remained a bilateral and relatively cold peace, it also changed regional politics dramatically. In the words of one of Jordan's foreign ministers, "Sadat's actions in 1979 changed the orientation of the entire region. It took the wind out of Syria. And it eliminated the military solution. But was it ever possible? Look at 1948, 1967, and even 1973 which wasn't exactly a glorious victory. Since then the entire Arab world was exposed to the elements with no cover."[7]

While the Hashimite regime may have longed for peace, it would not—and could not—conclude such a peace under these conditions. Sadat's Egypt was ostracized from the Arab world, expelled from the Arab League, and subjected to a pan-Arab economic boycott. In short, the costs of peace were severe for Egypt, far too severe for Jordan to follow suit. But years later, especially from 1987 to 1993, three key regional changes together provided the opening that the Hashimite regime had long sought in order to achieve a full peace agreement.

First, in 1987 the occupied Palestinian territories exploded in a massive grassroots uprising now known as the Intifada. Officials from Israel, Jordan, and indeed even the PLO seemed to have been caught equally off guard. As the unrest continued west of the Jordan river, King Hussein finally announced a decision that many policymakers had been urging for a very long time: Jordan's renunciation of claims to the occupied West Bank. The kingdom had taken control of the territory following the 1947 partition of Palestine and the 1948 Arab-Israeli war. Jordan later annexed the territory, only to lose it—including East Jerusalem—to Israel in the Six Day War of 1967. By renouncing ties and claims to the territory, the Hashimite regime had in effect turned the problem over to the Israelis and Palestinians. Like its later 1994 peace treaty with Israel, Jordan's 1988 move was intended at least in part to eliminate the "solution" to the Arab-Israeli conflict long discussed on the Israeli right: the so-called "Jordan Option," in which Jordan would become the Palestinian state, presumably eliminating the Hashimite Kingdom of Jordan.[8]

The second key event was the subject of the preceding chapter: the 1990–1991 Gulf crisis and war. While that crisis was clearly concentrated in the Persian Gulf region, it nonetheless affected the security of countries well beyond the Gulf, from Israel to Jordan, and from Egypt to Syria. The key factor affecting prospects for Arab-Israeli peace was not the war itself, but its aftermath. For Jordan's key peace negotiator, 'Abd al-Salam al-Majali, the after-effects and regional implications were critical:

> When the Gulf War took place, the strategy of the West changed. Israel was no longer the forefront of that strategy of the West. Despite ideas of a "Greater Israel" . . . in 1990 the West put its hands on the region's oil directly. There was no need for Israel as the frontline of the West, and also no longer any Soviet threat against the oil supplies of the Middle East. So 1991 provided for the revival of the Middle East peace process.[9]

In the aftermath of the war, the first multilateral peace talks were held in Madrid, Spain. With the Israelis refusing to speak directly to the PLO, a temporary solution was found in the form of sending a joint Jordanian-Palestinian delegation to the talks. Shortly after Madrid, however, Palestinian and Jordanian negotiators began holding separate talks with the Israelis.

The third key regional change, and the one that most directly affected Israeli-Jordanian peace, was at least as dramatic and unexpected as the previous two: the September 1993 announcement of the Israeli-PLO Accord in Oslo, Norway. The Jordanian government reacted at first with anger and frustration about being left out and not consulted by either party. The Hashimite regime was particularly annoyed at the PLO leadership. But what the Jordanians first viewed as a setback, effectively sidelining them in the peace process, on second glance appeared to them as a great opportunity. The Oslo Accords broke the taboo of direct Israeli-PLO negotiations, dramatically changing regional prospects for peace. "Oslo, to my mind, was a great earthquake," stated Jordan's lead peace negotiator, 'Abd al-Salam al-Majali, "it was the first recognition by the Zionist movement of the Palestinians and their unity on Palestinian soil."[10]

While the accord provided the important breakthrough of mutual recognition between Israel and the PLO, setting an agenda for full peace talks, the progress in the years that followed was slow and fraught with repeated setbacks and continuing violence in Israel and the occupied territories. Although this amounted to far less than a peace settlement between the Israelis and Palestinians, the accord nonetheless amounted to a green light for the Hashimite regime in its own dealings with Israel. By concluding its treaty with Israel, the regime would now be following not in the footsteps of Sadat—but in those of the PLO itself.

Prior to September 1993, the Hashimite regime had been unable to formalize its tacit understandings with Israel. Given their less than revolutionary credentials in inter-Arab politics, the Hashimites were far more vulnerable than Sadat had been to charges of breaking from the Arab camp and selling out the Palestinians. A unilateral Jordanian defection from Arab ranks toward a separate peace would have left the monarchy vulnerable to the wrath of more radically-oriented neighbors (and perhaps its own population). Both Syria and Iraq represented potential security threats, not so much in an external military sense, but more likely in terms of supporting or sponsoring domestic destabilization within Jordan.

Similarly, Jordan could hope for no relief from its southern neighbor, Saudi Arabia, should the Hashimite kingdom attempt to follow the pattern set out by Sadat. While the Saudi kingdom represented a minimal military threat, Saudi displeasure with Jordanian policy in the peace process was certain to carry with it the equally important threat of economic blackmail. Jordan's Gulf war experience had brought home the true depth of financial pain that an angry Saudi monarchy could inflict on the Hashimite state.

In addition to these external pressures to remain within the bounds of at least the idea of a united Arab front, the regime was even more aware of its domestic setting, in which more than half the population of the kingdom was of Palestinian origin. This demographic reality, coupled with regional vulnerability, essentially made a bilateral Jordanian-Israeli settlement politically impossible for the Hashimite regime, until some settlement of the Palestinian issue had been satisfactorily achieved. In the words of Jordan's Foreign Minister, Kamel Abu Jaber, who had led the joint Jordanian-Palestinian delegation to the 1991 Madrid Peace Talks:

Before 1993 and the Oslo Accord, the Arab states all committed to no separate agreements with Israel. Especially after Egypt. So Lebanon, Jordan, Syria, the Palestinians, we all agreed that there must be no separate agreements. So when the Palestinians went off by themselves, this made it possible for the Jordanians to sign a treaty and for that matter for the Syrians and for Lebanon. The others didn't work out, unfortunately, but Oslo gave all Arab parties the opportunity.[11]

While the Israeli-PLO accord by no means represented a full settlement, and indeed provided only a very spare beginning to more long-term peace settlement, it nonetheless broke down the main roadblock for the Jordanians—the roadblock in which the PLO had to make the first move. If the main political voice of the Palestinian nationalist movement had reached a direct understanding with Israel, then fear of being seen as a unilateral defector from Arab ranks was considerably reduced. Jordan could argue that it was moving with the flow of Arab nationalist sentiment, rather than against it.

By signing the accord with Israel, PLO leader Yasir Arafat had not only opened the way for King Hussein, but had also put the Jordanian regime on alert that its intermediary role was no longer needed. It should be noted, however, that although the Jordanians had been viewed by various Israeli and American administrations as the appropriate intermediaries for Palestinian aspirations, this view was never shared by either the PLO or most Arab governments. For more than twenty years, the Arab states had regarded the PLO as the "sole, legitimate representative of the Palestinian people." The Hashimites, however, had only supported this Arab consensus grudgingly and reluctantly, because the regime felt it simply had no other choice.[12]

Although Oslo cleared a major roadblock for the Jordanians, their role now appeared to be suddenly less vital than before. With Israel and the PLO negotiating directly, Jordan was no longer needed in any third-party capacity. And having renounced claims to the West Bank in 1988, Jordanian participation in talks over territorial settlement was also rendered less critical, perhaps unnecessary. But after spending his entire reign banking on Jordan's vital role in any future peace settlement, King Hussein and his regime—in order to keep the kingdom a main recipient of Western aid—were not about to allow themselves to become obsolete overnight.

If the Israeli-PLO breakthrough opened the way for real progress on the Jordanian-Israeli negotiating track, it also spurred the Jordanians into rapid activity. The Jordanian regime appeared to believe that only a dramatic breakthrough of its own would restore the kingdom's formerly favored geopolitical status with the "great powers," allowing Jordan to reap the economic and security rewards of reaching a settlement. Beyond the benefits of peace for its own sake, a full agreement with Israel would bring benefits from the United States in the form of greater economic assistance and enhanced military linkages, both of which would help ensure the long-term survival of the Hashimite regime and of Jordan as a state.

Regarding its Arab neighbors, Jordan did not have to worry about alienating them anew—since its relationship with Saudi Arabia had remained dismal since the 1991 Gulf war, its alliance with Iraq was steadily deteriorating, and its relations with Syria were frequently stormy. In short, the timing of the PLO move had found Jordan with few neighboring relationships to invest in, especially in inter-Arab relations. Jordan's drift away from Iraq would continue as the kingdom attempted to recoup close relations with Western states, also lost since the Gulf war. By moving in sync with the peace process designs of the United States, the Hashimite regime hoped to reestablish its firm relationship with the U.S. government, and also to use that relationship as a vehicle to restore its political and economic linkages to U.S. allies such as Saudi Arabia and the other Arab Gulf monarchies.[13] The only question that remained, for Jordan's foreign relations, was the possible reaction from Damascus.

While no Jordanian regime would wish to provoke Syrian hostility, King Hussein and his government appeared to have given up waiting for the Asad regime. The Jordanians may have judged that the timing was right for them to take the diplomatic initiative. The expected criticism of the Jordanian regime was to some extent lessened by the fact that the PLO had moved first, paving the way, and by the kingdom's vocal insistence that the final peace settlement would still have to be comprehensive and hence inclusive of Lebanon and Syria. But perhaps the most effective way the regime critics were outmaneuvered or countered was through the quickness with which the treaty itself was concluded. The Hashimite regime thus presented potential opponents, both within the kingdom and without, with a *fait accompli*. Waiting for the PLO to make its move may have been difficult enough, but with an Israeli-PLO accord already made, the Jordanians were simply not willing to wait for Syria to move before Jordan did. Indeed, they had long been questioning whether President Asad would ever move at all.[14]

In sum, several external factors appeared to influence the nature and timing of the Jordanian decision to make peace with Israel. First among these was the outbreak of the Intifada, followed by Jordan's renunciation of claims to the West Bank. Second, the aftermath of the 1991 Gulf War revived the Middle East peace process and provided Jordan with a means to end its brief period of ostracism in regional and global politics. Third, the Israeli-PLO accord, which at first appeared to leave Jordan on the sidelines, was quickly grasped by the Jordanians as offering them an opportunity to make their own, more comprehensive agreement. The presence of the Israeli-PLO negotiation muted previously dominant domestic and regional constraints on the regime's ability to conclude a full peace treaty.

In addition to the above three factors, Jordanian willingness to press ahead in the peace process was propelled further along by American political pressure coupled with economic incentives to achieve a major breakthrough on the Jordanian-Israeli track. Finally, the regime concluded that the economic opportunities would lead to tangible material gains that would, in turn, serve to mollify any domestic skepticism or criticism as well as outweigh any hostility from Syria.

These external factors each contributed to the Jordanian decision to break from its well-established pattern of tacit understanding with Israel, and to turn instead toward full and formal peace between the two countries. But for the monarchy to proceed with this project, it had to ensure that its domestic political and economic standing was solid enough to take the political risk that the treaty entailed.

Domestic Politics

Although Jordan's experience with the Gulf war had involved considerable economic hardship, King Hussein's regime did emerge from that conflict more popular domestically than it had ever been in its history. As discussed in the preceding chapter, the crisis had come at a particularly vulnerable time for the regime, following closely on the April 1989 riots and the nascent stages of political liberalization. But in the end, the regime had emerged with a far more solid base than before, and the king's stance during the crisis, while vilified in the Gulf and the West, had gained it a tremendous amount of popularity and legitimacy at home. It was with this strong domestic foundation that King Hussein's regime turned toward the post-Gulf war resuscitation of the Arab-Israeli peace process.

By opening the system to the return of parliamentary elections (beginning in 1989), establishing the National Charter (*Mithaq al-Watani*, 1991), and legalizing political parties (beginning in 1992), the Hashimite monarchy had in effect purchased for itself a new lease on life. The regime's opponents were out in the open and able to vent some of their grievances. Other elements of the population were easily co-opted into the new system of openness and parliamentary participation. Perhaps most importantly, the regime used the liberalization process—in both economic and political terms—to broaden the base of the dominant domestic coalition underpinning Hashimite rule. This pro-Hashimite coalition drew together business, political, and military elites with a common interest in opening Jordan to greater economic opportunities, from foreign investment to the revitalization of tourism and trade.

By establishing peace and formal political and economic linkages to Israel, many Jordanians hoped to create the basis for an economic boom in the kingdom and the region. Many looked to Israel for joint ventures and trade opportunities. The military may have viewed peace as the *quid pro quo* for gaining full restoration of American military aid as well as for the spare parts and materiel needed for Jordan's U.S.-supplied armed forces.[15] For the monarchy itself, a peace agreement might bring all these things, as well as much-needed debt relief. Indeed, as the peace agreement began to take shape, the Clinton administration agreed to cancel $702 million in Jordanian debt to the United States.[16]

Between 1989 and 1993, in short, the regime managed to co-opt or contain many of its critics, while expanding its own domestic support base. With the domestic situation firmly in hand, the regime had a window of opportunity to make inroads in the peace process that might add lasting economic stability to the political stability already achieved. Indeed, it was well understood by Jordanian government elites that the resuscitation of the peace process was vital to the revival of the Jordanian economy. In turn, economic stability was seen as key to long-term political stability.[17]

Having decided to proceed with a peace agreement, the regime was concerned mainly with how to market the agreement to its own people.[18] One Jordanian analyst summarized the dilemma:

The king's problem was that he and the Hashimites had preached for years that Israel was an aggressor state, and that Jordan was standing up to them. How then to now shake hands and make a peace agreement, especially given the public sense of Jordan working often against the Palestinians? Domestic politics matters profoundly here. Half the population is Palestinian, and half of that is made up of refugees. So economics became the selling point. It was the way to market the treaty, and it was also a way to fix Jordan's economic problems for good.[19]

During the 1990–1991 Gulf crisis and war, the Hashimite regime had run with, rather than against, its own people. In concluding the 1994 peace with Israel, the regime was to some extent doing the reverse, at least in terms of some communities, such as the large and powerful Islamist movement. Other constituencies—from the military to public and even some private sector elites—were willing to support the treaty. The enormous emphasis placed on economic rewards was intended to sell the treaty, ultimately, to both communities.

Comparing reactions to Jordan's decisions to sever ties to the West Bank and its later peace treaty with Israel, Lynch has noted the differences at the local, regional, and global levels, and also between the two events:

> The severing of ties produced a negative response in the international arenas, a strongly positive reception in the Arabist arena, and an ambivalent Jordanian response, which eventually transformed into a positive consensus. The peace treaty, on the other hand, generated an extremely positive consensus in the international public sphere, an ambivalent and muted response in the Arabist arena, and an ambivalent Jordanian response, which became increasingly negative over time.[20]

The dramatic changes in regional politics allowed the regime to finally "go public" with its interests in better Jordanian-Israeli relations. But the domestic political liberalization process allowed elements in the Jordanian public to "go public" as well, albeit in direct opposition to the treaty. The regime was attempting to sell the public on its foreign policy choice, but the steadily growing opposition suggests that the regime did not, after all, succeed in convincing many in the Jordanian opposition.

It is important to remember that, even at the outset, Jordanians were divided on the peace treaty. The regime did have a pro-peace treaty coalition to work with, but also an anti-treaty coalition to counter. Those hostile to the move, however, had very little time to organize between Oslo in 1993 and Jordan's full treaty barely a year later. Most of the anti-treaty organizing had to take place *after* the peace process had actually been concluded. In this sense, the regime accomplished its goal of presenting its domestic opponents with a finished product.

Thus, although the Hashimite regime enjoyed the enthusiastic support of a core domestic pro-peace coalition, numerous constituencies throughout the kingdom received the news of the accord with dismay or hostility. Some demonstrations, mainly by the Islamic Action Front (*Jabha al-'Amal al-Islami*), were organized against the agreement, although the regime curbed these particularly during U.S. President Bill Clinton's visit to the kingdom in October 1994. Unfortunately, these moves also signaled a broader trend in Jordanian domestic politics and in regime-society relations. The regime had moved with speed to achieve the peace treaty when its internal security dilemma was at its lowest possible point. But when this foreign policy and security decision generated significant opposition, reigniting the domestic security dilemma, the regime responded by constraining the domestic public sphere in an effort to curb dissent. Peace with Israel, in short, also entailed the return of domestic de-liberalization.[21]

Even in Jordan's private sector, many professional associations made clear their displeasure with the treaty, in contrast to the support for the agreement among many top financiers and commercial elites. Ten professional associations released a collective statement, which stopped short of outright condemnation, but noted their belief that the peace treaty represented "one of the Arab nation's several ill-omened days."[22] The statement purported to represent Jordan's professional associations for engineers, lawyers, dentists, doctors, pharmacists, veterinarians, nurses, writers, and geologists, and rejected the opening of any professional dealings with their Israeli counterparts.

The Jordanian press, for the most part, responded positively to the agreement. One of the two leading Arabic dailies, *al-Dustur*, welcomed the agreement in an editorial entitled "A qualitative step on the road to hope."[23] The English-language daily *Jordan Times* described the treaty as an "historic achievement" but warned Jordanians against having too high expectations, suggesting that slow and methodical progress in Jordanian-Israeli relations would be most palatable to a general public that had not been prepared for the abruptness of this major change.[24]

Within the Jordanian parliament (which followed the 1993 elections), the response was by no means as warm to the government's peace policy. Islamist, leftist, and Arab nationalist political parties all announced their opposition to the treaty, arguing that it represented a bad deal for Jordan, that the process was moving far too fast, and that the government had failed to defer to the parliament and hence to the representatives of the people. Led by the Islamic Action Front, these opposition parties argued that while the government was ready for a full peace treaty, the public was not.[25] After the agreement was initialed, but before the official signing, a coalition of seven opposition parties released a statement critical of the process of normalizing relations with Israel, arguing that the Palestinians were being left alone against a stronger Israel. The statement further lauded Hamas militant action against the "Zionist enemy."[26]

The Islamic Action Front's sixteen-member bloc boycotted President Clinton's speech to the Jordanian parliament, demonstrating its objections to the entire process. Yet the same bloc had also lost in its bids to have one of its members elected either speaker or deputy speaker of Jordan's lower house of parliament. The elections were instructive, for they showed that, although a strong and vocal bloc opposed the peace process, the counter-bloc of centrists and pro-regime conservatives remained the larger and dominant force in the Jordanian lower house of parliament. It is worth noting, however, that this imbalance is precisely how the regime's election laws were meant to work.[27] Thus, despite the opposition of Islamists, leftists, and Pan-Arab nationalists, the regime could still rely on the dominance of parliament's pro-regime and pro-peace elements to endorse the treaty with Israel and override the opposition.

While external events provided the political opening for Jordan to conclude its long-desired peace with Israel, the regime hoped above all that dramatic economic improvements would flow to the kingdom, smoothing over opposition in the long run. The regime was banking on a noticeable improvement in Jordan's economy, which would serve to vindicate the monarchy's peace decision while deflating much of the appeal of key oppositionists, such as Jordan's powerful Islamist movement.[28]

Political Economy

Both economically and politically, Jordan's entrance into the 1990s had been painful and costly. By 1990 Jordan had dug itself into an ever-deepening hole of indebtedness. The kingdom's foreign debt had increased from 233.73 million dinars in 1979, for example, to 1,356 million dinars in 1988.[29] It was precisely this situation that had led the IMF to impose the austerity package in return for debt renegotiation. And while the kingdom's debt steadily increased over time, Jordan also continued to run a chronic budget deficit. Between 1962 and 1990, the national deficit had increased from -710 thousand dinars to -95 million.[30] With its economic weakness and the political instability that had begun to accompany it, Jordan found little relief at the onset of the 1990s.

In the immediate aftermath of the 1991 Gulf War, most Jordanian citizens appeared willing to endure a certain amount of economic hardship for what they viewed as a principled stand during the Gulf War. But the costs of the war had been great, including the abrupt cessation of foreign aid from the United States, the United Kingdom, Saudi Arabia, and other Gulf states. Jordan's oil supplies from Iraq and its trade linkages had essentially dried up as a result of the embargo on Iraq. Jordan's port revenues at Aqaba also disappeared, while other industries such as tourism were written off as total losses during the war. Adding to the economic damage, almost half a million Palestinians and Jordanians expelled from Gulf states arrived in Jordan, putting additional stress on Jordan's housing and public services. Hasan al-Barari, a Jordanian analyst specializing in Jordanian-Israeli relations, has argued that the peace treaty was tied to this recent Gulf War experience, and in particular its impact on Jordan's economy and domestic politics:

> Jordan was isolated completely in the region. Plus there was an absolute flood of refugees to Jordan. Jordan felt extremely vulnerable. The peace treaty rehabilitated Jordan in the region. The king saw this as the only way to rehabilitate Jordan. The decision was driven by survival first, economics a close second. Jordan isn't fully a rentier state. But in 1993 and 1994, Jordan needed rents. Regime legitimacy was failing along with state services within domestic politics. So the negotiations focused on economic factors.[31]

With the revival of the peace process in the post-Gulf war era, Jordan was able to reestablish some of its economic and political ties to the United States, but not yet to the Gulf states. While the economic situation ultimately turned out to be far less dire than Jordanian policymakers had feared, the kingdom's increasing indebtedness and chronic deficit suggested the need for a longer-term solution. The connection between economic well-being and political stability was not lost on government officials, particularly since the unrest of 1989.[32] They knew that the atmosphere of positive feeling toward the monarchy following the Gulf war would not last long unless the economic situation quickly improved.

In sum, the Jordanians sought a real breakthrough in the peace process, not only for the sake of peace, but also for the economic windfall that they believed would follow from peace. The regime expected the economic payoff of peace to be especially high in terms of trade and joint ventures with Israel, including a boost to the Jordanian tourism industry, as well as increased U.S. economic and military aid, and possibly, through the mediation of the

U.S., increased aid flows from, and labor flows to, the Arab Gulf states. And that windfall was expected to mollify regime critics and provide the necessary economic "payoffs" to key constituencies—such as the public and private sector business elite as well as the armed forces—which were key elements within the ruling coalition on which the regime itself was based.

Effects of the Treaty on Jordanian Politics and Inter-Arab Relations

The above analysis has attempted to explain not only the move toward official peace, but also the stunning speed with which the Hashimite regime approached the treaty once the regime decided to pursue peace. The process moved so fast, in fact, that much of the Jordanian population was left well behind. This does not mean that most Jordanians were opposed to peace, as the Islamists charged, but neither was there the level of enthusiasm that the government claimed existed. Rather, the general view seemed to be in favor of peace and of economic gain, but considerably pessimistic about how favorable a deal the kingdom had received, and how likely it was that the hoped-for economic windfall would actually take place. Many, especially amongst the Palestinian population within Jordan, were primarily concerned with the treaty's implications for the Palestinian people, whether in the territories, in Jordan, or elsewhere.[33]

In the period immediately following the signing of the peace treaty, King Hussein's gamble appeared to have paid off, at least politically. There was no outpouring of hostility, no outbreak of street demonstrations, no rioting. Indeed, although the regime kept a close eye on these matters, the ingredients for domestic upheaval were not there. But neither was the economic windfall that many expected. Jordan's main architect of the treaty, former Prime Minister 'Abd al-Salam al-Majali, was candid in assessing both causes and effects of the treaty:

> In 1994 we negotiated with Israel because of five main things. One, Jordan, unlike other countries, has the highest per capita rate of refugees in the world. Two, there was the threat of Jordan as the Palestinian state. Three, our water was being taken by Israel. Four, the Israeli occupation of the Wadi Araba. Five, our economy was down because of the Iraqi problem. The treaty solved much of this, but not all of it . . . We made our peace treaty and the assorted smaller agreements. Like trade and so on. Unfortunately, not all went well. There is freer

movement of people, but the economic side is not good. It didn't fit the promises. Clinton especially promised solutions to many economic problems. For example, major water desalination projects transforming the Wadi Araba. No. It's still a desert. These didn't pan out.[34]

Having been unable to prevent the peace treaty, Jordan's main professional associations, led by elected Islamist leaders, orchestrated a national campaign to prevent normalization of relations between Jordan and Israel.[35] Their governments may have made peace, but their societies had not. As the situation for Palestinians worsened in the territories during the second Intifada, which began in September 2000, the anti-normalization campaign continued to grow in strength within Jordan.

In the years following the treaty, the continuing optimism of the regime contrasted with the more pessimistic assessments in the public at large. As suggested above, many expected quick and dramatic economic benefits that simply did not occur. For some Jordanians disappointment set in quickly, while others already opposed to the peace process may have felt that their negative predictions had come true.[36] For many in the heavily Palestinian private sector in Jordan, the treaty amounted to capitulation, plain and simple. Others, stressing the economic rather than political implications of normalized relations with Israel, feared that Jordanian business would not be able to compete against imported Israeli goods.

But if, in the Jordanian private sector, there was some reticence regarding economic interaction with Israel, there was no reticence in the public sector, where plans had been drawn up for various development schemes and joint ventures. These included a new airport between the port of Aqaba and Israel's Eilat resort city, as well as agreements for linking national electricity grids. Jordanian economic planners stressed the great potential for Jordanian-Israeli cooperation in the transportation and tourism industries. While the Jordanian government at least initially expected substantial material gains from normalized Jordanian-Israeli relations, it is worth noting that Israeli expectations may have been considerably more moderate. For Israel, the greater issue may not have been the opening to the Jordanian economy per se, but the potential to use Jordan as a gateway to the more lucrative economic potential of other Arab economies, such as those of the Gulf states.[37]

Despite the grand economic plans of the Jordanian public sector, opposition to the treaty continued to make itself heard within Jordan's relatively open domestic public sphere. But the government's response to its most vocal critics began to test the level of tolerance for dissent within Jordan— thus testing the liberalization and democratization process itself. The most dramatic episode in this context was the 1996 arrest (not for the first time) of outspoken Islamist leader Layth Shubaylat. But, as in a previous episode (in 1992–1993), the attempt by the government to silence Shubaylat served only to amplify his voice, not just in news coverage in the mainstream press, but also in Jordan's burgeoning weekly tabloids. In addition to being one of the most prominent voices of dissent among independent Islamists, Shubaylat also held a power base as leader of the Jordanian Engineers Association (JEA). If the arrest of Shubaylat had really been a signal from the regime to rein in the many critical voices emanating from Jordan's various professional associations, then the Engineers Association, at least, responded to the regime with a signal of its own. Despite his imprisonment, Shubaylat remained a candidate for reelection as leader of the JEA and garnered a full 82 percent of the vote.[38]

Shubaylat and other critics of the regime attacked not only the peace treaty and normalization of relations with Israel, but also the regime's increasing criticism of its former ally, Iraq, and its overt embrace of closer strategic partnership with the United States. These changes in Jordanian foreign policy were underscored by changes in the Jordanian government itself. In January 1995, with the peace treaty achieved, Prime Minister and top peace negotiator 'Abd al-Salam al-Majali was replaced by the same man who had preceded him, the king's cousin and former Field Marshal of the Army, Sharif Zayd Ibn Shakir. Ibn Shakir had served on many previous occasions as prime minister—usually at times of heightened regime insecurity, domestically, and in times of transition, when the palace felt the need to ensure order.

As on previous occasions, Ibn Shakir's caretaker role was brief. By February 1996 Jordan had a new Prime Minister, 'Abd al-Karim al-Kabariti, and a new cabinet. Both were announced with considerable fanfare, emphasizing the general idea of new management for a new era. In addition to furthering Jordan's political liberalization process, the Kabariti government was charged with pursuing precisely the policies that its Islamist opponents most virulently rejected: deepening the political and economic relationship with Israel as well as the strategic alliance with the United States, while distancing the kingdom from Saddam Hussein's Iraq.[39]

Despite the turnover of governments within Jordan since the peace treaty, even Jordanian policymakers themselves were far more concerned with the abrupt shift in Israel's government. Jordan had signed its peace treaty with the Labor government of Israeli Prime Minister Yitzhak Rabin, who was assassinated by a Jewish Israeli militant the following year. In 1996 Israeli elections sent a tremor across the Arab world, as Labor Prime Minister (and key Oslo negotiator) Shimon Peres was narrowly defeated by Likud leader Binyamin Netanyahu. Officials of both the Jordanian government and the PLO were stunned at the electoral outcome. But in the midst of all the gloomy predictions and assessments that followed Netanyahu's election, Jordan's king presented a sharp contrast in his unusually optimistic response.[40] During the hastily arranged Arab summit meeting held in Cairo to take stock of the new developments in Israel, Hussein urged his fellow Arab leaders "not to panic." In a television interview with the American Cable News Network (CNN) during the final day of the summit, Hussein continued his upbeat tone, calling for a deepening and broadening of the peace process, and for fulfillment of agreements already made.[41]

Given Jordan's regional position, the king's insistence on emphasizing the positive, especially in Jordanian-Israeli relations, made a great deal of sense. The regime had, after all, taken great risks to secure the peace and believed Jordan's economic future to be tied to the treaty. Within inter-Arab relations, the Arab summit underscored the warming of Jordanian relations with Egypt and even (if to a much lesser extent) Saudi Arabia, for the first time since the 1991 Gulf War. Jordanian relations with Syria and also with the PLO continued to oscillate between functional if not warm cooperation and outright hostility. A direct meeting between King Hussein and President Asad, arranged at the Cairo summit, served at least to maintain communication between the two leaders, and the most Jordanian officials could hope for was an agreement to disagree on policies toward Israel.

But it was the deterioration of Jordanian relations with Iraq that most closely corresponded to the deepening of the Jordanian-Israeli connection. Following the signing of the peace treaty, the Jordanian government had grown steadily and more publicly critical of Saddam Hussein's regime. By January 1996, concrete action was added to verbal criticism, as the government allowed Iraqi opposition groups to open offices in Amman. The kingdom had also granted asylum to Iraq's highest ranking defectors ever— including daughters and sons-in-law of Saddam Hussein. Yet the Hashimite regime was shocked when many of the same defectors decided to return to Baghdad, resulting in the violent deaths of all but Saddam's own daughters. The grisly episode said as much about the state of Jordanian-Iraqi relations as it did about Iraqi domestic politics. The Jordanian alignment with Iraq, which had lasted since at least 1979, had been severely tested in the 1990–1991 Gulf crisis, and had survived to at least some extent. But following Jordan's peace treaty with Israel, the chief casualty was Jordan's relationship with Iraq. Jordan had in a sense realigned once again, not to another Arab state, but to a kind of *entente* with Israel as well as to a renewed strategic partnership with the United States.

While the regime maintained its relationship with the United States through numerous challenges, the warm period of Jordanian-Israeli relations—and hence the only period that even resembled an actual alignment—lasted barely from 1994 to 1996. The peace treaty was maintained, but Jordanian-Israeli relations cannot truly be seen as an alignment outside of that two-year period, and certainly not as an alliance. In addition to large issues such as the failure of economic benefits to materialize, individual incidents divided the two countries back to proper but not warm relations. The most intense of these incidents involved Israeli Mossad agents attempting to assassinate Hamas leader Khalid Masha'al in Amman in broad daylight in 1997. The episode caused a major rift between Jordan and Israel's Likud government, ending the king's earlier optimistic assessments.[42] Jordanian-Israeli relations, it seemed, would not constitute an alignment after all.

Conclusions

This chapter has examined the Jordanian decision to conclude a peace treaty with Israel on the basis of external constraints and opportunities, economic considerations, and domestic political conditions. Regional changes provided Jordan with the opportunity for peace, and economic factors provided powerful incentives, but the domestic politics of regime security accounted for the urgency and rapidity of the Jordanian peace initiative toward Israel.

It is especially important to bear in mind here, however, that the 1994 peace treaty was not between the Israeli and Jordanian peoples, but between the Israeli government and the Hashimite monarchy. Given time, the idea of full peace may take firmer root. But in the years immediately following the signing of the pact, the gap between regime and populace remained.

By concluding the peace treaty, King Hussein ran well ahead of much of his population, believing that the treaty was the best choice for his country and for the longevity of his regime. Still, the decision to proceed with the treaty amounted to a gamble—a gamble that the treaty would be a ticket not only for lasting peace, but also for a large and sustained economic payoff which would boost the Jordanian economy, raise the level of revenue for the state, and restore the prominent regional role that the kingdom had lost in the bitter period during and after the 1991 Gulf war. Finally, by concluding the treaty with Israel, the Hashimites also reinserted themselves into an issue profoundly dear to their hearts—the future status of Jerusalem and particularly its holy places. Thus, much to the chagrin of the PLO, King Hussein's regime had managed to reassert the Hashimites' historic view of their own role as protectors of Jerusalem and its Holy places, despite having renounced claims to the entire West Bank in 1988.

While all these considerations and hopes were meant to benefit the country as a whole, the bottom line remained the long-term survival of Jordan as a Hashimite monarchy. And this point brings us back to the individual role played by King Hussein in shaping Jordanian foreign policy. It is very likely that King Hussein's forcefulness in achieving and defending the treaty reflected an awareness of his own mortality and a desire to achieve peace in his lifetime. This peace, in turn, was to help ensure a firmer foundation for the Hashimite monarchy as it approached the twenty-first century.

A certain amount of urgency may have preoccupied the Jordanian monarch and his inner circle, particularly given the king's recent problems with ill health. It would have been far more difficult for any successor, lacking Hussein's personal political clout and legitimacy, to conclude such an agreement. Hussein could make peace largely on his own terms, but a weaker successor government under his brother or one of his sons could not. This consideration, then, with domestic regime security—specifically in the form of mortality and the looming succession—is a final and essential part of the explanation for Jordan's 1994 decision to conclude a peace treaty with Israel.

Yet this consideration is also a bit of a twist to the broader idea of regime security. In most cases that concept refers to immediate internal pressures constraining foreign policy, but in this case the pressures had more to do with King Hussein's illness and sense that he had little time to conclude the treaty. The domestic pressures had yet to appear, yet King Hussein correctly sensed that they would emerge in the near future. Indeed, he seems to have realized that his successors would face greater domestic regime security constraints, and hence he made his decisive move at a moment of relative domestic strength, rather than at a moment of weakness. While this case is different from the other instances of domestic insecurity chronicled here, it does fit in a broader understanding of this framework. The bottom line was still Hashimite regime security, despite the unusual circumstance. Ultimately, Hussein's assessments regarding his personal health, and the political health of his successor regime, turned out to be accurate forecasts of the near future.

In 1999 King Hussein did succumb after his long battle with cancer. The question of maintaining the peace, then, would fall largely on the shoulders of his successor, his eldest son Abdullah. If Hussein's regime had initiated the political liberalization process, survived the Gulf crisis, and made peace with Israel, it would be up to King Abdullah's regime to revive the domestic reform process, maintain the peace, and re-establish Jordan's damaged relations with the Arab world. Under the new king, Jordan would turn again to inter-Arab relations in a concerted attempt to repair the various Arab relationships ruptured by Jordan's stances on either war with Iraq or peace with Israel.

PART III

Arab Alliances and Jordanian Foreign Policy under King Abdullah II

Ending the Jordanian-Syrian Cold War

Throughout their histories as independent states, Jordan and Syria have had at best a tenuous relationship, marked by temporary military alliances during wars with Israel, but more often by varying degrees of mutual hostility. These long periods of hostility were so extensive, in fact, that they amounted to a local "Cold War" in the midst of the many other conflicts already operating in the region. By 1999, however, a marked thaw had emerged in Jordanian-Syrian relations. While the thaw began only in 1999, within two years it had shifted already from a cold war to a cold peace and then to even more meaningful cooperation and coordination. By 2001 some officials were talking of the potential for a full Jordanian-Syrian alliance.[1]

The successful ending of the Jordanian-Syrian Cold War marked a new chapter in the history of these two states' bilateral relations. Relations between Amman and Damascus have more often than not been marked by acrimony. But, as chapter 6 demonstrated, the thaw in the cold war had actually happened once before, in the 1970s, when Jordan and Syria shifted from antagonism to full-scale alliance. By the end of that decade, however, the more familiar pattern of animosity had returned. In the more recent episode, regime changes in both Damascus and Amman facilitated the shift from hostility to rapprochement. Nonetheless, the hiatus between the two periods of alignment was long and difficult for both countries. It had taken twenty years for the two regimes to begin aligning toward one another again, in an attempt to end their cold war once and for all. This chapter examines the ending of the Jordanian-Syrian Cold War, and the Jordanian attempt to create a new Jordanian-Syrian alignment.

Regime Succession: From Hussein to Abdullah

With the death of King Hussein, in 1999, and the accession to the throne of King Abdullah II, Jordan had a new top foreign policymaker for the first time in almost half a century.[2] The new king was not, however, the decision maker that many had expected. But in the weeks just prior to his death, King

Hussein left his hospital bed in the United States, flew back to Jordan, and changed the line of succession—on the tarmac of Amman's international airport—before reboarding his plane and flying back to the United States. Hussein shifted the succession from then-Crown Prince Hasan (Hussein's brother and for more than thirty years his heir apparent) to his eldest son, Abdullah.

As one of the key advisors to the king and one of Jordan's main economic planners, Hasan was known to Arab and Western governments and indeed to Jordanians themselves. Abdullah was, comparatively speaking, a political novice. He had held no prior political office, and had instead pursued a successful career in the armed forces, eventually becoming commander of Jordan's elite special forces units. But, despite the surprise in Jordan and abroad regarding the abrupt shift in the royal line, the 1999 succession took place without incident, and Abdullah II ascended the Hashimite throne.[3]

Almost immediately after becoming king, Abdullah made clear his interest in foreign policy, his emphasis on economic development, and his insistence on mending fences broken over Jordan's frequently unpopular foreign policy stances—from earlier Persian Gulf wars to peace with Israel. With these themes in mind, the new king set out on a whirlwind tour of key capitals, introducing himself to many of the world's most powerful leaders and attempting to cement Jordan's key international relationships, which the regime identified as key to its own security and survival. In Jordanian foreign policy, then, the overriding concerns with regime survival did not vanish with the succession in the monarchy from King Hussein to King Abdullah II.

Within six months of ascending the throne, Abdullah had met with the leaders of the Group of Seven (G-7) countries, at each stop making the case for foreign aid, trade, and investment in Jordan.[4] Just as importantly, he led delegations to former enemies—such as Libya and Syria. Similarly, in personal visits to other monarchs, King Abdullah completed the process of reconciliation (after the 1991 Gulf War) with each of the Arab Gulf monarchies. In these latter visits too, the king and his ministers stressed the need to bolster the economic relations between Jordan and wealthier Arab regimes, in a conscious effort to shore up the Hashimite regime itself—all while maintaining their often unpopular ties to the United States, the United Kingdom, Turkey, and Israel.[5]

In its first full year in office, the new Hashimite regime appeared to have achieved all these goals with startling speed. In doing so, the regime appeared to have secured for itself a period of enviable domestic and regional stability from which to launch its many plans for economic development in the Hashimite kingdom. But regional and global politics soon took a dramatic turn for the worse—with conflicts in Israel, Palestine, Afghanistan, and Iraq—and the Abdullah regime was soon forced to respond to a series of crises that threatened to drag Jordan once again into the maelstrom of Middle East conflicts. At the same time, the Abdullah regime, by bringing to an end Jordan's longstanding Cold War with Syria, managed to secure a major realignment, of sorts, in Arab politics. The following sections examine how and why the Jordanian-Syrian Cold War was brought to an end, and why the attempt at a new alignment had only limited success.

External Security

Even though, with the death of Nasir in 1970, many regarded the Arab Cold War as over, Jordan and Syria managed more often than not to return to a bilateral version of this dynamic for much of the remainder of the twentieth century. Despite the temporary success of the Jordanian-Syrian alliance of the 1970s, by the start of the 1980s, the Jordanian-Syrian Cold War had returned in full force. Throughout the 1980s, Jordan supported Iraq while Syria supported Iran in the eight-year-long Iran-Iraq war. But, beyond throwing their support behind opposite powers in the first Gulf War, the tensions between Jordan and Syria also had profound domestic consequences, as each intervened in the domestic politics and stability of the other.[6]

It remains unclear how direct a role either government played in the destabilization that followed. Suffice it to say that each blamed the other for bombings in their capital cities. In 1985, just as Jordan and the PLO—and specifically King Hussein and Yasir Arafat—reached agreement on a joint stance toward future negotiations with Israel, a massive explosion tore through the lobby of the Intercontinental Hotel in downtown Amman. The mere suspicion that Syrian agents were behind the blast effectively scuttled the Jordanian-PLO accord. In Syria itself, a series of shootings and bombings by militant Islamists in various cities killed numerous Ba'th party officials. Jordanian agents were not directly implicated in any of these assassinations, but the Syrian government charged the Jordanians with providing aid, support, and sanctuary to Syrian Islamists.[7]

Even Jordan's own prime ministers do not agree on this point. Former Prime Minister Ahmad 'Ubaydat (1984–1985), for example, vehemently denied that any such subversion ever took place with support from the Jordanian government.[8] One of his rivals, also a former prime minister, suggested that Jordan did support the Muslim Brotherhood in Syria, but that this policy (a mistake in his view) was carried out without the knowledge of King Hussein.[9] Another former prime minister argued that Jordanian-Syrian problems remained broader still, and were rooted in disregard for the other's sovereignty and security:

> [The Syrians] have even, at times, claimed us as southern Syrians. Then again, we Hashimites have at times seen them as our northern inheritance. But Syria likes to be the power. It likes its hegemony. But Jordan could never accept this. Syria works through Lebanon or through Jordan to irritate Israel. But we resent this. It also affects our own security.[10]

Regardless of whether opponents of either regime received external support or not, the 1980s version of the Jordanian-Syrian Cold War appeared to have become a *mukhabarat* versus *mukhabarat* struggle (that is, a spy versus spy struggle between intelligence services), in a localized version of the global U.S.-Soviet Cold War and its associated espionage campaigns.

In the Arab-Israeli conflict, the two states also found themselves often at odds. In 1988, for example, Jordan gave up entirely its claims to the West Bank, paving the way for a full peace treaty with Israel in 1994. The Syrian government, again in contrast, prided itself on more than four decades of steadfastness and resolution, maintaining its claim to all of the Golan, with neither a peace treaty nor a meaningful peace process with Israel well into the twenty-first century.

Throughout these decades of policy differences and animosity, the Jordanian and Syrian regimes differed not only on relations with Israel, but also on relations with the PLO. One Syrian policymaker, a sometime advisor to President Hafiz al-Asad, emphasized this point. Regarding this time period, he argued that "the most important factor in inter-Arab relations is each country's relationship with the PLO. Jordan and Syria are the only two Arab states adjacent to Israel who are eligible—after Sadat's visit to Jerusalem—to 'control' the PLO, let's say. So the question is who will exercise more control over the PLO, Amman or Damascus?"[11]

In 1990, after Iraq invaded Kuwait, Jordan and Syria took almost opposite stands once again—but in each case surprising many observers. Syria elected to join the U.S.-led coalition against Iraq, while Jordan attempted (unsuccessfully) to mediate between the antagonists, calling for an inter-Arab solution rather than foreign intervention. Syria deployed more than 12,000 troops to Saudi Arabia as part of the U.S.-led coalition against Saddam Hussein's Iraq.

In the years following the 1991 Gulf War, significant strategic changes affected the regional system. The collapse of the Soviet Union and the resultant evaporation of the global Cold War, for example, made the localized Jordanian-Syrian version seem antiquated, to be sure. More importantly, the evaporation of the global Cold War eliminated Syria's main non-regional sources of aid and arms. In many ways, Syria used the earlier Gulf crisis as a means to realign within Arab politics, securing as allies Egypt and each of the monarchies in the Gulf Cooperation Council. Similarly, Jordan used the revived peace process as a means to reestablish local and global alliances, thereby reasserting the regime's geopolitical significance.

By 1999, even before the Hashimite succession, the Jordanian-Syrian Cold War appeared to be dying down. The various external security factors that may have driven this rivalry over the years—the Arab Cold War, the global Cold War, the Iran-Iraq War—had ended. Even the Arab-Israeli conflict, which had certainly not ended, transformed with the Jordanian-Israeli peace treaty. While the Syrian regime viewed the treaty as yet another Hashimite defection from the Arab order, the pact was nonetheless a done deal. Years of thwarting any Jordanian tendency to make a separate peace ended in 1994. In external security matters and in the regional strategic arena, little was left to fuel continued hostility. Indeed, one of the few factors accounting for the continued Jordanian-Syrian rivalry was, in a sense, personal.

Beyond the assorted strategic and ideological causal factors, the Jordanian-Syrian Cold War seemed to have developed its own tragic inertia. Beyond even policy differences, the level of mutual suspicion and distrust between the two regimes had become deeply entrenched in the persons of President Hafiz al-Asad and King Hussein. With the passing of these two powerful antagonists and the emergence of a new generation of leaders, Jordan and Syria were able to make a second attempt at ending their long-standing Cold War.

Thus, for decades, the prevailing trends in Jordanian-Syrian relations amounted simply to varying degrees of hostility—from diplomatic rifts to political threats to actual acts of military and civil violence. But both in the 1970s and again from beginning in 1999, the Jordanian-Syrian Cold War was brought to an end.

Domestic Politics

When King Hussein died in 1999, he and Syrian President Asad had never really reconciled. Yet Asad surprised Jordanians and indeed the world by arriving with a large entourage, including most top Syrian officials, to march in King Hussein's funeral procession and to pay his respects to the late king's son and heir, Abdullah. Jordanian-Syrian rapprochement, to some extent, began that very day. Just over a year later, in June 2000, President Hafiz al-Asad died in Damascus, having ruled for thirty years as head of the Ba'thist regime in Syria. Unlike Jordan, however, Syria was a republic, and an avowedly radical one at that. Yet here too a son had been anointed successor to his long-serving father. And here too the son, Bishar al-Asad, did succeed his father as ruler of the nation.

Adding to the general interest of the Jordanian and Syrian successions was the apparent similarity of the two new leaders. Their predecessors, King Hussein and President Hafiz al-Asad, had remained rivals throughout most of their respective tenures. In addition to personally disliking one another, the former leaders had been influenced by the local and global Cold Wars and had frequently taken opposite positions on the Arab-Israeli conflict and peace process. Throughout the reigns of Hussein and Asad, Jordan and Syria served virtually as archetypes for a conservative, pro-Western monarchy on the one hand and a radical, pro-Soviet nationalist republic on the other. Asad passed from the scene still steadfast in his stalled peace talks with Israel, while Hussein in 1994 rapidly pushed through a full and formal peace treaty with Israel. Given their ideological differences and their often opposite stances on major issues of war and peace, Jordanian-Syrian relations were, much of the time, understandably strained.

Unlike their fathers, President Bishar al-Asad and King Abdullah II can be seen as similar in at least a few ways. At the time of succession, both were in their mid-thirties; both were interested in computers and communications and changing their societies; and each was succeeding a leader who had served so long that most citizens remembered no other. But the thaw in Jordanian-Syrian relations began more directly as the result of the Jordanian, rather than the Syrian, succession. King Hussein died more than a year before Hafiz al-Asad passed away. Asad had made clear his desire for warmer relations through his good-will gesture of travelling to Jordan for Hussein's funeral. And, once the mourning period was over, King Abdullah wasted no time in attempting to shore up Jordan's relations not only with Syria, but also with other key Arab states from Morocco to Egypt to the

Gulf monarchies. Following the succession in Damascus, President Bishar al-Asad also seemed to embrace the idea of active rapprochement and even of alignment between Jordan and Syria.

To some extent, the energetic personal diplomacy of King Abdullah II can be credited with achieving the Jordanian-Syrian rapprochement. That achievement, however, is due not only to the presence of the new leaders, but also to the absence of the old ones. Interestingly, it was the passing of Hussein that seemed to allow for the warming of bilateral relations. One of Jordan's former prime ministers suggested that "for our relations with Syria, it's natural it would get better because the two old pillars have disappeared and with that came two new leaders, but without the same inhibitions. And they are the same age and generation."[12] He continued:

> The major issue that isn't noticed enough in our relations with other Arab countries was, well, King Hussein was an ambitious man. He inherited the philosophy of the Arab revolt, the ancestry of the Prophet Muhammad, and his grandfather's vision he shared of uniting the Arabs with Jordanian leadership and with the Hashimite family. King Abdullah does not claim to be the king of all the Arabs. Just the King of Jordan. So these people—Syria, Palestinians, Lebanon, Saudi Arabia—are not as edgy as they were with King Hussein. They are not threatened by Abdullah.[13]

In a similar vein, one of Jordan's former foreign ministers stressed the leadership transition and end of an earlier, more ideological era, explaining the Jordanian-Syrian shift:

> With our changed relations with Syria, you had the deaths of two characters: King Hussein and Hafiz al-Asad. They were [each] from a different generation and a different ideology. King Hussein was an Arab nationalist. He believed in the vision of Arab unity and the vision of the Great Arab Revolt. Other leaders therefore saw him as a danger to their separate interests. Asad too was the same, only from the Ba'thist perspective. The new generation of leaders understands the power of the West, and the terrible power of what Israel can do. These people are no danger to each other. [Bishar al-]Asad knows that Abdullah is not trying to unite Syria, and vice versa. Abdullah knows Bishar is not pushing for greater Syria. They are pragmatic. They are both Western educated. Both are not ideological as in the past sense. Abdullah's ideology, what he wants, is development of Jordan mainly. Not ideology.

Plus they [Abdullah and Bishar] have a personal relationship. They knew each other before either took power. . . . The new generation knows its limits. [Hafizal-]Asad and Hussein really did have agendas and goals that were ideological and toward the broader Arab world.[14]

This discussion certainly underscores key reasons for the ending of the Cold War between Jordan and Syria. But it is also true that both states, in the absence of the longstanding ideological and personal baggage, have more regional alignment options in general. For Jordan in particular, relations with Syria no longer hold instant implications for other inter-Arab relationships. Indeed, in the absence of the personal rivalries and the opposite stances that had characterized the Cold War and the Iran-Iraq War, Jordan apparently no longer has to choose between aligning with either Syria or Iraq.[15]

The personal familiarity between Bishar and Abdullah helped bring Jordanian-Syrian relations to their closest point since the alignment of 1975–1979. This rapprochement was further enhanced by strong pro-Syrian constituencies in Jordanian politics. I refer here not to Ba'thist sympathizers, but rather to Jordanians whose livelihood is rooted in business, trade, and transportation links between the two countries. Influential officials, such a former prime minister and President of the Senate Zayd al-Rifa'i, have long seen the various periods of the Cold War as the aberration, while warm Jordanian-Syrian relations are seen as the "natural" order of things. Syrian opposition exiles, in contrast, especially those affiliated with the Muslim Brotherhood, had been welcome in Jordan for decades, and hence were alarmed at this warming of relations. After President Bishar al-Asad assumed power in 2000, and in the context of warming Jordanian-Syrian relations, the kingdom deported a series of leading members of the Syrian Muslim Brotherhood.[16]

It was against the Muslim Brotherhood in 1982 that the Syrian state had used its most extreme force ever in crushing domestic opposition. Unlike the adversarial roles played by the Jordanian and Syrian *mukhabarat* during their decades of Cold War, now the two states seemed to be edging toward intelligence cooperation. Jordan's director of the *mukhabarat*, in fact, became a regular participant in most major bilateral meetings and agreements. While Jordan moved to expel select Syrian dissidents, the Syrian state conversely agreed to a modicum of media pluralism by allowing Jordanian newspapers to begin circulating in Syria for the first time in 20 years.[17]

Having apparently abandoned support for each other's opposition movements, and having instead concluded a series of political and economic agreements, the Jordanian-Syrian Cold War seemed to have come to an end.

Political Economy

What is most striking about the roles of individual governmental elites in the alignment-building process, perhaps, is the similarity in background of the officials themselves. In both Jordan and Syria, cabinet portfolios have been given increasingly to Western-educated technocrats, and particularly to elites with training in economics (substantially reflecting the central concerns of both regimes). As the two countries drew closer together in 1999, their respective prime ministers seemed to symbolize this pattern of elite change within the two regimes. Jordanian Prime Minister Ali Abu al-Raghib and Syrian Prime Minister Muhammad Mustafa Miru were both Western-educated economists noted for their technocratic expertise and their emphasis on economic development. And it is particularly telling that most of the bilateral meetings designed to end the Cold War featured large roles for ministers with economic portfolios. Furthermore, of the agreements signed between the two states to mark the beginning of their rapidly increasing cooperation, the great majority were explicitly about economic concerns.

In August 1999 Jordan and Syria signed a trade agreement eliminating tariffs on selected products in bilateral trade. More than two years later, in October 2001, the two countries pushed this process much further by formalizing a Free Trade Agreement (FTA). The Jordanian-Syrian FTA entered into force in 2002, lifting tariffs on most goods exported from either country to the other. Some items such as clothing and shoes were allowed a temporary tariff exemption, leaving tariffs as high as 60 percent, but with the intention of eventually eliminating these too in a series of reductions.[18]

Both countries had been undergoing processes of economic restructuring and adjustment in recent years, albeit in varying degrees. In the Jordanian case, adjustment began in 1989, when the kingdom was unable to meet its debt obligations and was forced to turn to the International Monetary Fund for economic aid. Since that time, the Jordanian government implemented a series of IMF programs, each time triggering political upheavals.[19] Thus Jordan's economic and political liberalization has been tumultuous, at times, and since the late 1990s has shown signs of an increasing disconnect between the political and economic sides of the project. Political liberalization has, if anything, stalled or slid backwards, precisely because economic adjustment has proceeded apace with corresponding political discontent.

For all its limitations, however, the Jordanian reform process has gone much further than that in Syria. This discrepancy led to a series of meetings between Jordanian and Syrian officials to explore paths toward reform. Jordan's foreign minister, 'Abd al-Illah al-Khatib, noted:

> Bishar started . . . on a very positive note in relations with Jordan. But maybe the power centers in Syria constrain him from moving too much. In the year 2001 we had several meetings at the Dead Sea, meetings about reform and so on. The Syrian delegation was very impressed with the changes in Jordan, but after that they were pulled back and contacts were strictly limited. Maybe more powerful figures in the regime limited these contacts. They feared too much influence for similar changes in Syria. Especially with two younger leaders who know the world. The ingredients of rapprochement were there. Other factors limited how close we could actually get, though. I think Bishar was pulled back, away from the progressive stance of Jordan. Still, they, the two leaders, do have good personal relations.[20]

Despite high expectations for political liberalization upon the accession of Bishar to the presidency, followed by a brief period known as "Damascus Spring," the Syrian state thereafter seemed to conduct business as usual in its essentially authoritarian fashion. Economic liberalization in Syria has been slow and limited, but has made inroads since the early 1990s and is certainly more visible than any political liberalization.[21] It is in this context of privatization, liberalization, and freer flow of goods that business elites in both countries increased their transnational links across the Jordanian-Syrian border.

As this book has shown, Jordan has seemed obsessive about achieving economic agreements. While Syria has been more reluctant, the Jordanian government has embraced the Bretton Woods institutions (the IMF, World Bank, and the World Trade Organization) while actively pressing for a free trade agreement with the United States. This request was particularly unusual since—aside from NAFTA—the United States had, at the time, a free trade agreement only with Israel. But King Abdullah was intent on securing the U.S.-Jordanian Free Trade Agreement, as a key economic factor solidifying Jordan's political and military alliance with the United States. The agreement might have received greater scrutiny or criticism within the United

States at some other time, but in the immediate aftermath of the terrorist attacks of September 11, 2001, on the United States, Congress quickly approved and ratified the deal.

Jordan may have cemented its image as the virtual poster-country for embracing globalization, when it hosted a special meeting of the World Economic Forum (WEF) in June 2003 and annually thereafter.[22] The WEF, gathering together the world's most powerful government and business elites (including the world's main creditors) meets in Davos, Switzerland, every winter. Bringing the WEF to Jordan's Dead Sea resort for what were becoming annual summer meetings was something of a diplomatic and perhaps economic coup for King Abdullah. But even before the WEF began meeting regularly in Jordan, the Jordanians strongly encouraged the new Syrian president to follow their economic lead, including Syria in discussions shortly after the succession. Jordanian Prime Minister Fayiz Tarawnah accompanied King Abdullah on his condolence visit to Damascus, but came away convinced that there were limits to how fast Bishar could move:

> We met for lunch on the fortieth day of the mourning period. Bishar asked many questions. He asked King Abdullah specific questions about privatization, investment, opening the economy. He clearly wanted to open up Syria. King Abdullah was very enthusiastic about this. He offered any and all experience and help Jordan could offer. He even encouraged Bishar to go to Davos to the World Economic Forum, possibly even as part of a joint Jordanian-Syrian delegation. He encouraged Bishar to introduce himself. He said they would be interested because "they don't know Syria or your father." The failures are not because of Bishar but because of structures . . . the old guard still surrounded him. All the president's men were still there.[23]

With Jordanian prodding, Syria sent its own representatives to the Jordan WEF meeting in 2003, having earlier applied for membership in the World Trade Organization. Syria's WEF delegation, however, was made up of private business people, rather than government and party officials, underscoring the regime's still tentative approach to such global capitalist institutions.

Besides economic interests in boosting bilateral trade and encouraging foreign investment, another key concern of both Jordan and Syria is water. Both countries experienced several years of droughts in the late 1990s. The problem was more severe for Jordan, with seven consecutive summer droughts and considerably less water than Syria. Jordan had already had to turn to Syria to supplement its water supply in 1999 and 2000. By 2001, the two countries concluded a new water agreement that increased the flow of Yarmuk river water to Jordan. In addition, the new agreement revived an earlier 1987 plan between Jordan and Syria to work jointly on the creation of the al-Wihdah dam, which is to create a reservoir along the Yarmuk river basin. In the meantime Syria (which many Jordanian officials accuse of diverting Yarmuk water away from Jordan) continued to divert or re-divert water to help alleviate Jordan's chronic drought problem.[24] Jordanian economist Riad al-Khouri has suggested that a certain symbiosis may develop here, in which Syria helps Jordan with its water supply while Jordan helps reform Syria's cumbersome and antiquated banking system—amounting, in his words, to "liquidity" of two very different types.[25]

Renewed Strains in Jordanian-Syrian Relations

The rapprochement and even emergent alignment between the two states was challenged almost immediately by regional and global crises: first, the second intifadah in the Palestinian territories; second, the attacks of September 11, 2001, on the United States and the resulting U.S. military campaign in Afghanistan and its global campaign against terrorism; and third, in 2003, the U.S. invasion of Iraq.

Given the rising intensity of regional crises, one might expect differences over high politics issues to drive a wedge between Jordan and Syria once again, especially over the Arab-Israeli conflict and peace process or over relations with Gulf states. But here, too, the regimes were in sync for the most part. Jordan had re-achieved its pre-Gulf War relations with all of the Arab Gulf monarchies, while Syria had become even more formally aligned with these states through the Damascus Declaration alignment.[26] Despite differences regarding relations with Israel, both states supported the Palestinian intifadah, both opposed Israel's violent suppression of that uprising, especially under the Sharon government, and both agreed even on many broader security issues throughout the region.

A key point, then, is that these are not the days of the old Arab Cold War, with states being distinguished as radical republics versus conservative monarchies. In some respects, Syria and Jordan might still fit these categories, but the radical republic and the conservative monarchy had drifted closer to alignment, showing no concern regarding the other's political system. More importantly, the distinctions between radical and moderate Arab states, as drawn by U.S. foreign policymakers, seem to apply less than they ever did. For example, on countless occasions Syria has made clear its opposition to the al-Qa'ida attacks on the United States, while also condemning U.S. and European double standards regarding Palestinian rights. But this is not just the position of a "radical Syria." Rather, it is the position of Syria and of Jordan, Egypt, the Gulf states, and indeed of most Arab countries. Jordan and Syria agreed further that the sanctions on Iraq (before the fall of Saddam Hussein) punished the Iraqi people and not the regime, and that they should have been lifted.

When the United States created its military buildup for an attack on Iraq, Jordan and Syria both opposed the invasion. President Bishar al-Asad was, admittedly, far more vocal and one of the strongest opponents of the invasion. Even on the thorny issue of terrorism, it is not just Syria that objects to the U.S. and the United Nations condemning terrorism without distinguishing between al-Qa'ida and national liberation movements. The Jordanian government maintained this viewpoint even as it closed down Hamas offices in the kingdom; Hamas could continue to operate, but not in Jordan.

As threats continued to emanate from the Bush administration against Syria in particular, Jordan and once again most Arab countries insisted that these threats must stop. Unlike Iraq, Syria was directly allied not only to states that the U.S. government opposed (such as Iran) but also to major U.S. allies (such as Egypt and all six Arab Gulf monarchies). Yet Syria's regional position had, without question, steadily deteriorated in the early twenty-first century. It is worth noting that the pressure to reassert this outdated sense of radical versus moderate Arab states came not from Jordan, but from the Bush administration in the United States. Jordan had, in a sense, benefitted from the "War on Terror" by receiving massive increases in U.S. foreign economic and military aid. The Hashimite regime consequently had to tread carefully to appease its American patrons, even as Jordan attempted to avoid any reassertion of the Jordanian-Syrian Cold War.

The U.S. invasion of Iraq led to an extensive insurgency and the rise of routine terrorism within Iraq. Foreign Islamist fighters, some of them Syrian, crossed into Iraq to join the fight against the U.S. occupation. While such fighters crossed into Iraq from several countries, presumably including Jordan, the Bush administration focused on Syria specifically, alleging Syrian support in facilitating such crossings and in supporting the Iraqi insurgency. The Syrian government strongly denied these allegations, but U.S. military attacks began to target towns on the Syrian-Iraqi border, while the administration continued to threaten the use of force against Syria. Since the Bush administration had already invaded and occupied two countries in the region, such threats had to be taken very seriously indeed.

Tensions grew stronger still when Lebanese Prime Minister Rafiq Hariri was assassinated by a car bomb in Beirut on February 14, 2005. Suspicion within Lebanon immediately focused on Syria. The resulting outrage in Lebanon led to vast street demonstrations calling for justice and for the ouster of Syrian forces from Lebanon. As the demonstrations and international condemnation of alleged Syrian complicity in the assassination developed into a crescendo, Syria was obliged to withdraw its remaining military forces from Lebanon. In October 2005, the first of a series of U.N. investigative reports charged Lebanese and Syrian intelligence agencies with complicity in Hariri's murder, leading the U.S. administration to call for action from the U.N. Security Council. In short, Syria's diplomatic and security position continued its steady and demeaning decline. This included domestic intra-regime insecurity, as Bishar loyalists and older hard-liners appeared to engage in struggles for the soul of the party, the regime, and the nation.

The Jordanian regime, meanwhile, had supported U.N. calls for full Syrian withdrawal from Lebanon. Jordan maintained its post-cold war relations with Syria, but given the overwhelming series of crises and of Syrian missteps, the damage was sufficient to prevent a full-scale Jordanian-Syrian alliance from forming after all, despite all the groundwork already achieved. Yet, just as importantly, there was no sign that Jordan and Syria were returning to their earlier hostility. Jordanian policymakers and policy advisors seemed to have reached a kind of consensus: that Bishar still held real possibilities, that the problem in Syria (and hence the impediment to Jordanian-Syrian relations warming still further) was rooted in old guard Ba'thists, and that the various policy mistakes were leading to a showdown within Syria—if U.S. threats didn't in the meantime strengthen the hands of regime hardliners.

In the view of Jordan's former Foreign Minister Kamel Abu Jaber, "Today, despite Bishar, the old guard is still in power in Syria, but Jordanian-Syrian relations are at least on an even keel, somewhere between warm and tepid."[27] Jordanian Senator Layla Sharaf, Chair of the Senate's Foreign Relations Committee, emphasized that "Jordan and Syria have settled our minor border questions, our minor little tiffs; and Bishar is a much better person than his regime."[28] Similarly, a former prime minister stated flatly that "the old man has died. His son is more progressive. A reformer. But I don't know if he will be able to change the powerful people around him."[29] Another former prime minister agreed, but also, while offering Jordan as a bridge between Syria and its U.S. detractors, expressed the disappointment that many Jordanian officials felt:

> Syria could have leaned on us, but maybe they still don't think we are a country. Just Southern Syrians maybe. But still our relations are not hostile. We have regular meetings. There is the higher committee on Jordanian-Syrian relations, which meets regularly. I would say luke-warm relations, but no hostility. Jordan remains ready with its good offices for Syria.[30]

One of Jordan's key foreign policy advisors argued, however, that even Syria's debacles might actually provide the means for Bishar to truly create his own regime, rather than struggle with the one he inherited from his father:

> I have a hunch that a struggle for power is beginning in Syria. The Bishar school versus his brother-in-law (in charge of military intel-ligence) and others who are more conservative. Bishar may be able to use their debacle in Lebanon to take policy into his own hands. With-drawal may even strengthen his hand in domestic politics.[31]

At the 2005 Ba'th Party Conference, minor changes did appear, leading to the retirement of long-time hardliner 'Abd al-Halim al-Khaddam. But as has been the case with reform in Syria in general, the various changes were minor and incremental. And Khaddam himself, in a particularly bizarre twist, became a leader-in-exile of the anti-Ba'thist opposition to Bishar's regime.

Conclusions

As this chapter has made clear, much of the history of modern Jordanian-Syrian relations has consisted of political and at times even military con-frontation. The mutual animosity between the two countries increased with changes in the regional system over time, especially concerning the Arab-Is-raeli conflict. The animosity was also affected, however, by changes in their respective domestic systems. Since at least the early 1950s, with the onset of the Hussein regime in Amman and a series of ideological military "strong-men" in Damascus, bilateral relations were for years marked by rivalries of radicalism versus conservatism, country-nationalism versus Arabism, and revolutionary republicanism versus traditional monarchism. The two states had also maintained vastly different approaches to the Palestinian-Israeli issue. While Jordan secured a peace treaty with Israel in 1994, Syria and Israel remained officially in a state of war well into the twenty-first century. Jordan and Syria even backed opposite sides in the Persian Gulf Wars of 1980–1988 and 1991, while leaning in opposite directions throughout the U.S.-Soviet global Cold War. Yet, on merely two occasions since independence, the two states have succeeded in ending their acrimonious relationship—their localized cold war—and achieved rapprochement.

The 1975–1979 period saw the creation of a fairly strong alliance between Jordan and Syria, based on changing strategic, domestic, and economic factors. That alliance, however, ultimately collapsed. The real question for the present, then, is whether the more recent rapprochement will amount to a more substantial alignment or even a full alliance in the near future, and, more importantly, whether the warming of bilateral relations will last. The circumstances, I would argue, are significantly different this time around, especially under new leaderships with scant linkages to the headier ideological rifts that long characterized inter-Arab relations. The Jordanian and Syrian regimes are both run, for now, by leaders with at least some similar goals and interests, especially in terms of economic development, access to foreign aid, and debt relief.

From the start the new Jordanian-Syrian relationship, like the earlier rapprochement, was built on functional transnational ties and agreements in "low politics"—from cultural exchange through economic agreements. In both rapprochements, contrary to Neorealist expectations, the main causal factors were rooted heavily in domestic politics and political economy, and only slightly in external security concerns or structural changes in the regional balance of power. Regime change in both capitals provided the opening for rapprochement, but the drive in each case came from using this opening as an opportunity to shore up the domestic security of both regimes.[32]

With major political transitions within both countries in the post-Hafiz al-Asad and post-King Hussein eras, both countries also went through transitions in their very state identities. While many outside Jordan and Syria persist in seeing these countries as the virtual embodiment of their late leaders, and hence see the countries as the binary and eternally opposite social constructs alluded to above, the reality is far different and perhaps more mundane. For all their differences, the regimes of Bishar al-Asad and King Abdullah II are mainly pragmatic. Neither is as ideological as its predecessor. And perhaps more importantly, the two states agree on many of the major issues of the day. A key question, however, is whether the Jordanian-Syrian Cold War is over for good.

Despite the emerging U.S.-Syrian crisis, the Jordanian-Syrian rapprochement (if not alliance) has managed to hold. In addition to their many shared economic interests—from trade, to water access, to joint aid lobbying toward the Gulf monarchies—Jordan and Syria have agreed even on some of the most contentious regional security issues of the day. And these lines of agreement are reinforced by frequent direct contacts between regime officials, including bilateral summitry between President Asad and King Abdullah. In November 2007, for example, the two heads of state met in a bilateral summit to revive the groundwork for an alignment. This meeting was followed by a host of agreements on Jordanian-Syrian cooperation regarding trade, industry, water resources, and border issues, as well as exchanges in education, cultural affairs, and even sports. In these agreements the two governments returned (at least rhetorically) to discussions of "integration" and working together "to defend Arab causes and serve common interests."[33]

It is probable that this rapprochement will lead to a more lasting positive relationship between Jordan and Syria than has heretofore been possible since the late 1970s. Even though bilateral relations are no longer likely to lead to a full-scale alliance, at least one fact is clear: the Jordanian-Syrian Cold War is—once again—over.

12

Jordan and the Second U.S.-Iraq War

The years after the Hashimite succession from Hussein to Abdullah were an especially tumultuous and violent period, even in the context of Middle East politics. The early years of the new century saw the collapse of the peace process, an increase in Jihadist terrorism, and U.S. wars against both Afghanistan and Iraq. This chapter provides an analysis of Jordan's foreign policy and its alignment decisions, as the regime responded to a severe challenge to the security of the region, the kingdom, and the Abdullah II regime: the second U.S. war against Iraq.

In September 2000, following the failure of Israeli-Palestinian negotiations at Camp David, a second intifada began as Palestinians rose up against Israeli occupation in the West Bank and Gaza. A year later, on September 11, 2001, al-Qa'ida terrorists hijacked planes and flew them into the Twin Towers of New York City and the Pentagon building in Washington, DC. A fourth plane was also hijacked but crashed in a field in Pennsylvania. All told, almost 3,000 people died in the attacks. Closer to home, Jordanian intelligence services charged that al-Qa'ida had also intended to attack Jordan at that time, and to assassinate the king and his family.[1]

Within months, U.S. military forces began bombing Afghanistan, attacking both al-Qa'ida forces as well as those of the Taliban regime ruling Afghanistan. In contrast to its later stance on the U.S.-Iraq war, the Hashimite regime supported the U.S. war on the Taliban and al-Qa'ida in Afghanistan. Jordan's former Prime Minister Fayez Tarawnah noted the impact of the September 11, 2001, attacks for Jordan:

> September 11th changed much. The king felt that that was beyond inhumane. He was concerned also with the image of Islam and of the Arabs, and of human tragedy. Emotionally and politically, we stood with the United States. The king was often on US television . . . He made clear he and Jordan were definitely with the US in the international war on terrorism. We did not field troops in Afghanistan but

did send field hospitals, to make clear our support and our stance. There was no controversy about it. We had never recognized the Taliban regime anyway and had suffered from the "Afghani Arabs."[2]

But as the Palestinian uprising and the war in Afghanistan continued (even after the fall of the Taliban regime), the United States government threatened to invade Iraq.

The Bush administration had invoked the nebulous phrase "War on Terror" to justify a wide range of military operations, from Afghanistan to Iraq, with additional threats of military action against Iran, North Korea, and Syria. While Afghanistan had provided shelter for al-Qa'ida militants, Iraq was a secular socialist dictatorship with a long history of hostility toward Islamist movements of any kind. Still, despite most available evidence, the U.S. administration insisted that invading Iraq would be part of the "War on Terror," even as critics charged that the invasion would undermine efforts to combat global Islamist terrorism. Administration officials argued that Iraq was linked to al-Qa'ida in some way, and continually invoked the horrific memories of the terrorist attacks of September 11, 2001, despite the absence of Iraqi involvement in those attacks. The U.S. charges against Saddam Hussein's regime changed over time. Originally the Bush administration insisted that Iraq possessed an arsenal of weapons of mass destruction, and that Saddam's regime constituted a direct threat to the United States. The focus later shifted to the person of Saddam Hussein and to the idea of regime change in Baghdad, and even holding a new democratic Iraq up as a model for the rest of the region to follow.

Thus, following one relatively placid year in office, the Abdullah regime in Jordan was thereafter buffeted between a series of regional crises, each of which directly affected the regime: violence in Israel and Palestine, al-Qa'ida terrorism, a U.S. invasion of Afghanistan, and then the threat of war on Iraq (and hence on Jordan's eastern border) as well. For Jordanian policymakers, however, the wars on Afghanistan and on Iraq were very different. Former Foreign Minister Kamel Abu Jaber summarized the Hashimite regime's view, noting that:

> The Afghan war was an altogether different situation. The Taliban were a pre-primitive political order. It was an embarrassment to the whole Islamic world, what they were doing to women, and banning music, dancing, and so on. Jordan supported getting rid of that regime. Some Islamists opposed it, but not all did. It was different from Iraq.[3]

The regime had many times in the past confronted threats and challenges emanating from either the Arab-Israeli conflict or recurrent conflicts in the Persian Gulf. This time, however, the new Hashimite regime of King Abdullah II faced both conflicts at the same time. Yet, as had so often happened before, the regime was torn between competing interests and allies. As a second U.S. war on Iraq appeared to be inevitable, would Jordan join a U.S.-led coalition? Would the regime attempt to mediate between the U.S. and Iraq, or—as in the 1991 Gulf War—would Jordan be accused of allying with Saddam Hussein against the U.S.?

External Security

As preceding chapters have made clear, Jordan's relations with Iraq have shifted dramatically over the years. This instability becomes especially clear in the light of how close the two countries' relations were for more than a decade preceding the ill-fated Iraqi military onslaught against Kuwait.

As recounted in chapter 9, while the United States recruited Arab countries to join its coalition against Iraq in the first U.S.-Iraq War in 1991, Jordan tried to steer a middle course between Baghdad and Washington. In the end, Jordan's Gulf War position alienated most of the kingdom's allies and especially damaged relations with the United States, the United Kingdom, and the Arab Gulf monarchies. The latter states further penalized the kingdom not only by cutting off oil and aid supplies, but also by expelling hundreds of thousands of Jordanian and Palestinian guest workers.[4] Given the severe economic, social, and political costs that Jordan incurred for its 1991 Gulf war decision, it is not surprising that the shadow of that episode has loomed large over Jordanian foreign policy ever since. And certainly that shadow remained in place in 2003, as the Hashimite regime was once again confronted with a U.S. war against its Iraqi neighbor and former ally.

Despite the duration of the 1979–1991 Jordanian-Iraqi Alliance, the mid-1990s had marked a new low point in Jordanian-Iraqi relations. As discussed in chapter 10, by 1995 King Hussein had broken publicly with Iraq and allowed Iraqi opposition groups to organize and set up offices in Amman. As has occurred during every Jordanian-Iraqi rift, regional rumor mills and assorted tabloids carried the theory that Jordan intended to revive Hashimite claims to Iraq—an intention the Jordanian government has always denied, and would again feel compelled to deny as late as 2003.[5] The 1990s Jordanian-Iraqi rift, however, proved nonetheless to be short-lived and in the final years of King Hussein's reign, Jordanian-Iraqi relations began to smooth over.

Following the 1999 succession in the Jordanian monarchy, Jordan became the first Arab country to officially break the United Nations embargo on Iraq. In his first speech to the Jordanian parliament, King Abdullah emphasized his view (shared by many throughout the Arab world) that the sanctions and embargo were far too severe and were hurting the Iraqi people without really harming their regime. Jordanian civilian planes began to land in Baghdad, carrying with them much-needed medical supplies. Official delegations soon followed, not only from Jordan but also from other Arab countries, as these too began to break the embargo. The war of words that had accompanied the earlier Iraqi-Jordanian rift appeared to be over.[6] Most importantly, Iraq agreed to resume shipments of oil to Jordan, at the customary concessionary prices. While the two countries were by no means re-establishing their former alliance, Jordan re-emerged as Iraq's economic lifeline (mainly through the Jordanian port of Aqaba) to the rest of the world.[7]

Yet, even in the worst periods of the diplomatic rift of the mid-1990s, the Jordanian-Iraqi relationship had managed to maintain pragmatic and functional economic ties. Jordan's former Foreign Minister 'Abd al-Illah al-Khatib argued, however, that Jordanian-Iraqi relations were poorly understood by outside powers:

> There was no common ground between Jordan and Saddam. It was a marriage of convenience. Not even a marriage really, but of necessity not of choice. Jordan relied heavily on Iraq, especially for our oil needs. People misunderstood that as charity by Saddam. But it was not. In exchange, (Iraq) could breathe through Jordan. Jordan was the only legal transaction for Iraq outside of the oil for food plan of the UN, under article 50 of the UN Charter, and the UN acquiesced. That was the basis for Jordan sustaining its relations with Iraq. But it was not otherwise a genuine relationship. Jordan never condoned Iraq's policies or its behavior. In 1998, when I took the position of foreign minister of Jordan, there was Saddam fatigue in the region. We continue to suffer economically even now because of his wars.[8]

Despite the extensive damage to the political side of Jordanian-Iraqi relations—caused by the 1991 Gulf War, Jordan's peace with Israel, and Jordan's decision to host Iraqi opposition groups—the symbiotic economic relationship between the two states had managed to survive after all.[9]

The tendency to prioritize such economic ties, and hence to rebuild the many bridges ruptured in Jordan's inter-Arab relations in the 1990s, quickly became cornerstones of Abdullah's foreign policy. Yet, as Palestinian and Iraqi casualty tolls continued to mount, the regime's strong ties to Western states, and especially to the United States, carried with them ever-larger domestic costs. Regime and society appeared to be pulling in opposite directions, at least on the issue of the U.S.-Jordanian relationship. This polarization, while it led many regime officials to fear domestic unrest, only added to a series of fears hinging on major demographic threats to domestic stability, such as the fear of large numbers of refuges fleeing to Jordan from either the West Bank or Iraq, or both simultaneously.[10]

Jordanian policymakers also feared that war to the East would actively undermine Jordanian interests to the West, specifically interests of achieving a peaceful settlement between Israel and the Palestinians. King Abdullah had repeatedly noted that the Arab-Israeli issue remained the core obstacle to broader Middle East peace, rather than any issue concerning Iraq. As the traditional English-language pun phrased it, Jordan remained wedged "between Iraq and a hard place." And as one of Jordan's former prime ministers put it:

> Since mid-2002 the king expressed fears of war on Iraq. He was not fond of Saddam. He never even saw the guy. But we were at the point, in the region, where we had all the ingredients to solve the Arab-Israeli issue. This [war in Iraq] would be a huge distraction. The worries were not about the war as a military operation, but about its consequences and aftermath . . . The US decision to announce support for a Palestinian state was a plus, and Bush used to be vocal on the settlements issue. The roadmap emerged, the Arab summit, but then the Iraq invasion and destruction. The Americans can only work one issue at a time, it seems. The Iraq war shelved all of this potential.[11]

For these reasons, King Abdullah and the Hashimite regime repeatedly communicated their opposition to any strike on Iraq. The Jordanians' protests were joined by a veritable chorus from other U.S. regional allies such as Egypt, Tunisia, and Saudi Arabia, and by even more fervent opposition from Syria.

Indeed, King Abdullah angered the Bush administration during his July 2002 visit to the United States. While the king would later be more cautious in his wording, in that visit he referred to the war planning as "ludicrous" and further described it as a "tremendous mistake."[12]

Contradictory press reports charged that the regime absolutely opposed any strike, and also that the regime was negotiating secret deals to allow strikes to take place from Jordanian soil.[13] These latter reports also charged that economic factors remained a major sticking point, with the regime making clear the need for an alternative oil supplier if Iraqi supplies were to be disrupted.[14] In the end, Jordan did allow the deployment of U.S. Patriot anti-missile batteries in its eastern desert, but the regime insisted that no U.S. combat operations were launched from Jordanian soil and that the U.S. military deployment was minimal, defensive, and temporary. As noted earlier, the memory of the 1991 Gulf War loomed large during the 2003 crisis. King Abdullah was determined not to have Jordan suffer the same outcome that had occurred after that earlier crisis and war.

In January 2003, when the World Economic Forum held its annual meeting in Davos, Switzerland, King Abdullah was the only Arab head of state asked to address the conference. In doing so, the king reaffirmed Jordan's opposition to war with Iraq, but also expressed his skepticism that war could be avoided, given U.S. military preparations. He also reiterated, however, his concern that the real unresolved issue in Middle East politics was the Palestinian-Israeli conflict, and not any issue in the Gulf region.[15]

External security concerns appeared to be deeply connected to the regime's fears for domestic stability. The regime's close relations with the United States had become a fairly severe domestic liability, just as Jordan's extensive economic ties to both the United States and Iraq tore the regime in opposite directions. Finally, Jordanian policymakers were deeply concerned with the regional security situation in a post-war Iraq. Former Prime Minister 'Abd al-Salam al-Majali specifically noted Jordan's opposition to the break-up of Iraq, as well as the kingdom's fear that a war might destabilize the entire region. "We were afraid," he argued, "of Iraq being Balkanized."[16]

Attempting to clarify Jordan's position on the U.S.-Iraq war, one of Jordan's former foreign ministers argued that

> The king took the right position. Nothing could be done to stop the invasion, regardless of Jordanian foreign policy. Jordan cautioned against the war. Once again, Jordan can say, I told you so. After the war, King Abdullah was one of the first to say the U.S. won the war,

but not the peace. We thought war would bring more disaster to the region. We did not support Saddam. But we did not support invasion either.[17]

Another former foreign minister echoed this point, but also added an assessment broadly shared throughout the region:

> Jordan did not support the U.S. war against Iraq. King Abdullah advised Bush and the Americans not to go to war. But the American plan had been made much earlier. Even during the 2000 campaign. It was a bulldozer not to be stopped for any reason. And then all the excuses for the war turned out to be false and so they had to focus on Saddam's personality . . . Jordan feared that war might drag in Turkey, Israel, and others, creating a black hole sucking the whole region in. [Another] fear was the dismemberment of Iraq. And now, in effect, that has taken place. Bush has opened a Pandora's box for a long time to come. And this applies not just to Iraq, but to the whole region. They have created a bleeding festering wound.[18]

Given the many regional security concerns noted above, Jordan was not in a position to choose between conventional options such as balancing and bandwagoning vis-à-vis regional threats. Which external power was the threat to bandwagon with, or balance against? For all its problems with Saddam Hussein's regime, the Hashimite monarchy did not fear Saddam's regime as an external threat per se. The monarchy feared, if anything, the Iraqi regime's impact on domestic security.

Similarly, the only nation issuing overt military threats was the United States, but these threats were directed at Iraq, and later even at Syria and Iran, not at Jordan. Here too, the conventional expectations simply don't apply to the Jordanian position. If anything, the regime may have been practicing its longstanding approach of "omnibalancing" between internal and external threats. Jordan refused to join the United States and the United Kingdom in their attack on Iraq, but maintained economic ties and frequent diplomatic exchange with both countries, thereby bandwagoning in perhaps the mildest possible economic—but not military—sense. For the most part, Jordanian policy was marked mainly by damage control and in that sense resembled hurricane preparation. The regime attempted to maintain its political and economic links to its key allies, but otherwise bolted down in an attempt simply to survive yet another regional disaster.

Domestic Politics

As Jordan's efforts to avert war appeared to be bearing no fruit, the regime began to brace for the domestic unrest that many officials believed would result from a U.S. attack on Iraq. Domestic crackdowns had accompanied many other regional crises, including the regime's decision to make peace with Israel. In this sense the Hussein and Abdullah regimes appear to be similar. In terms of priorities, the Abdullah regime, like that of Hussein before it, placed paramount importance on economic links and security concerns, often at the expense of the program of domestic political liberalization. All controversial foreign policy moves were accompanied by further retreat from Jordan's domestic political liberalization process.[19]

In the political climate of this series of regional crises, Jordan's parliamentary elections were repeatedly postponed. National parliamentary elections had been held in 1989, 1993, and 1997, with a fourth round due in November 2001.[20] Those elections were rescheduled to the summer, then to the fall of 2002, and were soon more than a year overdue. The elections finally did take place, however, in June 2003, after the fall of Saddam Hussein's regime in Iraq, and in the context of attempts to revive the Israeli-Palestinian peace process.

In her analysis of de-liberalization in Jordan, Jillian Schwedler has suggested that these electoral postponements would have occurred even without the additional security concerns that followed the attacks of September 11, 2001, on the United States. Indeed, the de-liberalization process seemed to be well underway in the immediate aftermath of the 1994 peace treaty with Israel.[21] The renewed Palestinian uprising, coupled with fears of renewed war in the Persian Gulf, only added to that process. In Schwedler's view, "the events of September 11 did not so much change the course of domestic politics in Jordan as accelerate them by providing a Washington-friendly justification for increased political repression."[22] Jordanian foreign policy, therefore, must be seen as walking the tightrope between internal and external security challenges. But by the same token, the regime's interest in the maintenance of its own security tends to take precedence in both domestic and foreign policy over all other considerations. The external security environment was so insecure that the regime in effect attempted to deal with the only realm it had more control over: by preempting any revival of its internal security dilemma.

Indeed, external ties are seen as so vital to the kingdom that the regime has at times exhibited limited tolerance for domestic opposition to its foreign policy decisions. Tolerance has appeared especially limited in the rift between the government and its political opponents over the latter's continuing campaign to prevent normalization of relations with Israel, despite the 1994 peace treaty.[23] With the second intifada beginning in 2000, that campaign steadily gathered more domestic political support and soon came to encompass public anger over U.S. threats against Iraq. As Lynch has argued, this development in Jordanian domestic politics led to an unusually powerful and pervasive consensus against U.S. support for Israeli occupation and against U.S. military threats to neighboring Iraq. The consensus in turn led to a boycott of U.S. goods in the kingdom, including the many U.S. fast-food restaurants that had multiplied especially across Amman. The level of popular dissatisfaction, and of government unease, was reflected in the increase of Jordanian military deployments in civilian areas where unrest was anticipated, in what some opposition leaders described as "occupied Amman."[24]

King Abdullah's domestic and foreign policy may best be summarized in the regime's own slogan: "Jordan first" (al-Urdun Awalan). While this slogan suggests a strong nationalist (rather than pan-Arabist) approach to foreign policy, it has also been used to counter "foreign" influences within Jordanian domestic politics. King Abdullah has, for example, personally criticized the international ties of many of Jordan's core opposition parties, from both pro-Syrian and pro-Iraqi Ba'thist Parties within the kingdom, to the communist party, to the Islamic Action Front. In King Abdullah's words:

> The programs, objectives, membership and financing of every party operating in Jordanian territory ought to be purely Jordanian . . . In recent decades, Jordan has given priority to Arab interests and not to its national interests . . . We have a right to be concerned first for our own people, as every country in the world does, which is where our "Jordan first" slogan comes from.[25]

The nationalist tone applies not just to foreign policy, but also to domestic politics. In actual practice, however, this means that many forms of political opposition, whether secular left or religious right, can potentially be categorized as "un-Jordanian." Even before the "Jordan first" public relations campaign began, dissident voices have at times been silenced through arrests of journalists, political party activists, and professional association officials critical of the regime. Dissidents as diverse as independent Islamist Layth Shubaylat and feminist activist Tujan al-Faysal (the only woman elected to parliament prior to 2003) were in separate cases arrested, convicted of various anti-regime remarks, and later released. But having been convicted, neither major opposition figure was thereafter eligible to run for a seat in parliament.

In August 2002, signaling the limits to its tolerance of criticism aired by the satellite television station al-Jazeera, the regime shut down the station's Amman office. The offending program involved an interview with U.S. scholar Asad Abu Khalil, who criticized the late King Hussein for being too close to Israel and the United States even before the 1994 peace treaty. According to Muhammad Afash Adwan, Jordan's minister of information, al-Jazeera crossed a line in a way that "continuously intends to harm Jordan and its national stands whether directly or indirectly" and "in a way which confirms that its main goal is to create disturbance . . . and provoke sedition."[26]

Within the kingdom, meanwhile, unrest re-emerged once again in the south of Jordan, particularly in the city of Ma'an—the scene of widespread rioting against IMF austerity programs in 1989 and 1996, as well as the scene of widespread demonstrations against the U.S. bombing of Iraq in 1998. In 2002 Ma'an was once again a focal point for opposition. Interestingly, the city has been seen by the regime at times alternatively as a bedrock of traditional Hashimite support, a hotbed of Islamist activity, or a center for pro-Iraqi Ba'thist activity. Despite the apparent contradictions, Ma'an is, in short, continually socially reconstructed, but always with emphasis on external sources of opposition.[27]

Jordan's intelligence service, or mukhabarat, apparently believes that this opposition is not just a matter of indigenous Islamist activity, but rather of outside agitators. These were represented as either al-Qa'ida-influenced Saudis, who had crossed from the nearby Saudi border, or as veterans of Afghani fighting who had re-emerged in Jordan after the fall of the Taliban regime in the 2001–2002 U.S.-Afghani war. During earlier unrest in 1996 and 1998, the mukhabarat charged that local pro-Iraqi Ba'thist agents were stirring unrest and violence in Ma'an. As before, the regime response involved not only the police, but also the regular army. Troops sealed off the town completely before moving through key neighborhoods in force, killing six people and arresting more than 100.[28]

Given the level of force used to quell Ma'an, the Hashimite regime may have been attempting to rein in dissent in general, in anticipation of the looming U.S. war against Iraq. For some Jordanian officials, the Ma'an incidents appeared to foreshadow a far worse bout of domestic unrest that would surely follow a U.S. invasion of Iraq. In the context of rising regional crises, many Jordanian officials feared the nightmare scenario of an Israeli mass expulsion of Palestinians from the West Bank across the Jordan river. Similarly, to the east, the regime feared being dragged into a U.S.-Iraq war.[29] Among many other objections, they feared that massive numbers of Iraqi refugees might flow westward into the kingdom, joining hundreds of thousands of dissident Iraqis already there. As it happened, the dire Jordanian warnings were, if anything, underestimates of the depth of the problem. In the years following the U.S. invasion of Iraq, the Iraqi refugee population in Jordan alone swelled to almost one million, with another million having fled to Syria.

In press interviews Jordanian Foreign Minister Marwan Muasher made Jordanian fears quite explicit:

> We do not want to see a situation where the Israeli government might make use of a war on Iraq in order to transfer Palestinians to Jordan . . . We already have a war going on in the West Bank and we don't need another war going on to our East. It is easy for outsiders to try to solve the problem from the outside. They are not living here. We're living in the midst of Iraq and the Palestinian conflict, and our ability to handle two wars, for a country like Jordan, is extremely limited.[30]

Some Jordanian officials stressed their fear that Iraqi intelligence agents already resided in the kingdom and could stir up trouble, acting as a kind of "fifth column" against the Hashimite regime. Jordanian policymakers further feared being pressured to allow American forces to launch combat missions from the Jordanian desert into western Iraq. The domestic implications of the regime joining an unprovoked attack on another Arab country, especially one that had suffered so much under the sanctions regime, were dire to say the least.

While Jordan refused to allow a U.S. invasion to take place from its territory against Iraq, the government did allow the temporary placement of U.S. Patriot anti-missile batteries, staffed by U.S. military personnel, in its eastern desert. This issue was so domestically sensitive, however, that the government was forced to repeatedly deny rumors that thousands of U.S. or even Israeli troops had deployed within Jordan. Given its fears of internal unrest and domestic regime insecurity, the government repeatedly issued decrees with new restrictions on publications, public demonstrations, and various other aspects of civil society. From 1999 to 2003 alone, the government issued well over 100 such "temporary" laws. In Jordan, as elsewhere, the state emphasis on security and the "War on Terror" was used to justify numerous aspects of de-liberalization.

In sum, these moves should be seen as emblematic of the deep level of *domestic* insecurity that was felt by the regime even before the U.S.-Iraq war, yet—ironically—that was caused by the regime's fears regarding *regional* insecurity. In other words, by adopting foreign policy positions that appeared to bandwagon with U.S. foreign policy in the region, the regime became more vulnerable at home. In fairness, the regime did oppose the U.S. attack on Iraq and warned the U.S. repeatedly against it. Yet, having failed to dissuade its U.S. ally, the Jordanian regime thereafter worked to ensure that there would be no U.S.-Jordanian rift as had accompanied the earlier U.S.-Iraq war. The Ma'an affair suggests that the regime was bracing for far more unrest than actually occurred during the Iraq war and later U.S. occupation. While de-liberalization seemed to be the order of the day, security and intelligence services remained on alert, in effect forming a barrier between the monarchy and those within Jordanian politics who continued to push for a return to the deep levels of political liberalization in Jordan that had so inspired Jordanians in the 1989–1994 period. In its attempt to avoid the external security dilemma, the regime emphatically held on to its external alliances virtually as life lines, thereby triggering the internal security dilemma, with its so often ironic and even tragic results.

Political Economy

While external security factors pressed the regime from the outside and domestic politics pressured the regime from within, both threatened the broader political economy of Hashimite regime security. Like most developing countries, Jordan is subject to a certain redundancy of pressures built into the global political economy, as key sources of public and private economic aid overlap. The major governmental donors of economic aid (the United States, the European Union countries, and Japan) have the majority of votes within powerful global economic institutions such as the International Monetary Fund and the World Bank. The redundancy of pressures continues in the world of private banking or corporate foreign investment, since most global banks and indeed most of the world's foreign investment capital is also concentrated in the United States, Western Europe, and Japan. In short, small indebted countries such as Jordan tend to be inherently constrained in their foreign policy decision making. Jordan, to be blunt, cannot afford to alienate its creditors and its sources of foreign aid.

Jordan under King Abdullah has placed even more stock in these external economic relationships than did King Hussein. Abdullah, for example, pursued with vigor the idea of a U.S.-Jordan Free Trade Agreement—the first U.S. free trade agreement with any Arab country. The events of September 11, 2001, may have unintentionally solidified that agreement, as the U.S. Congress quickly ratified the U.S.-Jordanian FTA, despite assorted misgivings. But after "9–11," King Abdullah announced that Jordan would support the U.S. policy of a global "War on Terror," including its invasion of Afghanistan.[31] Precisely because Jordan had positioned itself as a key "front-line state" in this global anti-terror campaign, the kingdom even managed to secure a *doubling* of its foreign aid package from the United States. Jordan thus became one of the top recipients of U.S. aid, behind Israel, Egypt, and Colombia.

Yet Jordan's economy, like all economies, still runs on oil. And hence an additional economic concern is the kingdom's oil supply source. In the context of the 2003 U.S. war on Iraq, however, the economic pressures were contradictory, since all of Jordan's oil came from Iraq, while the kingdom depended on U.S. and British foreign aid. But for Jordan the oil issue was not just a matter of entirely depending on a single country as a source; rather, the issue also turned on the lucrative nature of the Jordanian-Iraqi oil deal. Iraq provided Jordan with 100 percent of its oil supply; just as importantly, half that supply was provided at no charge, while the other half was provided at severely reduced prices, usually half price.

For Jordan, the question then became not only one of alternative oil suppliers, but also one of whether any other supplier would provide the kingdom with this kind of concessionary deal—and the kingdom's budget was not set to accommodate any other kind of arrangement. In addition, one top Jordanian official argued that Jordanian-Iraqi ties included personal links between political elites in Jordan and the regime in Baghdad, complicating matters still further. "Much of the Jordanian political and economic elite was bought by the Saddam regime," he argued, "both the public and private sector; and the (United Nations) oil-for-food scandal included Jordanian names, and there are probably more."[32]

The kingdom was intent on preserving not only its extensive economic ties to Iraq, but also its economic links to global powers, and was just as intent on restoring and deepening its economic connections to regional states such as the "oil kingdoms"—the Arab monarchies of the Gulf. King Abdullah appeared particularly determined to ensure that a political-economic rift would never again occur in Jordan's relations with the West or with the Gulf. It took several years for Jordan to reestablish its relations with the Arab Gulf states after the 1991 Gulf War. Jordan restored full diplomatic relations with Qatar in 1994. In 1995, King Fahd of Saudi Arabia refused to meet with King Hussein when the latter was in-country on the *haj* (pilgrimage) to Mecca. It was not until 1996 that the first face-to-face meetings occurred between the Jordanian and Saudi monarchs since the 1991 Gulf War. In sum, Jordanian government officials remained wary of future diplomatic—and, just as importantly, economic—rifts with major external benefactors. These overriding concerns with political economy continued to severely constrain Jordanian foreign policy before, during, and even long after the U.S. invasion of Iraq.

King Abdullah, however, attempted to lessen Jordan's dependence on foreign aid by increasing the domestic productive capabilities of the economy. This led the king's teams of economic planners to focus especially on foreign investment, joint ventures, trade, and tourism as the key factors in Jordan's economic development. The very makeup of the Jordanian government reflected these priorities, as more and more top officials were neoliberal technocrats who shared King Abdullah's vision of a Jordan rich in information technology and productive private capital. Thus, as important as economic factors have been in Jordanian policy in the past, they are even more important under King Abdullah II. According to one of Jordan's former cabinet ministers, "it is development that defines King Abdullah. And that right there explains Jordan's relations with the Gulf countries. It's about development."[33]

The oil issue also weighed heavily on Jordanian policymakers as it, in turn, affected all other economic plans. Jordan's former prime minister, Fayez Tarawnah, noted,

> Oil supplies were a critical factor to us. Oil was flowing to us at good terms and with the approval of the United Nations. Plus Iraq is our most natural market. And all this interrupts our reform program, which is all about direct foreign investment and export-oriented development. We have advantages we can sell. We are in the World Trade Organization, we have the Free Trade Agreement with the United States, and linked trade association with the European Union. All of these prove that Jordan has done its homework. Now a war on our eastern border will disrupt all this.[34]

War directly threatened the regime's economic interests; but, given the ideological convictions of the Bush administration, war appeared inevitable, though unnecessary. If war could not be avoided, then Jordanian policymakers meant to at least soften the economic blow to the kingdom and avoid (this time) a damaging loss of aid and oil supplies from any of Jordan's local or global allies.

The Jordanian regime secured increased levels of U.S. and European Union aid—in the words of Finance Minister Bassem Awadallah—"in order to mitigate the impact on the budget and the economy."[35] The kingdom further secured pledges of oil from Saudi Arabia, should its Iraqi oil supply be shut off. In sum, Jordan was torn between its two largest aid donors and its two largest trading partners—the United States and Iraq. But even here, regime officials were especially mindful of the damage that their wealthiest and strongest global ally could wreak on Jordan's economy. One of Jordan's former top policymakers stated, "The United States remains the largest donor to Jordan, so all this remains key to Jordanian security." He added, "Jordan can be destabilized by the Americans very quickly . . . if they want to do it."[36]

The Effects of the War on Jordanian Politics and Inter-Arab Relations

After the U.S. invasion, many Iraqis, including many opposition figures now elevated to government positions in the post-Ba'thist regime, charged Jordan with aiding and abetting the long reign of Saddam Hussein. Jordan's prior close relations with Iraq now came back to hurt Jordan's relations with the new Iraq. The Hashimite regime's relations were particularly and mutually hostile with Ahmad Chalabi, the leader of the U.S.-backed Iraqi National Congress, formerly an opposition group in exile. As a corporate executive, Chalabi had presided over the collapse of Jordan's Petra Bank in 1989, devastating the life savings of many Jordanians. He had later fled the country. Within Jordan, Chalabi was indicted, tried in absentia, and convicted of fraud and negligence in the banking disaster. This episode became diplomatically awkward, to say the least, when Chalabi was elevated to the post of temporary oil minister of Iraq and later became deputy prime minister, with special responsibilities for—of all things—finance.

To make matters still worse, Jordanian officials in December 2004 made a series of unfortunate comments that only increased the Jordanian-Iraqi rift.

Jordanian Foreign Minister Hani al-Mulqi, for example, warned of a growing Shi'a-dominant regime in Baghdad "decorated with a Persian scent."[37] King Abdullah spoke of the dangers of a "Shi'a axis" or "Shi'a crescent" from Lebanon to Iraq to Iran. The extent of the globalization of media and information was clearly indicated when the king—in numerous interviews with Jordanian, Arab, and international media—was pressed to clarify his remarks. The king and foreign ministers officials retracted their earlier comments and insisted they had no special concerns with Shi'a "dominance" in Iraq, nor were they hostile to neighboring Iran.

Yet the Jordanian-Iraqi rift did not extend to the entire Iraqi government. In 2004 Iraq's new president, Jalal Talabani, embarked on a tour of key regional capitals, pointedly making Amman his first stop. Talabani led the Patriotic Union of Kurdistan (PUK) which, like the Kurdish Democratic Party (KDP), had long opposed Saddam Hussein's regime. In the mid-1990s, King Hussein had allowed the PUK, KDP, and other Iraqi opposition groups (but not Chalabi) to open offices in Amman, establishing the final break between the Hashimites and Saddam Hussein. Talabani reminded the media of these facts during his 2004 visit, and again in his return to Jordan in 2005. The Iraqi president insisted that Jordanian-Iraqi ties were "strategic and excellent," and promptly began discussing with Jordanian officials a return to more extensive economic ties between the two countries.[38] Jordan, meanwhile, provided the training for more than 35,000 new police officers in Iraq and supported rebuilding efforts, hoping to gain some of the lucrative rebuilding contracts.

In terms of Jordan's broader international relations, as this chapter has made clear, Jordan under King Abdullah II placed a premium on stabilizing and strengthening its inter-Arab and other regional relations. These endeavors included establishing stronger ties with its traditional Western allies and with the main global economic institutions. These key international alignments are based in large part on the regime's perceptions of Jordan's economic interests. In many respects, the official message from the Jordanian regime, at venues such as the World Economic Forum and elsewhere, is that Jordan is open for business.[39]

Jordanian policy under King Abdullah has stressed the idea of rebuilding and maintaining bridges in inter-Arab relations and beyond. The regime has even showed a kind of impatience with any emphasis on earlier inter-Arab rivalries, especially those viewed as overly ideological. Despite the extensive regional unrest and insecurity surrounding Jordan, the kingdom has established more stable and substantive inter-Arab relations than perhaps at any other time in Jordanian history, while simultaneously deepening its links to key global powers and international institutions.

Yet none of these alliances and alignments have fully insulated Jordan from the ripple effects of the resurgent Palestinian uprising against Israeli occupation, terrorist attacks on the United States, or U.S. war with Iraq. And none of these alignments, despite the economic gains that they sometimes entail, can shield the regime from its own population, should stability in the region continue to collapse. Since as early as 1994, external crises have often provided the cause, or the excuse, for stagnation of the political liberalization process within the kingdom, and even for active de-liberalization.

Thus, in the context of severe regional instability, the regime's already-established tendency to allow political liberalization to take a back seat to all other priorities has only exacerbated the regime's troubles, rendering the successes in foreign policy dubious in the end. "Jordan first," in short, may also amount to "regime security first." But long-term regime security cannot be purchased through external alliance alone, nor solely through foreign aid or foreign investment. To achieve real security, for both state and society in Jordan, a revitalization of the political liberalization process is absolutely essential. In that regard, the kingdom's resumption of parliamentary elections, in both 2003 and 2007, were steps in the right direction.[40]

In this context of emphasizing economic development over other concerns, and on external alliances over domestic support, the regime risked triggering an internal security dilemma of profound proportions. The close U.S.-Jordanian relationship, for example, carried with it not only economic benefits, but also serious domestic political costs in terms of undermining the legitimacy of the regime itself. It also left Jordan increasingly vulnerable to the kind of terrorism that was being directed at the United States. On November 9, 2006, suicide bombers set off explosives simultaneously in three crowded upscale hotels in the Jordanian capital, Amman. More than sixty people were killed, and hundreds wounded. While security officials at first feared that the attackers were Jordanian, al-Qa'ida quickly claimed responsibility. The suicide bombers turned out to be ethnic Iraqis who had crossed the border, on the orders of Abu Musab al-Zarqawi, a militant Jordanian Islamist who was at that time a leader of the al-Qa'ida movement in Iraq. The actions of al-Qa'ida's Iraqi contingent did not, however, gain the support of Jordan's own Islamist movement. Before the rubble had been cleared, massive anti-al-Qa'ida demonstrations were staged across the capital—organized in part by Jordan's indigenous Islamist movement: the Muslim Brotherhood and its political party, the Islamic Action Front.

While Jordanians of all political persuasions rallied against terrorism, they remained far more divided on the issue of U.S.-Jordanian ties, and whether these ultimately amounted to an asset or a liability for the kingdom. Under the administration of George W. Bush, the political clout and image of the United States had plunged to an all-time low—and one that threatened to tarnish the Hashimite regime as well. To be blunt, the relations with the U.S., especially under President Bush, when combined with public perceptions of corruption and cronyism in the economic development process—and combined with anger over various aspects of political de-liberalization—together threaten the regime's legitimacy and security in a more direct way than any external threat from any neighbor.[41]

Jordan cannot change its neighbors. Indeed, it has little ability to change outright the policies of powerful allies such as the United States. But despite these constraints, the regime could achieve a new legitimacy—and a new security—by leading the way toward a deeper and more genuine form of political liberalization than Jordan, or indeed the region, has yet seen. If the Abdullah regime were to pursue political liberalization with the same zeal and passion with which it has pursued economic development, then the possibilities would appear to be endless. The overriding concern with regime security, however, may continue to curb such enthusiasm. In the meantime, the regime of King Abdullah II has been well positioned to play a productive regional role, both in reviving a more meaningful peace process and in helping dissuade the United States from still further wars in the region. But in concert with such key foreign policy challenges, the greater security of the Hashimite regime hinges on its commitment to reviving and deepening the once-impressive political liberalization process at home.

Conclusions

In the second U.S. war on Iraq, Jordan found itself once again torn between regional and global interests, between major economic partners, and between domestic political constraints and foreign policy expediency. Jordan was not, as it had been in the 1991 Gulf crisis, formally allied with Iraq. Yet neither was Jordan an enemy of Iraq, as both states had maintained extensive economic ties despite increasing political differences. Jordan was, on the other hand, allied with the main belligerent in the crisis: the United States. Within Arab politics, meanwhile, the crisis had led Jordan to drift steadily closer to Egypt, especially as the two U.S. allies issued the same dire warnings against the war. Having reestablished political and economic rela-

tions with each of the oil-rich Arab Gulf monarchies, the Abdullah regime
was also averse to any policy that would alienate these regimes as King Hussein's regime had done in 1991.

In external security terms, the regime did not balance against either Iraq
or the United States. Nor did Jordan bandwagon in any real sense. Jordan
may not have been able to stop the war, but the regime certainly tried. The
regime focused instead primarily on its domestic front, so to speak, an-
ticipating intense public reactions once the U.S. attack began. In domestic
politics, public opinion in Jordan and elsewhere throughout the Arab world
remained vigorously opposed to any U.S. attack. In the Jordanian and Arab
public spheres, and especially in pan-Arab media such as al-Jazeera, this opposition resulted in vigorous discussions and an overwhelming consensus
against the war.[42]

In his press conference during the first month of the U.S. assault, the
Jordanian Prime Minister Ali Abu al-Raghib captured the overall mood of
Jordanian policymakers and of many Jordanian people, saying "Jordan has
done all it could to avert war . . . now that hostilities have erupted, we have
been witnessing an excessive use of force and the casualties are increasing
tremendously . . . There will be no winners in this war, everybody will be
a loser in this war."[43] The Hashimite regime opposed the war and argued
strenuously against it. Mindful of regional security concerns, the regime
emphasized that Iraq was not actually an external threat, and that it had not
threatened its neighbors since the 1990–1991 war, much less provided a direct threat to the United States. Jordanian officials insisted that an invasion
would destabilize the region further, while undermining regimes closest to
the United States.

In economic terms, Jordan faced either the loss of its oil imports from
Iraq, or its major economic and military aid package from the United States.
Since the former appeared inevitable, the regime focused on preserving
the latter. Economic factors were central to the regime's conception of its
security, and hence to its alignment and crisis decision-making, but they
nonetheless remained indeterminate in the sense that all roads led to economic loss. The regime opted here simply to risk the loss of Iraqi economic
relations (including oil supplies), believing that these could be recouped
through other Arab states. In contrast, the regime viewed the prospect of a
second rupture in U.S.-Jordanian relations as catastrophic and therefore to
be avoided at all costs.

Given the above considerations, the regime attempted to head off the
war and made clear at all opportunities that it opposed an invasion. But

once it became clear that nothing would stop the U.S. assault, the regime maintained its public stance of opposition while attempting to soften the economic blow and—above all—while maintaining its most economically vital ties to the United States, the United Kingdom, and the Arab Gulf monarchies, as Jordan had not been able to do in the 1991 Gulf War. When the second U.S.-Iraq war loomed, Jordan attempted to preserve *all* of its regional and global alignments.

Once the invasion began, protests erupted throughout the kingdom. The regime allowed more than sixty to take place before beginning to clamp down and break them up. Prime Minister Ali Abu al-Raghib, very much on the defensive, felt compelled once again to repeatedly deny that Israeli troops were operating on Jordanian soil, and to defend the regime's controversial and unpopular decision to allow Patriot anti-missile batteries and small numbers of U.S. special forces in its eastern desert.[44]

The regime attempted, in short, to simply survive the domestic unrest and the regional turmoil, grasping all the while its most treasured international economic relations, while fully intending—in a post-war scenario—to return to its strategy of rebuilding bridges in its inter-Arab relations, including its relations with a post-Saddam Iraq.

13

Regime Security and Shifting Arab Alliances

The international relations of the Middle East have often baffled casual observers and led to assumptions that, of all the world's regions, this one must be an exception to the norms of global politics. And within Middle East politics, inter-Arab relations have seemed perhaps most baffling of all.

While the above statements apply to much punditry and commentary about Middle East politics, they do not apply to serious scholarship about the region. To the contrary, the Middle East is no more baffling or arcane than any other region. Sadly, it may simply be lingering orientalism that would suggest otherwise. This book has presented a specific model for understanding the dynamics of inter-Arab relations and shifting Arab alliances, positioned against the broader context of what is too often a Western-centric literature on alliances and international relations.

Indeed, the very notion of alliance must be considered more broadly in order to be made relevant to the politics not only of the Middle East, but also throughout much of the post-colonial world. If one focuses only on alliances in a narrowly conceived way, that is, as formal defense pacts only, then one will find few "alliances" in the history of modern Middle East politics. Yet looser alignments and alliances between Arab states, committed to political and economic support (but not necessarily including formal military commitments), are routine and indeed key features of regional political life. But here, too, we must consider *who* the "state" actually is, and who is actually allying with whom. In inter-Arab politics, I have argued, alliances and alignments are best seen as transnational support coalitions between ruling regimes, rather than as combinations of states allying together as unitary rational actors. The latter conceptualization, so common in the Neorealist discourse on alliances and international relations, neglects the dynamics of domestic politics and internal insecurity that, as this book has shown, are often essential to understanding Arab alliance politics. I have offered an alternative approach here, the regime security approach, which examines ruling regimes and their insecurities at the nexus of domestic and international politics. This approach examines regime decision making and perceptions of threats from multiple sources—internal and external, military and economic, normative and material. In this way the regime security approach does not abandon the traditional focus on states, security, and external military threats; but neither is the approach limited to these variables alone. Rather, it expands beyond each of these variables in order to be more in tune with the empirical realities of Arab and Middle East politics, and of the politics in many other areas of the world.

This book, therefore, has presented an alternative theoretical framework to the dominant paradigm in the alliance literature, in an effort to provide an alternative explanation for shifting inter-Arab alignments, one that is both more theoretically nuanced and empirically accurate. While Kenneth Waltz's work[1] is among the cornerstones of neorealist theory, Stephen Walt's work[2] has become a key representative of that tradition in the alliance literature. As discussed at the outset of this book, Walt argues that alliance formation is driven by state attempts to balance against changing constellations of external threats. In effect, Walt offers a uni-causal theory that is parsimonious in its specific attention to external military threats. For Walt, alliances form in response to these external stimuli, as states attempt to maneuver amidst powerful systemic constraints. Neorealist parsimony, however, has in this case sacrificed considerable empirical detail, by being too theoretically narrow, and hence missing key variables determining international alignment behavior.

I have argued that, particularly in the Arab states system, a too-strict application of Walt's assumptions is at best misleading, since it leaves out key domestic and economic variables. These variables are indeed important, and have received (largely separate) treatments in the literature. Laurie Brand, for example, has provided a detailed economic analysis and hence a political economic model of regional alliance-making based on budget security. States make and break alliances, in this model, mainly on the basis of concerns for the security of the state's revenue and economic resources.[3] While this book does emphasize political economy as a key component of regime security, political economy remains just that: a part of a broader and a more complex set of issues. Economic factors have, for example, proven to be very important in most of the cases examined here, but in none of the cases are they solely or mainly causal. Thus, as important as external security and budget security are, as models they remain too narrow, and too uni-causal, for a complete explanation of inter-Arab alliance politics.

Constructivist theorists, meanwhile, have emphasized the importance of ideas and dialogues in regional politics over the meaning of Arabism as well as state and regional interests and identities. In doing so, scholars such as Lynch and Barnett have underscored the need to examine domestic politics, and hence to see interests not as objective and externally determined, but rather as highly subjective and internally generated in a contested domestic public sphere.[4] In the context of limited liberalization in Jordan and elsewhere, and in the context of increasing globalization of media and information, this emphasis on the domestic politics behind foreign policy decisions has only grown in importance.

In this book, I have tried to be mindful of the many contributions noted above, while avoiding some of the pitfalls and limitations. The *regime security* approach that I present in this book offers an explicitly multi-causal perspective as an alternative to the more uni-causal approaches of Walt and others. This book attempts to move past artificial theoretical divides — such as those between Realism and Constructivism — toward a more integrated approach to security, alliances, and international politics.

The regime security perspective retains external security threats as an important variable, but it also adds two more key factors facing Arab regimes: (1) domestic politics, including perceived internal security threats, and (2) political economy. The attention to domestic politics and political economy is essential, I argue, for it is here that one finds the real material underpinnings of the maintenance, security, and political survival of Arab regimes. Alliance politics for Jordan and other Arab and Third World states do have strong material bases; economic factors are regarded by all developing states as central components of national—and, more importantly, *regime*—security. But, just as importantly, based on the perceptions of ruling elites, these alliances and alignments are designed to adjust to changing sets of internal and external threats and challenges to the stability and continued survival of individual regimes. Sometimes these threats are to the economic viability of the state and regime. Sometimes they take the form of domestic opposition. And sometimes they take the more traditional form of external security threats.

As this book has made clear, external security threats and budget security considerations rise and fall in the calculations of alliance and alignment making; hence, relying solely on either approach will be at best misleading. Yet, in all cases examined here, the paramount consideration has been the *domestic politics of regime security and survival.* Beyond even the useful concept of "omni-balancing" between domestic and regional security challenges, this book has demonstrated that Arab politics is often plagued by a more complex notion of the security dilemma.[5] In traditional International

Relations Theory, the security dilemma refers to the all-too-frequent dynamic of states attempting to enhance their security largely through arms, but unwittingly provoking fears among their neighbors who also re-arm, yielding a less secure situation despite the bolstered defenses. In the Arab states system, Arab states confront not only this traditional version of the security dilemma, but also find themselves wedged between both internal and external security dilemmas, in which shoring up security at one level often triggers insecurity at another, with similarly ironic and even tragic results. The regional emphasis on alliances, alignments, and extensive armaments, for example, has in effect militarized the region—and hence the regimes themselves. Even the civilian regimes, in short, rest heavily on the dual pillars of the armed forces and the internal security services or *mukhabarat*.

The resultant security states engage in constant regional security assessments and in the politics of alignment and realignment. In doing so, these regimes often find themselves further removed from their own societies. The very emphasis on external alliances and alignments may lay partly in the fact that it is easier for regimes to switch alliance partners than it is to carry out significant domestic reform. The internal security dilemma too often undermines hopes for greater liberalization or democratization, as states hunker down against domestic opposition rather than risk the more open approach of domestic reform.

Yet regimes remain obsessive about legitimacy in domestic as well as regional politics, largely because domestic legitimacy can be read as a barometer of regime security. Thus regimes continue to use the language of Arabism and Islam in efforts to bolster their legitimacy and security vis-à-vis their societies and their neighbors. Ideology is therefore a key marketing tool used by sometimes cynical regimes to justify whatever decisions they have made domestically and internationally, including alliance choices. Since Arab states are engaged at almost all times in the politics of alignment and realignment, they are also subject to still another security fear: the alliance security dilemma, in which states fear being either abandoned by an ally or entrapped by that ally into an unnecessary conflict.

Are we better advised, then, to view changing international alignments through the lens of an external balance of threats, or as a function of budget security, or as a regime's response to a combination of external, domestic, and economic challenges to its security and survival? In an effort to provide an empirical answer to this theoretical question, this book has analyzed almost forty years of Jordanian alliance and alignment policies in Arab regional politics. As noted at the outset of this study, the assessments offered here are qualitative, and cannot be regarded as formal hypothesis testing. Nonetheless, the strength of this analysis lies in the depth of empirical evidence from which the theoretical inferences are drawn. The case studies in key foreign policy decisions are based on detailed field research and extensive interviews—conducted over a fifteen-year period—with policy makers and their critics as well as with analysts and activists. In most cases it is the present and former political officials who have gone on record and hence are named in the endnotes, while analysts and activists and other critics have more often preferred anonymity.

The eight case studies presented here provide a diverse set of alignment situations, from alliance in the course of war to alignments aimed first at economic integration and only later at security cooperation. These cases thus run the gamut from wartime-security pact to customs union. The theoretical implications of the eight cases detailed in this book are particularly important, suggesting that both the balance-of- threats and budget-security approaches are too narrow to fully explain alliance and alignment choices. The regime security perspective, however, is able to account for all the diverse forms of alignment behavior found in each of the eight cases. In none of the cases were external threats found to be the sole or even the main factor in the alignment decision. Even in the cases of regional crises and war—whether in 1973 or 1991 or 2003—the evidence suggests that domestic politics and political economy are critical parts of the alignment equation. In other words, even in instances where an external balance of threats would most be expected to dominate, domestic regime security factors prove to be the key explanatory variable.

The cases analyzed in this book thus underscore the need to move beyond uni-causal explanations of alliance and alignment behavior. Even cases as different as Jordan's decision regarding the October War coalition (1973) and its later decision to ally with Syria (1975–1979) both reveal a greater complexity of causal influences than one can see through the limited scope of the external balance of threats. By focusing instead on the regime itself and seeing it at the intersection of domestic and system-level security arenas, while also broadening our conceptualization of security to include economic and even normative factors, we are able to account more fully for the empirical realities of international alliances and alignments, and for inter-Arab relations.

While this book has presented a detailed examination of almost forty years of Jordanian foreign policy, it has also provided an analysis of key political dynamics in the Arab state system. Yet the implications of this analysis are not limited either to the Jordanian experience or even to Arab regional politics. The implications of this analysis extend far beyond Jordan or even the entire Arab system. The alliance and alignment politics examined here are rooted in dynamics that are familiar and comparable to those facing all developing countries, and hence this analysis can be usefully applied well beyond the Middle East. Indeed, the framework and approach to this study of alliances and alignments may be generalizable to developing states in many other regions of the world. The regime security approach can be usefully applied to the analysis of any state or states that are precarious domestically and are economically dependent internationally—a characterization that would seem to apply to a majority of the world's countries. Other developing countries could be examined in the same way as I have done here for Jordan. And in explaining inter-Arab politics and shifting Arab alignments—aspects of Middle East politics that have too long remained shrouded in a kind of self-fulfilling mystique—we do not have to resort to deterministic ideas about Arab political culture or the psycho-biographies of individual leaders. Nor is there any reason to restrict empirical analyses to uni-dimensional theories of any kind.

By focusing on the ruling elite itself as simply a regime, rather than assuming the country to be a unitary actor, we are able to tap into the crosscurrents of influences and constraints on that regime: internal as well as external security challenges, and also the economic as well as traditional military underpinnings of a regime's security. Thus, by using the regime security approach, and by focusing on the regime itself and its security concerns vis-à-vis each of these quarters, we can better explain and understand a complex and vital area of world politics.

Notes

Chapter 1. Regime Security, Alliances, and Inter-Arab Politics

1. Egyptian President Anwar al-Sadat's peace overtures to Israel were followed by his trip to Jerusalem in 1977, the Camp David Accords in 1978, and the Egyptian-Israeli Peace Treaty in 1979. The Iraqi-Kuwaiti crisis involved the Iraqi invasion of Kuwait in August 1990 and the outbreak of war between Iraq and a U.S.-led coalition in 1991. In both cases, bilateral war or peace initiatives led to major regional crises and radical realignments among Arab states.

2. For a discussion of alliance theory and the Gulf War realignment, see Garnham, "Explaining Middle Eastern Alignments During the Gulf War," 63–83. On the Gulf crisis and war, see Ryan and Downie, "From Crisis to War," 491–510. For reactions and analysis from Arab scholars and policymakers, see the collection of essays in Markaz Dirasat al-Wahda al-'Arabiyya, *Azmat al-Khalij wa Tada'iyatiha 'ala al-Watan al-'Arabi* (The Gulf Crisis and its Challenges to the Arab Nation).

3. King Hussein later asserted that sponsorship of terrorist activity had been carried out without his knowledge. The Prime Minister (and former director of the Jordanian intelligence and security forces), Ahmad 'Ubaydat, denied any such policy directed toward Syria, but was nonetheless sacked by the king. 'Ubaydat's replacement, Prime Minister Zayd al-Rifa'i, and Syrian Ba'th party officials interviewed were still agitated by the episode more than a decade later, and raised the accusations once again. Interviews in Amman and Damascus, February to April 1993.

4. Snyder, "Alliances, Balance, and Stability," 123.

5. Liska, *Nations in Alliance*.

6. Snyder, "Alliances, Balance, and Stability," 123 and Snyder, "Alliance Theory: A Neorealist First Cut," 105. Snyder remains one of the most prolific scholars ever to write on alliances. See in particular his book *Alliance Politics*.

7. This definition follows closely Snyder's distinction between alliance and alignment, in which "Alliances . . . are only the formal subset of a broader and more basic phenomenon, that of 'alignment.' Alignment amounts to a set of mutual expectations—between two or more states that they will have each other's support in disputes or wars with particular other states . . . [T]heir political reality lies not in the formal contract, but in the expectations they support or create." Snyder, "Alliance Theory," 105.

8. Alliances as formal security pacts are more often between Middle East states and outside powers, rather than between Middle East states themselves. The Syrian alliance with the Soviet Union and the Israeli alliance with the United States are examples. Interregional alignments, on the other hand, tend to avoid formal military commitments. Jordan, for example, was widely regarded as an ally of Iraq during the 1990–1991 Gulf

Crisis, yet, despite previous cooperation in security affairs, the Jordanian-Iraqi alignment included no formal commitments to the other's defense. Individual Jordanian citizens volunteered to help defend Iraq, but the Jordanian armed forces did not come to Iraq's aid—nor did the Iraqi government expect them to do so.

9. Kerr, *The Arab Cold War*; Maddy-Weitzmann, *The Crystallization of the Arab State System*; Porath, *In Search of Arab Unity*; Seale, *The Struggle for Syria*.

10. Taylor, *The Arab Balance of Power*.

11. Barnett, *Dialogues in Arab Politics;* Gause, "Balancing What? Threat Perception and Alliance Choice in the Gulf," 273–305; Lynch, *State Interests and Public Spheres*; Mufti, *Sovereign Creations*; and Sela, *The Decline of the Arab-Israeli Conflict*. There are also several excellent studies of specific bilateral relationships in inter-Arab politics. See in particular Gause, *Saudi-Yemeni Relations* and Kienle, *Ba'th v Ba'th: The Conflict Between Syria and Iraq*.

12. See the review of the alliance literature by Ward, *Research Gaps in Alliance Dynamics*.

13. One of the leading works in this genre is J. David Singer and Melvin Small, "Alliance Aggregation and the Onset of War."

14. Liska, *Nations in Alliance*; one of the classics in this genre remains Waltz, *Theory of International Politics*.

15. For a penetrating critique of Western-centrism in both Neorealist and Complex Interdependence theories, see Escude, *International Relations Theory: A Peripheral Perspective*.

16. Walt, "Alliance Formation and the Balance of World Power," 3–43. See also Walt, *The Origins of Alliances*.

17. Walt, *The Origins of Alliances*.

18. Waltz, *Theory of International Politics*.

19. Christensen and Snyder, "Chain Gangs and Passed Bucks: Predicting Alliance Patterns in Multipolarity," 137–68.

20. Siverson and Starr, "Regime Change and the Restructuring of Alliances," 145–61.

21. Morrow, "Arms Versus Allies: Trade-offs in the Search for Security," 207–33.

22. Snyder, "Alliance Theory," 103–23 and Snyder, "Alliances, Balance, and Stability," 121–42. See also his *Alliance Politics*.

23. Barnett and Levy, "Domestic Sources of Alliances and Alignments," 369–96; Barnett, "High Politics Is Low Politics," 529–62; Lawson, "Domestic Conflict and Foreign Policy;" Lawson, *The Social Origins of Egyptian Expansionism During the Muhammad 'Ali Period*; Levy, "Domestic Politics and War," 653–73; J. Snyder, *Myths of Empire*; and Yorke, *Domestic Politics and Regional Security: Jordan, Syria and Israel*.

24. McKeown, "The Limits of 'Structural' Theories of Commercial Policy," 43–64. The lack of attention to process is particularly glaring in Waltz's theory, but has been addressed by Snyder. See Snyder, "Process Variables in Neorealist Theory."

25. David, "Explaining Third World Alignments," 233–56 and also David, *Choosing Sides: Alignment and Realignment in the Third World*.

26. Harknett and Vandenberg, "Alignment Theory and Interrelated Threats."

27. Barnett and Levy, "Domestic Sources of Alliances and Alignments."

28. She argues that "foreign policy in general, and alliance formation, in particular, may well constitute an integral part of the state-building or regime-consolidation process. In this way, national security at its most basic may, in fact, be budget security, understood in terms of reproducing the conditions necessary for the ruling coalition to afford to maintain its position." Brand, "Economics and Shifting Alliances: Jordan's Relations with Syria and Iraq," 394.

29. Brand, "Economics and Shifting Alliances," p. 394.

30. In the first use of Habermasian public sphere theory within international relations, Marc Lynch provides a detailed theoretical and empirical examination of changing Jordanian identity, interests, and policy in the late 1980s through the mid-1990s. See Lynch, *State Interests and Public Spheres*.

31. Along similar lines, see Putnam's discussion of the linkages between domestic politics and international relations. Putnam, "Diplomacy and Domestic Politics: The Logic of Two-Level Games," 427–60. Even more recent work has attempted to expand beyond Putnam's two-by-two approach by bringing in third parties. See Knopf, "Beyond Two-Level Games: Domestic-International Interaction in the Intermediate-range Nuclear Forces Negotiations," 599–628.

32. While this chapter is highly critical of systemic theories and stresses the need to consider domestic politics, it does not "err on the other side" by ignoring systemic constraints. For a critique of "innenpolitik" approaches along these lines, see Zakaria, "Realism and Domestic Politics: A Review Essay," 177–98.

33. Wolfers some time ago noted the malleability of national security as a concept in international relations and as a justification for state policies. Wolfers, "'National Security' as an Ambiguous Symbol," 481–502. For another discussion, see Sonderman, "The Concept of the National Interest," 121–38.

34. Brand, "Economics and Shifting Alliances," 393–413.

35. See Bates and Lien, "A Note on Taxation, Development, and Representative Government," 53–70.

36. See the classic study on the effects of perception and misperception in global politics by Jervis, *Perception and Misperception in International Politics*.

37. Gause, "Balancing What?" 273.

38. Gause, "Balancing What?" 303.

39. Gause, "Balancing What?" 303.

Chapter 2. Security Dilemmas in Arab Politics

1. Like many other theoretical and conceptual contributions to the study of comparative politics, the concept of bureaucratic-authoritarianism emerged from studies of Latin America. See in particular the original work on this topic by O'Donnell, *Modernization and Bureaucratic-Authoritarianism*.

2. Korany, Noble, and Brynen have remarked on the "multidimensional" character of security in Arab politics. See their conclusions in their co-edited volume, *The Many Faces of National Security in the Arab World*.

3. For a sampling of scholarship representative of both sides of this paradigmatic debate in international relations theory, see Baldwin, *Neorealism and Neoliberalism*.

4. For insightful discussions of the need to reexamine security in a broad sense, see, for example, Mathews, "Redefining Security," 162–77; Nye and Lynn-Jones, "International Security Studies: A report of a Conference on the State of the Field," 5–27; and Ullman, "Redefining Security," 129–53.

5. For an excellent critique of the state of Middle East studies within the discipline of Political Science, noting the tendency to emphasize unique political culture at the expense of more generalizable theory-building, see Anderson, "Policy-Making and Theory-Building: American Political Science and the Islamic Middle East," 52–80.

6. While the analysis presented here may well be generalizable to the various other post-colonial states of Latin America, Africa, and Asia (and hence to a far larger part of the world than that occupied by North America and Europe alone), the discussion in this chapter—for the sake of brevity and manageability—will focus on Arab regional politics alone.

7. On the emergence of the modern Arab state system, see Maddy-Weitzman, *The Crystallization of the Arab State System* and Fromkin, *A Peace to End All Peace: The Fall of the Ottoman Empire and the Creation of the Modern Middle East.*

8. These problems are even more acute in Africa, where economic stagnation, lack of political legitimacy, and external forces from colonialism to the Cold War have contributed to increasing instability and degeneration of largely artificial political units. The cases of Angola, Burundi, Mozambique, Rwanda, Sierra Leone, Somalia, and Congo/Zaire in the 1990s and early twenty-first century are particularly extreme examples of this phenomenon of the "hollowness" of states. See Herbst, "Responding to State Failure in Africa," 145–76; Jackson and Rosberg, "Why Africa's Weak States Persist," 1–24; and Jackson, *Quasi-States: Sovereignty, International Relations, and the Third World.*

9. See Barnett, "Institutions, Roles, and Disorder: The Case of the Arab States System," 271–96.

10. A classic discussion of the legitimacy problem in Arab politics can be found in Hudson, *Arab Politics: The Search for Legitimacy.*

11. Indeed, we might regard the Arab territorial state (*al-dawla al-qutriyya al-'arabiyya*) as artificial in some respects, and yet remarkably resilient into the early twenty-first century. On this issue see, for example, Korany, "National Security in the Arab World: The Persistence of Dualism"; Faour, *The Arab World After Desert Storm*; and Luciani, *The Arab State.*

12. See the review and discussion by Ayoob, "The Security Problematic of the Third World," 257–83.

13. Steven David, in an analysis of the alliance choices of developing countries, refers to this dynamic as "omnibalancing." See David, "Explaining Third World Alignments," 233–56.

14. See, for example, Thomas, *In Search of Security: The Third World in International Relations*; Azar and Moon, *National Security in the Third World*; Ball, *Security and Economy in the Third World*; Job, *The Insecurity Dilemma: National Security of Third World States.*

15. For several cuts at various aspects of security in Arab politics, see the collection of

essays in Korany, Noble, and Brynen, (eds.), *The Many Faces of National Security in the Arab World.*

16. On the different uses of the term "state" in international relations theory, see Halliday, "State and Society in International Relations: A Second Agenda," 215–27.

17. Ayoob also emphasizes the security of the ruling regime before that of the country itself, and notes the differing levels of security threats facing regimes. Mohammed Ayoob, "Perspectives from the Gulf: Regime Security or Regional Security?" 92–116. On the variable nature of the concept of "national security," see the classic discussion by Wolfers, "'National Security' as an Ambiguous Symbol," 481–502.

18. On these points, see also Ayoob, "Perspectives From the Gulf" and Job, *The Insecurity Dilemma: National Security of Third World States.*

19. Buzan is among the leading theorists examining different levels of security threats confronted by states; his "security complexes" approach focuses on domestic, regional, and systemic/global levels of security. In the framework I outline here, the regime's position is precisely at the intersection of these security complexes. See Barry Buzan, *People, States and Fear.* See also Cottam, "Levels of Conflict in the Middle East," 17–41.

20. On the politics of state-society relations in the Third World, see Kamrava, "Conceptualizing Third World Politics," 703–16 and Kamrava, *Politics and Society in the Third World.* The literature on state-society relations in African politics is particularly rich. See, among others, Spalding, "State-Society Relations in Africa," 65–96; Bratton, "Beyond the State: Civil Society and Associational Life in Africa," 407–30; Migdal, *Strong Societies and Weak States*; and Rothchild and Chazan, *The Precarious Balance: State and Society in Africa.*

21. For classic discussions of the security dilemma, see Jervis, "Cooperation Under the Security Dilemma," 167–214 and Herz, *Political Realism and Political Idealism.*

22. The seminal study of misperception in international relations remains that of Robert Jervis, *Perception and Misperception in International Politics.* On security-dilemma dynamics, and in particular reciprocal strengthening of self-images and images of the other, see especially chapter three.

23. Glenn H. Snyder insightfully extends the security-dilemma dynamic beyond adversary relationships to relations between allies, noting that the key fears of states in an alliance security dilemma are those of either abandonment or entrapment (into an unwanted conflict) by one's own ally. See Snyder, "The Security Dilemma in Alliance Politics," 461–95.

24. Fred Lawson, for example, argues that several factors add to the security dilemma in the Arab world: the continuous process of state building; contradictions within ruling regime coalitions; the late development of industrialization; and, finally, asymmetrical interdependence within the world political economy. See Lawson, "Neglected Aspects of the Security Dilemma."

25. On security complexes in general, see Buzan, *People, States and Fear.*

26. To quote Michael Barnett, "high politics is low politics." See Barnett, "High Politics is Low Politics: The Domestic and Systemic Sources of Israeli Security Policy," 529–62.

27. For a study of the security dilemma and international conflict in the Middle East, see Stein, "The Security Dilemma in the Middle East."

28. Sadowski, *Scuds or Butter? The Political Economy of Arms Control in the Middle East.*

29. On the evolution of these hyper-securitized states, see Halliday, *The Middle East in International Relations*; Heydemann, *War, Institutions, and Social Change in the Middle East*; and Mufti, *Sovereign Creations.*

30. Robert Jervis, "Cooperation Under the Security Dilemma," 167–214, and Snyder, "The Security Dilemma in Alliance Politics," 461–95.

31. See, for example, Reich, *The Powers in the Middle East: The Ultimate Strategic Arena.*

32. Some Arab states (such as Egypt, Iraq, and Saudi Arabia) did attempt to develop their own domestic arms industries, but mostly with limited effects. Despite the hopes that these industries would generate economic growth and some degree of military self-sufficiency, these states still remained in varying degrees dependent on external patrons and allies for both military and economic support. See Sayigh, "Arab Military Industrialization."

33. Jordanian officials readily acknowledged this disproportion, but argued that Jordanian armaments were still not enough. Interviews with the author in Amman, Jordan, April 1993. For an analysis of Jordan's strategic position and its military capabilities, at least up to the 1980s, see Cordesman, *Jordanian Arms and the Middle East Balance.* Jordan's armaments may indeed be disproportionate to its geographic and demographic size, but this circumstance appears less unusual when one notes the even more extensive armaments of neighbors such as Israel, Syria, and Iraq.

34. Barnett, *Dialogues in Arab Politics.*

35. A notable exception was Syria, whose armed forces were heavily dependent on Soviet arms and supplies. For Syria, therefore, the cutoff in Soviet arms and aid necessitated a major foreign-policy shift toward the West—including participation in the U.S.-led Gulf war coalition against Iraq and at least intermittent involvement in an Arab-Israeli peace process that they believed was stacked against them. Author interviews with Syrian officials in Damascus, Syria, March and April 1993.

36. For insightful reappraisals of the security challenges faced by Arab states, see the essays collected in Korany, Noble and Brynen, *The Many Faces of National Security in the Arab World.* On the Third World in general, see also Job, *The Insecurity Dilemma.*

37. On the cyclical nature of militarization and increasing economic insecurity, see Sadowski, *Scuds or Butter? The Political Economy of Arms Control in the Middle East* and Hewedy, *Militarization and Security in the Middle East.* Hewedy argues that regional militarization and its consequences for domestic economies are the single most important variables explaining the persistence of authoritarian states in the region. Sadowski, making similar arguments, also notes the importance of the Cold War in fueling these vicious cycles, and suggests that, because the post-Cold War Middle East can literally no longer afford such policies, the loss of Soviet support has led to acquiescence to regional peace talks and domestic demands for more political liberalization and perhaps even democratization.

38. This argument or lament was made by numerous civilian economic planners

in Jordan. Author interviews in Amman, Jordan, February and March 1993, and June 2001.

39. The term "*rentier* state" refers to those states that draw the overwhelming majority of their state revenue from non-tax resources. In this regard, the classic *rentier* states of the Arab regional system are, of course, the oil-producing Gulf monarchies. But even states elsewhere in the region—those that rely heavily on the political economy of oil to generate inter-Arab aid and income from worker remittances—are sometimes referred to as "semi-*rentier*" states. See Beblawi and Luciani, *The Rentier State*.

40. In a statistical analysis of the effects of military spending on the Physical Quality of Life Index (PQLI), Adeola argues, "While education and health variables are allied and positive predictors of PQLI, the influence of the military variables examined is clearly detrimental to human health and the quality of life. It is noteworthy that external debt burden and military expenditures combine to inhibit the social welfare of Third World people." For the details of this study, see Adeola, "Military Expenditures, Health, and Education: Bedfellows or Antagonists in Third World Development?" 441–67.

41. On the issue of domestic politics and state expansionism, see Lawson, *The Social Origins of Egyptian Expansionism During the Muhammad 'Ali Period*. Despite what the title suggests, this work examines far more than Egyptian political history and offers a provocative explanation for state expansionism in general. See in particular the conclusion for Lawson's application of the model to the Iraqi invasion of Kuwait.

42. In contrast to the experience of the Western democracies—especially the United States—that spent more than four decades in an arms race with the Soviet Union and Warsaw Pact, the experience of these states suggests that arms racing alone cannot explain the growth of authoritarian states. But the issue is not so much one of creating authoritarian militarized regimes as it is one of sustaining them, and of thwarting chances for political liberalization; in the Arab states system, as this chapter demonstrates, these factors cannot be addressed without reference to the internal and external security dilemmas. It is also worth underscoring that none of the Western industrial democracies have faced or faces the same level of domestic insecurity as that of most Arab regimes.

Chapter 3. Ideology and Political Economy in Inter-Arab Alliances

1. Hudson, *Arab Politics: The Search for Legitimacy*, 20.

2. See the classic study on Arab political philosophy—both Islamist and nationalist—by Albert Hourani, *Arabic Thought in the Liberal Age, 1793–1939*. On Pan-Arabism, Arab nationalism, and ideology in Arab politics, see Dawn, *From Ottomanism to Arabism*; Farah, *Pan-Arabism and Arab Nationalism*; Chelkowski and Pranger, *Ideology and Power in the Middle East*; Hourani, *A History of the Arab Peoples*, 401–33; Kedourie, *Politics in the Middle East*, 268–346; Khalidi, Anderson, Muslih, and Simon, *The Origins of Arab Nationalism*; Mufti, *Sovereign Creations: Pan-Arabism and Political Order in Syria and Iraq*; Owen, *State, Power and Politics in the Making of the Modern Middle East*, 81–107; Tibi, *Arab Nationalism*; and Zeine, *The Emergence of Arab Nationalism*.

3. Throughout this study, the terms "Pan-Arabism," "Arab nationalism," and "Arabism" will be used interchangeably. Each connotes the *qawmiyya* type of nationalism

which identifies with the broader "Arab nation," and hence these are distinct from the *wataniyya* type of nationalism which identifies with a particular Arab country.

4. On the struggles that helped to create the modern Middle East from the ashes of the Ottoman Empire, see Fromkin, *A Peace to End all Peace*.

5. Kerr, *The Arab Cold War*.

6. The United Arab Republic was a brief attempt at formal political unification between Egypt and Syria, and later included Yemen. The U.A.R. experiment, however, lasted only from 1958 to 1961.

7. See Fouad Ajami's study of Arab politics since the 1967 war, *The Arab Predicament: Arab Political Thought and Practice Since 1967*.

8. As late as 1993, Jordanian and Syrian officials still bristled at the mention of Sadat's actions. Some Jordanian officials charged that Sadat had talked them out of joining the war effort, only to blame them later for not coming to Egypt's aid. Even more anger was expressed by many Syrian officials, who argued that Sadat had unilaterally ended the war without warning Syria and, perhaps even worse, had persuaded Syria to enter a conflict that he, Sadat, had no intention of pursuing to its end. Regardless of where the truth lies, the key issue for this study is that, although Jordanian and Syrian policy makers disagreed on what had happened, all put their objections in explicitly Pan-Arab terms. Author interviews in Amman, Jordan (February and March 1993) and Damascus, Syria (April 1993).

9. On the process of political fragmentation and the shift from Egyptian hegemony, see Noble, "The Arab System: Pressures, Constraints, and Opportunities," 49–102.

10. See Taylor, *The Arab Balance of Power*, 49–82.

11. For a discussion of Pan-Arabism and state sovereignty as rival "institutions" in Arab politics, see Barnett, "Institutions, Roles, and Disorder: The Case of the Arab States System," 271–96. See also Gause, "Sovereignty, Statecraft, and Stability in the Middle East," 441–67.

12. Lynch, "Taking Arabs Seriously," 81–94.

13. Barnett, *Dialogues in Arab Politics*.

14. Barnett, *Dialogues in Arab Politics*, 251.

15. Lynch, *Voices of the New Arab Public*.

16. Lynch, *Voices of the New Arab Public*, 3.

17. For Lynch, this media revolution offers myriad possibilities for increasingly pluralist politics in the region, including a rejuvenation of civil society and more serious public accountability. In sum, the media revolution may provide a "foundation for reform and liberalization." Lynch, *Voices of the New Arab Public*, 3.

18. Gause, "Balancing What?" 274.

19. While Islam and political movements such as Islamism have deep local roots, they are not as exclusive to the Arab world as Arab nationalism is. The majority of the world's Muslims, for example, are not Arab or from the Middle East. It should be noted, however, that many "fundamentalist" Muslims in the Middle East see their ideology as more indigenous than Pan-Arabism; they argue that the latter is still a nationalist movement, and nationalism itself is a Western ideological import to the region.

20. Walt, *The Origins of Alliances*, 181–217. On the rivalry between Nasirists and

Ba'thists, see Kerr, *The Arab Cold War,* and on the conflict between Syrian and Iraqi Ba'thists, see Kienle, *Ba'th v Ba'th.*

21. While still "alive," Pan-Arabism's utility in this capacity may at least have decreased since the Gulf War, as both rulers and the ruled question the longstanding norms of Arab politics. See the discussion by Ibrahim Karawan, "Arab Dilemmas in the 1990s," 433–54.

22. See, for example, Ajami, "The End of Pan-Arabism," 355–73.

23. Yet even Syrian officials acknowledged that "disturbances" had occurred in towns near Syria's border with Iraq, but had been promptly put down. Interviews with the author in Damascus (April 1993).

24. On the rise of territorial nationalism, see the discussion in Faour, *The Arab World After Desert Storm,* 55–75.

25. Barnett, "Institutions, Roles, and Disorder," 271–96.

26. This re-emergence is despite the role of Islamism as the state ideology in post-revolutionary Iran and in Sudan. But precisely one of the problems facing these regimes has been how to transform an anti-state and anti-establishment ideology into one that supports the new Islamic state and its institutions.

27. The Muslim Brothers were specifically part of the *Sunni* Islamist revival. Shi'a Islamism rose at the same time, inspired especially by the writings and activism of Ayatollah Ruhollah Khomeini. Khomeini even helped inspire the Iranian revolution, which resulted in the downfall of the last Shah of Iran and the rise of the only theocracy in the region: the Islamic Republic of Iran. On Islamism see, inter alia, Ayubi, *Political Islam;* Enayat, *Modern Islamic Political Thought;* Esposito, *Unholy War,* Hunter, *The Politics of Islamic Revivalism;* Gerges, *The Far Enemy;* Gilles Kepel, *Muslim Extremism in Egypt;* Kepel, *Jihad;* Sivan, *Radical Islam;* and Piscatori, *Islam in the Political Process.*

28. As Luciani has observed, "the regional dimension influences the stability of Arab states, and regimes seek legitimacy through their regional role to an extent that is uncommon elsewhere in the world." Giacomo Luciani (ed.), *The Arab State,* xxx. In the same volume, see in particular the chapter by Adeed Dawisha, "Arab Regimes: Legitimacy and Foreign Policy," 284–299.

29. See Fromkin, *A Peace to End All Peace,* and Yapp, *The Making of the Modern Near East.*

30. See the analysis by Ibrahim, "Oil, Migration and the New Arab Social Order," 17–70, and Ibrahim, *The New Arab Social Order: A Study of the Social Impact of Oil Wealth.*

31. Ibrahim, "Oil, Migration and the New Arab Social Order," p. 58.

32. The World Bank, *World Development Reports.*

33. See Richards and Waterbury, *A Political Economy of the Middle East,* 381–83, 390.

34. Author interviews with Jordanian and Syrian policymakers in Amman (March 1993, June 2001) and Damascus (April 1993). See also Wilson, "The Economic Relations of the Middle East," 268–87.

35. Author interview in Amman, April 1993.

36. Among analyses of Third World security, one that moves well beyond military

concerns to include economic and even environmental variables is that of Thomas, "Third World Security," 90–114. As Thomas notes, much of the insecurity of regimes is due to the domestic legitimacy crisis of the state, which is linked to underdevelopment, indebtedness, and ecological crises.

Chapter 4. The Case Studies and Jordanian Policy in Context

1. For further analysis of Jordan's political liberalization, monarchical succession, economic adjustment, and foreign policy changes since 1989, see Ryan, *Jordan in Transition: From Hussein to Abdullah.*

2. Author interview with Marwan al-Qasim. Amman, Jordan, April 6, 1993.

3. Wilson, *King Abdullah, Britain, and the Making of Jordan.* Regarding various aspects of the emergence of modern Jordan, see Abu Jaber, *Pioneers Over Jordan: The Frontiers of Settlement in Transjordan*; Fishbach, *State, Society, and Land in Jordan*; Lewis, *Nomads and Settlers in Syria and Jordan*; Massad, *Colonial Effects: The Making of National Identity in Jordan*; and Rogan and Tell, *Village, Steppe and State: The Social Origins of Modern Jordan.*

4. Stephens, "Jordan and the Powers," 39–60. See also Brand, *Jordan's Inter-Arab Relations,* 39–83.

5. On U.S.-Jordan relations, see Madfai, *Jordan, The United States and the Middle East Peace Process.*

6. Among the biographies of King Hussein, see Dallas, *King Hussein*; Lunt, *Hussein of Jordan*; and Snow, *Hussein: A Biography.*

7. The period of the 1950s and 1960s—a period that saw two major Arab-Israeli wars (1956, 1967) as well as the inter-Arab Cold War, discussed in chapter 3—is sometimes referred to as the Nasir era, after the influential Egyptian president. This book begins its historical and political analysis precisely at the end that period. The Nasir era came to an end only with the death of the Egyptian president—who, ironically, was attempting to mediate an end to the Jordanian civil war when he died of a heart attack in September 1970.

8. The term "East Banker" refers to the "traditionally Jordanian" segment of the country's population, distinguishing this sector of the population from the "West Banker" or Palestinian segment of the population. This East Bank/West Bank cleavage has long been a prominent feature within Jordanian domestic politics, made problematic by the fact that the ruling regime has always been dominated by East Bankers, while the population itself is estimated by most people to be at least 60 percent Palestinian. This social cleavage was never so pronounced as during the civil war of 1970–1971. On the relations between the Hashimite regime and the Palestinian community in Jordan, see Brand, *Palestinians in the Arab World,* 149–220.

9. On the 1970–1971 confrontation between the Hashimites and the PLO, see Bailey, *Jordan's Palestinian Challenge,* 27–64.

10. Bailey, 13.

11. Jordan, in this economic context, is often seen as a "de facto oil economy," despite the fact that it is not itself a major oil producer. Similarly, Jordan is sometimes viewed in the literature as a rentier state, or alternatively as a "semi-rentier" or "secondary rent-

ier" state. See, for example, Brand, "Economic and Political Liberalization in a Rentier Economy: The Case of the Hashemite Kingdom of Jordan," 168–70. Regardless of which specific label is used, each underscores the dependent linkage of countries such as Jordan to the political economy of oil, aid, and labor migration. And each of these issues is accordingly viewed by policymaking elites as nothing less than vital to their security interests.

12. On Jordan's increasing security concerns with Persian Gulf stability over the years, see Cordesman, *Jordanian Arms and the Middle East Balance.*

13. On the British withdrawal from the Gulf and its implications, see Kuniholm, *The Persian Gulf and U.S. Policy,* 15–18.

14. On the Jordanian military, including these external linkages to Western powers, see Day, *East Bank/West Bank: Jordan and the Prospects for Peace,* 75–93, and Cordesman, *Jordanian Arms and the Middle East Balance.*

15. Author interview with Ahmad al-Lawzi, Amman, April 20, 1993.

Chapter 5. Jordan and the October War Coalition

1. On the domestic economic determinants of Egyptian alignment policies in this period, see Barnett and Levy, "Domestic Sources of Alliances and Alignments: The Case of Egypt," 369–96.

2. This issue was stressed by multiple Jordanian and Syrian government officials. Interviews in Amman and Damascus, January through April 1993.

3. Walt, *The Origins of Alliances.*

4. See Walt's general discussion of the alliance politics surrounding the October war, pp. 114–25. Jordan is listed as "tacitly bandwagoning with Israel" in table 11, p. 173. Similarly, Walt interprets Israeli threats to intervene in the Jordanian civil war (against the PLO and the Syrian invasion) as amounting to a Jordanian-Israeli "alliance." See table 8, pp. 150–51 and table 10, p. 159.

5. Author's interviews with Jordanian government officials. Amman, March 1993.

6. Details supporting this argument are given in the sections that follow, but draw largely on extensive interviews with Jordanian policymakers. Amman, January through April 1993.

7. As one long-time observer of Jordanian politics noted, "If one were to rank the periods of King Hussein's reign, the seven years from 1967 to 1974 has to fall at the very bottom." See Gubser, *Jordan: Crossroads of Middle Eastern Events,* 99.

8. Author's interview with Ahmad al-Lawzi, Jordanian Prime Minister from 1971 to 1973. Amman, April 20, 1993.

9. Herzog, *The Arab-Israeli Wars,* 302.

10. On the dynamics of the alliance security dilemma, see Snyder, "The Security Dilemma in Alliance Politics," 461–95.

11. Author's interviews with Jordanian government officials. Amman, February and March 1993.

12. This point was emphasized particularly by Lt. General 'Amr Khamash. Author interview, Amman, March 30, 1993.

13. Author interview with Lt. General Khamash. Amman, March 30, 1993.

14. Author interview with Ahmad al-Lawzi. Amman, April 20, 1993.

15. Author interview with Ahmad al-Lawzi. Amman, April 20, 1993.

16. See Clinton Bailey's discussion of these domestic as well as international aspects of the Hashimite regime's security concerns. Bailey, *Jordan's Palestinian Challenge*, 65. For further discussion of challenges to the Hashimite regime from Palestinian and other sources, see Satloff, *Troubles on the East Bank: Challenges to the Domestic Stability of Jordan*.

17. This assessment of Jordanian policy is drawn from interviews with Jordanian officials ranging from then-Prime Minister Ahmad al-Lawzi to lower level officials. Author interviews in Amman, January through May 1993.

18. Author interview with Lt. General Khamash. Amman, March 30, 1993.

19. Author interview with Ahmad al-Lawzi. Amman, April 20, 1993.

20. Dann, *King Hussein's Strategy of Survival*, 33.

21. International Monetary Fund, *International Financial Statistics Yearbook*, 1991: 466.

22. Author's interviews with Jordanian policymakers. Amman, March and April 1993 and July 2001. On Jordanian-Palestinian relations after the 1973 war, see Bailey, *Jordan's Palestinian Challenge*, 65–90.

Chapter 6. The Jordanian Alliance with Syria

1. In their appraisal of regional politics at the close of the 1970s, Jureidini and McLaurin noted that, "particularly from 1975 to 1979, the single cohesive alliance in the Middle East was the Jordanian-Syrian entente." Jureidini and McLaurin, *Beyond Camp David: Emerging Alignments and Leaders in the Middle East*, 60.

2. On Syrian foreign policy, see al-Ja'fari, *al-Siyasa al-Kharijiyya al-Suriyya* (Syrian Foreign Policy); Hinnebusch, "Revisionist Dreams, Realist Strategies: The Foreign Policy of Syria," 374–409; Hinnebusch, "The Foreign Policy of Syria," 141–65; and Lawson, *Why Syria Goes to War: Thirty Years of Confrontation*.

3. On the political development of Jordan and its national identity, see Massad, *Colonial Effects: The Making of National Identity in Jordan* and Lynch, *State Interests and Public Spheres*. On Syria, see Mufti, *Sovereign Creations: Pan-Arabism and Political Order in Syria and Iraq*.

4. The joint committee was to alternate its meetings between Amman and Damascus, and included specialized subcommittees focusing on trade, electrical power, industry, transportation and communications, and water (specifically cooperation regarding the Yarmuk River basin). See Taylor, *The Arab Balance of Power*, 70, and Brand, "Economics and Shifting Alliances: Jordan's Relations with Syria and Iraq," 396.

5. And this time, underscoring the increasing seriousness and depth of the bilateral ties, the co-chairs of the committee were to be the Jordanian and Syrian prime ministers themselves. Brand. 398–99 and Taylor, 70.

6. Author interview with Zayd al-Rifa'i, Jordanian prime minister from 1973–1976 and 1985–1989. Amman, March 29, 1993.

7. Even years later, in interviews with Jordanian and Syrian government officials, it

was clear that mutual suspicion still lingered. Author interviews in Amman and Damascus, February through April, 1993.

8. Author interviews with Syrian government officials. Damascus, March 1993. See also the discussion by Patrick Seale, *Asad: The Struggle for the Middle East*, 185–225.

9. Author interviews with Jordanian foreign ministry officials. Amman, March 1993.

10. Author interviews with Syrian government officials including advisors to President Hafiz al-Asad. Damascus, April 1993. See also Jureidini and McLaurin, *Beyond Camp David*, xv.

11. Jureidini and McLaurin, "The Hashemite Kingdom of Jordan," 298, fn 26.

12. Although Jordan made clear its military support of Syria in the Syrian-Iraqi confrontation, its role vis-à-vis Lebanon was purely diplomatic, and Jordan at no time contemplated sending its own forces.

13. Author's interviews with Jordanian and Syrian government officials. Amman and Damascus, February through April, 1993.

14. Taylor, *The Arab Balance of Power*, 70.

15. On the specific rivalry between the two Ba'thist regimes in Damascus and Baghdad, see Kienle, *Ba'th v Ba'th: The Conflict Between Syria and Iraq*.

16. See Jureidini and McLaurin, *Beyond Camp David*, 51, and Jureidini and McLaurin, "The Hashemite Kingdom of Jordan," 160.

17. See the discussion of this changing bilateral relationship in Baram, "Baathi Iraq and Hashimite Jordan: From Hostility to Alignment," 51–70.

18. Others have since argued that Asad actually had a key role in the botched invasion. On Asad's role as defense minister and commander of the air force during the invasion, and on his later seizure of power, see Patrick Seale, *Asad*, 154–65.

19. The prominence of the Rifa'i family in Jordanian politics dates back to the foundation of the Hashimite state. Zayd al-Rifa'i first assumed the prime minister's post in 1975 and would return to it again in the mid-1980s. Likewise, both his father and grandfather had previously served in the same post. Even after the succession from King Hussein to King Abdullah II, Rifa'i remained influential as Speaker of the Jordanian Senate.

20. Author's interview with Zayd al-Rifa'i. Amman, March 29, 1993.

21. Brand, "Economics and Shifting Alliances," 398–99.

22. Author's interviews with Jordanian and Syrian foreign ministry officials. Amman and Damascus, March and April 1993. See also Brand, "Economics and Shifting Alliances," 397.

23. Author's interview with Dr. Jawad al-'Anani, former deputy prime minister of Jordan. Amman, April 10, 1993. An economist, Anani also held numerous political positions including Minister of Industry and Trade, Minister of Finance, and Chief of the Royal Hashimite Court. See also Brand, "Economics and Shifting Alliances," 397.

24. Author's interview with Zayd al-Rifa'i. Amman, March 29, 1993.

25. The rapprochement rapidly developed into a Syrian-Iraqi unification project and seemed, as a result, to mark the beginning of far more than an alignment or even an alliance: a full political union between the two states. The project was short lived, however,

as Iraqi authorities claimed to have found evidence of a "plot" by Syrian Ba'thists to overthrow their counterparts in Baghdad. Despite Iraqi claims, it seems likely that the brief warmth between the two countries was primarily intended as a device to consolidate Saddam Hussein's own regime as he emerged in 1979 from his ten-year position as the "strong man" behind the regime to assume the presidency for himself. For their part, the Syrians felt that they had been duped; that they had been used as reluctant pawns in a Machiavellian ploy within Iraqi domestic politics. Almost overnight, the unification project deteriorated into hostility and polemics between the two regimes. Although the union had quickly become a dead letter, the official end did not come until 1980, when the two Ba'thist states expelled each other's diplomats. See Mufti, "The 1978–1979 Syrian-Iraqi Unification Plan," and Taylor, *The Arab Balance of Power*, 88.

26. Taylor, *The Arab Balance of Power*, 86.

27. Author interview in Amman, March 1993.

28. Author interview in Damascus. April 29, 1993.

29. Author interviews with Jordanian foreign ministry officials. Amman, March and April 1993. See also Taylor, *The Arab Balance of Power*, 93–95.

30. Author's interview with a former prime minister of Jordan. Amman, 1993.

31. Author interviews with former prime ministers Mudar Badran and Ahmad 'Ubaydat. Amman, (respectively) March 31, 1993, and April 15, 1993.

32. Day, *East Bank/West Bank: Jordan and the Prospects for Peace*, 85, and Taylor, *The Arab Balance of Power*, 93–94.

33. Author interview in Damascus. April 1993.

Chapter 7. The Jordanian Alliance with Iraq

1. On the revolution in Iraq see, for example, Sluglett and Sluglett, *Iraq Since 1958: From Revolution to Dictatorship*, pp. 47–76.

2. King Hussein documented his own views of these events, from the Jordanian coup attempt through the Iraqi revolution, in his autobiography, *Uneasy Lies the Head: The Autobiography of His Majesty King Hussein I of the Hashemite Kingdom of Jordan*, 151–208.

3. Bailey, *Jordan's Palestinian Challenge*, 7–15; Day, *East Bank/West Bank: Jordan and the Prospects for Peace*, 27–33.

4. Trends in Jordanian-Iraqi relations are traced in Baram, "Baathi Iraq and Hashimite Jordan: From Hostility to Alignment," 51–70, and Baram, "No New Fertile Crescent: Iraqi-Jordanian Relations, 1968–92," 119–60.

5. Baram, "Baathi Iraq and Hashimite Jordan," 51.

6. Author interviews with Jordanian policymakers. Amman, March and April 1993, and May 2005.

7. Several of King Hussein's top national security policy advisors, interviewed for this project, were familiar with contemporary Likud views in some detail, and several had taken to heart readings of the memoirs of then Israeli Prime Minister Menachim Begin. Interviews in Amman, January through April 1993. Israeli invasions of Lebanon in 1978 and 1982 only served to confirm Jordanian suspicions of Israeli intentions.

8. Dan Schueftan, "Israel's 'Jordan Option.'"

9. Author interviews with Jordanian government officials. Amman, February and March 1993, and June 2001.

10. See Mufti, "The 1978–1979 Syrian-Iraq Unification Plan."

11. See Taylor, *The Arab Balance of Power*, 55 and 73–96.

12. Author interview in Damascus. April 29, 1993.

13. On Jordan's political and economic support role in the Iraqi war effort, see Terrill, "Saddam's Closest Ally: Jordan and the Gulf War," 43–54.

14. Yorke, *Domestic Politics and Regional Security: Jordan, Syria and Israel*, 265.

15. Interviews with officials in the Jordanian Prime Ministry and with Jordanian economists. Amman, February and March 1993.

16. Terrill, "Saddam's Closest Ally," 46–50.

17. Gubser, *Jordan: Crossroads of Middle Eastern Events*, 121.

18. Author interviews with officials in the Jordanian Foreign Ministry. Amman, March 1993.

19. Author interview in Amman. March 1993.

20. Author interview with former Foreign Minister Marwan al-Qasim. Amman, April 6, 1993.

21. Yorke, *Domestic Politics and Regional Security*, 255.

22. In interviews with the author, this difference was emphasized by former Prime Ministers Zayd al-Rifa'i, Ahmad 'Ubaydat, and Mudar Badran. Interviews conducted (respectively) in Amman: March 29, 1993, April 15, 1993, and March 31, 1993. All three prime ministers also made clear that King Hussein's read of the situation was far more attuned to Jordan's domestic and regional interests than was the popular or "street" reaction to the Iranian revolution.

23. For a discussion of Islamism in Jordan at this time, particularly in response to the Iranian Revolution, see Satloff, *They Cannot Stop Our Tongues: Islamic Activism in Jordan*, 4–5.

24. Author interviews with Zayd al-Rifa'i, March 29, 1993, and Mudar Badran, March 31, 1993.

25. Author interviews with Jordanian journalists. Amman, November and December 1992. As Brand notes in her study, Iraqi government donations in 1979 ranged from relatively small gifts to social work groups, homes for the elderly, and scholarship funds, for example, to large grants for the Aqaba free trade zone (U.S. $13.6 million) and the civil aviation center (U.S. $500,000). She states that "despite its involvement in the war with Iran, Iraq paid U.S. $92 million to both Jordan and the PLO, a sum representing both its Baghdad [summit] commitment and the promise it had made at the 1980 Amman summit to pay the sums that Libya had declined to pay for the years 1979 and 1980." Brand, "Economics and Shifting Alliances," 407.

26. Gubser, *Jordan: Crossroads of Middle Eastern Events*, 120.

27. International Monetary Fund, *Direction of Trade Statistics Yearbook*, 1991: 243.

28. While Jordan's alignment with Iraq and its corresponding linkages to Saudi Arabia did result in increased aid, nonetheless the oil glut in the 1980s would quickly temper these short term gains. Unfortunately for Jordan's economic planners, much of this money had in effect been spent before it arrived, as budgets were formulated on the

assumption of radical aid increases. The 1986–1990 five-year plan, for example, specifically notes the failed aid forecasting of the previous plan, but the plan also makes clear
what Jordan thought it would get out of its new alignment partners. Hashimite Kingdom
of Jordan, Ministry of Planning, *Five Year Plan for Economic and Social Development,
1986–1990* , 46.

29. Author interviews with Jordanian government officials. Amman, March and
April, 1993. Gubser, *Jordan*, 121. This point is also underscored in Brand's analysis. She
notes that "in pushing for the 1978 summit and in focusing on aid to the confrontation
states, Saddam had rendered Jordan a very valuable service. The fall of the Shah only a
few months later and the threat of Khomeini served as an additional, but not the original, stimulus to move Jordan closer to Iraq." Brand, "Economics and Shifting Alliances,"
404.

30. Gubser, *Jordan*, 121.

Chapter 8. Jordan and the Arab Cooperation Council

1. This chapter draws on an early version of this analysis: Curtis R. Ryan, "Jordan and
the Rise and Fall of the Arab Cooperation Council," 386–401.

2. Author interview with a former prime minister of Jordan. Amman, March 1993.

3. Author interview with Mudar Badran, former Jordanian prime minister (1976–1979,
1981–1984 and 1985–1989). Amman, March 31, 1993.

4. Author interview with a former prime minister of Jordan. Amman, March 1993.
On the IMF riots, see Ryan, "Peace, Bread, and Riots: Jordan and the International Monetary Fund," 54–66.

5. For samples of this discussion, see "Arab Cooperation: Getting Together, in Bits,"
38–41; Stephen Brookes, "Two New Blocs Amid Shifting Sands," 36; Alan Cowell, "Arabs
Are Forming 2 Economic Blocs," *New York Times*, February 17, 1989.

6. The socio-economic agreements and achievements of the ACC are documented
in its one and only annual report. Imana al-'Am li Majlis al-Ta'awun al-Arabi (General Secretariat of the Arab Cooperation Council), *Majlis al-Ta'awun al-Arabi: Nasus
al-Itifaqiyat wa al-Qararat al-Muqa'a Khilal al-Am al-Awal 1989–1990* (Text of the Agreements and Decisions Signed During the First Year).

7. *Middle East Economic Survey* (hereafter cited as *MEES*) 32, no. 20, A8.

8. Economist Intelligence Unit, *Jordan: Quarterly Economic Report*, no. 2 (1989): 6.

9. *MEES* 32, no. 38, A7.

10. Wahby, "The Arab Cooperation Council and the Arab Political Order," 66.

11. Some have seen the ACC as an Iraqi-initiated as well as Iraqi-dominated bloc. See
the analysis of the purpose and outlook for the ACC by John F. Devlin, "The Purposes
and Effect of the Arab Cooperation Council," 4–7.

12. Terrill, "Saddam's Closest Ally: Jordan and the Gulf War," 43–54.

13. Author interviews with Jordanian foreign ministry officials. Amman, March and
April 1993. See also Economist Intelligence Unit, *Jordan: Quarterly Economic Report*, no.
2 (1989): 7.

14. Author interviews with former national security advisor to the king, Adnan Abu

'Awdah (Amman, February 29, 1993), and with Prime Ministers Mudar Badran (Amman, March 31, 1993) and Ahmad 'Ubaydat (Amman, April 15, 1993).

15. Jordanian officials interviewed tended to stress the desire to bring Syria into the ACC. Syrian officials interviewed, however, tended to be skeptical or outright suspicious of Jordanian intentions. Interviews in Amman (foreign ministry) and Damascus (foreign ministry and People's Assembly), February to April 1993.

16. Author interviews with Syrian government officials. Damascus, March and April 1993. Some Saudi leaders would even charge later that the establishment of the ACC had been the first step toward the invasion of Kuwait. Author interview with Jordan's former Prime Minister Zayd al-Rifa'i, Amman, March 29, 1993.

17. Wahby, "The Arab Cooperation Council," 62. Commenting on this development, one analyst remarked cryptically that "just why a non-aggression treaty should be necessary at this particular juncture—or why, if one is necessary, it should not be equally necessary for, say, Kuwait—is not entirely clear." *MEES* 32, no. 26, C3.

18. Nasrallah, "The ACC and Arab Regional Problems," 19–20.

19. Author interview at the Jordanian Foreign Ministry. Amman, April 1993. See also Lamis Andoni, "Arab Cooperation Council: Allaying Fears," 8, and *MEES* 32, no. 20, C2.

20. Author interview with Zayd al-Rifa'i. March 29, 1993.

21. Author interviews with officials in the Syrian Foreign Ministry and People's Assembly. March and April 1993.

22. Author interviews at the Jordanian Foreign Ministry. Amman, March and April 1993.

23. "It's Reckoning Time for Jordan," 26.

24. Both the Islamist and the secular leftist political activists who were interviewed for this study tended to use the term *intifada*.

25. This point was noted, with some satisfaction, by Dr. 'Abd al-Latif 'Arabiyyat, a leading member of the Muslim Brotherhood and speaker of Jordan's lower house of parliament (1990–1993). Interview in Amman, February 25, 1993.

26. On the political liberalization process, see, for example, Brynen, "Economic Crisis and Post-Rentier Democratization in the Arab World: The Case of Jordan," 69–97; Mufti, "Elite Bargains and the Onset of Political Liberalization in Jordan," 100–129; Robinson, "Defensive Democratization in Jordan," 387–410; and Ryan, "Elections and Parliamentary Democratization in Jordan," 194–214.

27. For Jordanian assessments of the kingdom's emerging party spectrum during this early period of liberalization, see Abu Khusa, *al-Dimuqratiyya wa al-Ahzab al-Siyasiyya al-Urduniyya* (Democracy and Jordanian Political Parties); 'Abdalat, *Kharita al-Ahzab al-Siyasiyya al-Urduniyya* (Map of Jordanian Political Parties); Sways, "Kharita al-Ahzab al-Siyasiyya fi al-Urdun," (A Map of Political Parties in Jordan), 122–41; 'Iyad, *al-Tayarat al-Siyasiyya fi al-Urdun wa Nas al-Mithaq al-Watani al-Urduni* (Political Tendencies in Jordan and Text of the Jordanian National Charter). Note that each of these studies was published even before the political parties law finally emerged in 1993. It had long been anticipated. After 1993 the al-Urdun al-Jadid Research Center began publishing a

series of studies of parties, elections, civil society, and democracy in Jordan, including Hourani, et al., *al-Ahzab al-Siyasiyya al-Urduniyya* (The Jordanian Political Parties). For Jordanian assessments of the democratization process more generally, see, among others, Abu Rumman, ed., *'Aqd Min al-Dimuqratiyya fi al-Urdun* (A Decade of Democracy in Jordan); Khulayfat, *al-Dimuqratiyya fi al-Urdun* (Democracy in Jordan); and Khuri, *Mustaqbal al-Urdun: al-Dimuqratiyya, al-Huwiyya, al-Tahdiyyat* (The Future of Jordan: Democracy, Identity, Challenges).

28. For a detailed analysis of the economic as well as political aspects of the liberalization program, see Brand, "Economic and Political Liberalization in a Rentier Economy: The Case of the Hashemite Kingdom of Jordan," 167–88.

29. Author interviews with Jordanian policymakers. Amman, March and April 1993, July 2001, and May 2005.

30. See the discussion in Piro, "The Domestic Bases of Jordan's Foreign Policy: State Structures, Domestic Coalitions, and the National Interest." See also Piro, *The Political Economy of Market Reform in Jordan*.

31. Piro, "The Domestic Bases of Jordan's Foreign Policy," 15.

32. Wahby, "The Arab Cooperation Council," 61.

33. Rodenbeck, "Egypt: Alignments," 8–9.

34. Rodenbeck, 9.

35. *MEES* 32, no. 20, A8.

36. *MEES* 32, no. 19, B1.

37. Economist Intelligence Unit, *Jordan: Quarterly Economic Report*, no. 1 (1989): 1.

38. Economist Intelligence Unit, *Jordan: Quarterly Economic Report*, no. 2 (1989): 10–11.

39. Economist Intelligence Unit, *Jordan: Quarterly Economic Report*, no. 3 (1989): 13.

40. One of the leading critics in this regard was a member of parliament and a former minister in the Rifa'i government, Dhuqan al-Hindawi. Economist Intelligence Unit, *Jordan: Quarterly Economic Report*, no. 1 (1990): 8–11.

41. Interviews with Jordanian foreign ministry officials and former cabinet ministers, March and April 1993. See also Ben Lynchfield, "Cairo Shies Away from Iraqi Military Alliance," *Jerusalem Post*, April 23, 1990.

42. Author interviews in Amman, April 1993.

Chapter 9. Jordan and the First U.S.-Iraq War

1. For a discussion of the anatomy of international crises, and particularly of the events in the Gulf as two crises—one local, the other global—see Ryan and Downie, "From Crisis to War: Origins and Aftermath Effects of the 1990–91 Persian Gulf Crisis," particularly pp. 491–92. This discussion of international crises draws on the classic work by Snyder and Diesing, *Conflict Among Nations: Bargaining, Decision-Making, and System-Structure in International Crises*, especially pp. 6–21.

2. For an assessment of the growing local crisis, written just prior to the invasion itself, see Graz, "Iraqi Sabers Rattle in the Gulf," 3–5.

3. "al-Hussein: hal an-niza'a fi al-itar al-arabi faqat" (Hussein: Solution to conflict in an Arab framework only), *al-Dustur*, August 5, 1990.

4. Author interview with former Foreign Minister Marwan al-Qasim. Amman, April 6, 1993.

5. Author interview with Marwan al-Qasim. Amman, April 6, 1993.

6. Author interview with former national security advisor Adnan Abu 'Awdah. Amman, February 29, 1993.

7. Author interview with Adnan Abu 'Awdah. Amman, February 29, 1993.

8. "Statement by the Foreign Minister of Jordan to the Arab League Meeting of Foreign Ministers, August 2–3 , 1990," in Hashimite Kingdom of Jordan, *White Paper: Jordan and the Gulf Crisis, August 1990–March 1991*, 3.

9. "Resolution 195 adopted at the Extraordinary Arab Summit," August 10, 1990, Cairo, in Hashimite Kingdom of Jordan, *White Paper: Jordan and the Gulf Crisis*, 23–24.

10. The official government statements on this topic can be found in Hashimite Kingdom of Jordan, *White Paper: Jordan and the Gulf Crisis*, 3.

11. Author interview with Marwan al-Qasim. Amman, April 6, 1993.

12. Author interview with former Prime Minister Mudar Badran. March 31, 1993.

13. Author's interviews with Jordanian policy makers. Amman, November 1992, February to April 1993, and May 2005.

14. Hence the revival in Jordan of the English-language pun that Jordan lay "between Iraq and a hard place." Indeed, many Jordanians compared their country's situation to that of Belgium between the European "Great Powers" of France, Germany, and Britain in the first half of the twentieth century. Author's discussions with Jordanians during the Gulf crisis. Irbid and Amman, Jordan, August 1990.

15. Author interview with Marwan al-Qasim. Amman, April 6, 1993.

16. Author interviews with Jordanian policymakers. Amman, March and April 1993, July 2001, and May 2005. Many roundly condemned the regime in Baghdad for initiating the crisis, while others questioned whether the Bush administration would have settled for any type of peaceful settlement. Despite the polarity of these views, they clearly reflect the lingering anger in Jordan over the Gulf crisis.

17. Walt, *The Origins of Alliances*.

18. Among analyses of the Gulf crisis, one that moves beyond balancing and bandwagoning to include omnibalancing (between internal and external threats) is that of Garnham, "Explaining Middle Eastern Alignments During the Gulf War," 63–83. On Jordan's role in particular, see Harknett and Vandenberg, "Alignment Theory and Interrelated Threats: Jordan and the Persian Gulf Crisis," 112–53. On omnibalancing see David, *Choosing Sides: Alignment and Realignment in the Third World*.

19. This was particularly the argument of former Prime Minister Ahmad al-Lawzi (1971–73), who also served as speaker of Jordan's upper house of parliament during the Gulf Crisis. Interview with Ahmad al-Lawzi. Amman, April 20, 1993.

20. For an analysis of the politics of political and economic liberalization in Jordan, see Ryan, *Jordan in Transition: From Hussein to Abdullah*, 15–63.

21. Author interview with Dr. 'Abd al-Latif 'Arabiyyat, Speaker of the lower house

of parliament from 1990 to 1993 and a leading member of the *Jabha al-'Amal al-Islami* (Islamic Action Front). February 25, 1993.

22. See Abu Jaber and Fathi, "The 1989 Jordanian Parliamentary Elections, 67–86, and Ryan, "Elections and Parliamentary Democratization in Jordan," 194–214. For profiles of the members of this parliament, see Riedel, *Who is Who in Jordanian Parliament 1989–1993*.

23. The Jordanian National Charter was concluded in 1991 and committed the regime to greater pluralism and democratization; but it also required all those who helped draft the Charter (a large, diverse grouping intended to represent every religious, ethnic, class, or ideological grouping in Jordanian society) to agree to certain conditions in order for political liberalization to proceed. Among these key agreements were acceptance of the legitimate nature of the Jordanian state as a monarchy, and more importantly, as a Hashimite monarchy.

24. Author interview with a top Jordanian policymaker during the Gulf crisis. Amman, February 1993.

25. Brand, "Liberalization and Changing Political Coalitions," 29.

26. Lynch, *State Interests and Public Spheres: The International Politics of Jordan's Identity*, 159.

27. Author interview with Dr. 'Abd al-Latif 'Arabiyyat. Amman, February 25, 1993.

28. As Baram noted, "By mid-1990 a de facto Iraqi-Jordanian federation had come into existence, but it was not a federation of equals because the king, the prisoner of his own policies since 1979, was no longer at liberty to withdraw. Jordan could not detach itself from the large Iraqi economy and, politically, it could no longer risk a breach with Baghdad." Baram, "Baathi Iraq and Hashimite Jordan: From Hostility to Alignment," 67.

29. Economist Intelligence Unit, *Jordan: Country Profile 1991*, 28.

30. As Stanley Reed observed at the height of the Gulf crisis, "Jordan has become so dependent on Iraq as a market for its exports and as a source of cheap oil that destruction of the Iraqi economy by either military means or blockade threatens to destroy Jordan's economy as well." See Reed, "Jordan and the Gulf Crisis," 23.

31. Author interviews with Jordanian policymakers. Amman, March and April 1993, June 1999, July 2001.

32. See the early report by the Economic and Social Commission for Western Asia (ESCWA), *The Impact of the Gulf Crisis on the Jordanian Economy*, and the later report on the global economic impact, including a brief analysis of Jordan, by Abdalla, "Impact of the Gulf Crisis on Developing Countries."

33. Terrill, "Saddam's Closest Ally: Jordan and the Gulf War," 43–54.

34. Economist Intelligence Unit, *Jordan: Quarterly Economic Report*, no. 4 (1990): 9.

35. Baram, "Baathi Iraq and Hashimite Jordan," 69.

36. Brand, "Liberalization and Changing Political Coalitions," 2–3.

Chapter 10. Beyond Arab Alliances?

1. This analysis draws in part on an earlier examination of Jordan's peace treaty with

Israel: Curtis R. Ryan, "Jordan in the Middle East Peace Process: From War to Peace with Israel," 161–77.

2. In what was referred to as a "six plus two" framework, the Damascus Declaration Alliance grouped together two militarily powerful states, Egypt and Syria, with the six states of the Gulf Cooperation Council (Bahrain, Kuwait, Oman, Qatar, Saudi Arabia, and the United Arab Emirates).

3. For an analysis of Jordanian-Israeli peace that looks closely at the Israeli side of this process, see Lukacs, *Israel, Jordan, and the Peace Process*.

4. See, for example, Shlaim, *Collusion Across the Jordan: King Abdullah, the Zionist Movement, and the Partition of Palestine*.

5. Dan Schueftan, for example, sees the Jordanian-Israeli relationship as having long amounted to a *de facto* alliance. Dan Schueftan, "Jordan's 'Israeli Option,'" 254–82. Jordanian political officials, in contrast, tend to vigorously reject this type of interpretation. Author interviews with Jordanian policymakers. Amman, February to April 1993, July 2001, and May 2005.

6. 'Arabuti, *Fikr al-Hussein fi al-Mizan* (Hussein's Thought in the Balance); Dann, *King Hussein's Strategy of Survival*; Faddah, *The Middle East in Transition: A Study of Jordan's Foreign Policy*; and Mutawi, *Jordan in the 1967 War*.

7. Author interview in Amman. May 2005.

8. See, for example, Israeli, "Is Jordan Palestine?" 49–66. For a detailed examination of these debates including Jordanian-Palestinian relations and questions of Jordan's national identity, see Lynch, *State Interests and Public Spheres: The International Politics of Jordan's Identity*, especially 71–139.

9. Author interview with former Prime Minister 'Abd al-Salam al-Majali. Amman, May 11, 2005.

10. Author interview with 'Abd al-Salam al-Majali. Amman, May 11, 2005.

11. Author interview with former Foreign Minister Kamel Abu Jaber. Amman, July 13, 2001.

12. Author interviews with Jordanian policymakers. Amman, May 2005.

13. Author interviews with Jordanian policymakers. Amman, June 1999, July 2001, and May 2005.

14. Author interviews with current and former Jordanian cabinet officials, Amman, February to April 1993, July 2001, and May 2005.

15. Author interviews with Jordanian policymakers. Amman, June 1999 and July 2001.

16. Zunes, "The Israeli-Jordanian Agreement: Peace or Pax Americana?" 60.

17. Author interviews with Jordanian policymakers. Amman, June 1999 and May 2005.

18. For an analysis of this process, see Astorino-Courtois, "Transforming International Agreements into National Realities: Marketing Arab-Israeli Peace in Jordan," 1035–54.

19. Author interview in Amman. May 2005. Marc Lynch has also discussed this problem of Israel's dual identity in the Jordanian public sphere, noting that "the sharp con-

tradiction between the demands of identity (Israel as enemy) and of interest (Israel as necessary partner) has long been of central concern." Lynch, *State Interests and Public Spheres*, 166. See also his full analysis of public sphere debates and the Jordanian-Israeli peace process, 166–97.

20. Lynch, *State Interests and Public Spheres*, p. 169.

21. For a detailed analysis, see Brand, "The Effects of the Peace Process on Political Liberalization in Jordan," 52–67.

22. *al-Ra'y,* 28 October 1994, Foreign Broadcast Information Service (hereafter cited as FBIS), 28 October 1994: 43.

23. FBIS, 19 October 1994: 46.

24. FBIS, 18 October 1994: 51.

25. In a news analysis of the opposition charges, Ayman al-Safadi noted that the Islamists had not produced any evidence to back up their claims that the public was with them and not with the government, and further, that the initialing of the agreement had prompted little reaction in the streets of Jordan. *Jordan Times* 18 October 1994, FBIS, 18 October 1994: 50–51.

26. Interestingly, the statement condemning the peace process was carried in the same issue of *al-Dustur* (18 October 1994) that praised the process in its own editorial. FBIS, 19 October 1994: 46–47.

27. On the debates over the electoral laws and their varied outcomes across several elections, See Ryan, *Jordan in Transition: From Hussein to Abdullah*, 15–42.

28. On this aspect, see also the discussion by Brand, *Jordan's Inter-Arab Relations*, 295–97.

29. International Monetary Fund, *Government Finance Statistics Yearbook,* 362.

30. International Monetary Fund, *International Financial Statistics Yearbook,* 466–67.

31. Author interview with Dr. Hassan Barari, Center for Strategic Studies, University of Jordan, Amman. May 12, 2005. For an insightful analysis of the Jordanian-Israeli relations and an assessment of the treaty in its tenth year, see Barari, *Jordan and Israel: Ten Years Later.*

32. Author interviews with Jordanian government officials, Amman, February to April 1993.

33. Author's discussions with Jordanians throughout the kingdom during 1997, 1999, 2001, and 2005.

34. Author interview with 'Abd al-Salam al-Majali. Amman, May 11, 2005.

35. See Scham and Lucas, "'Normalization' and 'Anti-Normalization' in Jordan: The Public Debate," 141–64.

36. Shahin, "Jordan: Not Yet a Comfortable Partnership," 8–9.

37. Albrecht, "Where is all the Business? Jordanian-Israeli Economic Ties Start Slowly," 13–15.

38. Andoni, "Jordan: First Test Case for Kabariti," 10–12.

39. Andoni, "Jordan: First Test Case for Kabariti," 10–12.

40. Jordanian frustration with the lack of an economic peace dividend may explain this muted response at least in part. Asher Susser, for example, has argued that "Jorda-

nian officials complained that Peres had spoken much about the economic underpinnings of peace while Israel had in fact implemented policies that were overprotective of Israeli business interests . . . Given their criticism of Peres, the Jordanians were not particularly dismayed by his defeat in Israel's May 1996 elections." Susser, *Jordan: A Case Study of a Pivotal State*, 97.

41. The contrast between Hussein's (at least public) assessment of the elections, as opposed to that of most Arab leaders, is clear in his statement, "I think there was too much reaction to the Israeli elections. I believe that it wasn't a question of the peace camp losing. An example is our Jordan-Israeli peace treaty, which passed by an overwhelming majority in the Israeli Knesset at the time, across the board. So peace is sought by all. It was wrong to try to display this election as one of peace or the abhorrence of peace. Everyone seeks peace and security. If this is their goal, then this is exactly what we would wish upon them and for ourselves in the future." King Hussein in interview with Christane Amanpour, CNN, June 23, 1996.

42. On this incident and its broader implications, see P.R. Kumaraswamy, "Israel, Jordan and the Masha'al Affair," 111–28.

Chapter 11. Ending the Jordanian-Syrian Cold War

1. Author's interviews with officials in Damascus, June 2001, and Amman, May 2005.

2. The discussion in chapters 11 and 12, on Jordanian foreign policy under King Abdullah II, draws in part on an earlier first cut at this topic: Curtis R. Ryan, "'Jordan First': Jordan's Inter Arab Relations and Foreign Policy under King Abdullah II," 43–62.

3. For a more thorough discussion of the Jordanian succession, see Ryan, *Jordan in Transition*, 87–107.

4. The Group of Seven refers to the world's most industrialized powers and includes Canada, France, Germany, Italy, Japan, the United Kingdom, and the United States. With the addition of Russia, following the collapse of the Soviet Union, the G7 began to meet as the G8.

5. Author's interviews with Jordanian policymakers. Amman, Jordan. May 2005.

6. Nevo, "Syria and Jordan: The Politics of Subversion," 140–56.

7. Author interviews with Syrian government officials. Damascus, April 1993.

8. Author interview with Ahmad 'Ubaydat. Amman, 1993.

9. Author interview. Amman, 1993.

10. Author interview in Amman. May 2005.

11. Author interview. Damascus, April 1993.

12. Author's interview in Amman, July 2001.

13. Author's interview in Amman, July 2001.

14. Author's interview with Kamel Abu Jaber, former foreign minister. Amman, July 13, 2001.

15. See, for example, Ryan, "Between Iraq and a Hard Place: Jordanian-Iraqi Relations," 40–42, or Ryan, "Jordan's Changing Relations," 83–87.

16. Reported in *al-Majd* (Jordanian newsweekly) July 23, 2001. BBC World Monitoring, July 23, 2001.

17. *al-Sharq al-Awsat,* August 28, 2001.

18. Rana Awad, "Jordan, Syria sign FTA," *Jordan Times,* October 9, 2001.

19. Andoni and Schwedler, "Bread Riots in Jordan," 40–42; Ryan, "Peace, Bread, and Riots: Jordan and the International Monetary Fund," 54–66.

20. Author interview with 'Abd al-Illah al-Khatib. Amman, Jordan. May 14, 2005.

21. On questions of liberalization, under Bishar and Hafiz al-Asad, see Ghadbian, "The New Asad: Dynamics of Continuity and Change in Syria," 624–41; Kienle, ed., *Contemporary Syria: Liberalization Between Cold War and Cold Peace;* and Perthes, *The Political Economy of Syria Under Asad.*

22. Moore, "The Newest Jordan: Free Trade, Peace, and an Ace in the Hole."

23. Author interview with Fayiz Tarawnah. Amman, Jordan. May 16, 2005.

24. Saad G. Hattar and Dana Charkasi, "Jordan asks Syria to hike flow of Yarmouk," *Jordan Times,* April 19, 2001.

25. Riad al-Khouri, "Syria and Jordan both look for liquidity, but of a different kind," *Daily Star,* August 28, 2001.

26. The Damascus Declaration emerged in 1991 in the aftermath of the second Gulf War, and consists of the "Six plus two" framework linking Syria and Egypt to the six states of the Gulf Cooperation Council (Bahrain, Kuwait, Oman, Qatar, Saudi Arabia, and the United Arab Emirates).

27. Author's interview with Kamel Abu Jaber. Amman, Jordan. May 15, 2005.

28. Author's interview with Senator Layla Sharaf. Amman, Jordan. May 17, 2005.

29. Author interview. Amman, Jordan. May 2005.

30. Author interview. Amman, Jordan. May 2005.

31. Author interview. Amman, Jordan. May 2005.

32. Greenwood, "Jordan's 'New Bargain'" and Ryan, "Jordan: The Politics of Alliance and Foreign Policy."

33. *Jordan Times,* December 20, 2007, and December 31, 2007.

Chapter 12. Jordan and the Second U.S.-Iraq Gulf War

1. *Jordan Times,* October 8, 2001.

2. Author interview with former Prime Minister Fayez Tarawnah, at the time serving as Deputy Speaker of the Senate. Amman, Jordan. May 16, 2005.

3. Author interview with former Foreign Minister Kamel Abu Jaber. Amman, Jordan. May 15, 2005.

4. This section on Jordanian-Iraqi relations draws in part on Ryan, "Jordan's Changing Relations," 83–87.

5. These charges also found their way into Western news media. See for example the essay by Amir Taheri, "Jordan's Choice: Taking the Right Side this Time," *National Review,* February 3, 2003.

6. For a detailed analysis of the public sphere debates within Jordan regarding the ups and downs of Jordanian-Iraqi relations, see Lynch, *State Interests and Public Spheres: The International Politics of Jordan's Identity,* 231–54.

7. See also Ryan "Between Iraq and a Hard Place: Jordanian-Iraqi Relations," 40–42.

8. Author interview with former Foreign Minister 'Abd al-Illah al-Khatib. Amman, Jordan. May 14, 2005.

9. Nimri Aziz, "Iraq and Jordan—A Partnership Restored.."

10. Author interviews with Jordanian policymakers. Amman, Jordan. June 2001 and May 2005.

11. Author interview. Amman, Jordan. May 2005.

12. Peter Hermann, "Iraq-U.S. Strife Adds to Jordan's Difficulties," *The Baltimore Sun*, August 25, 2002: 1.

13. See, for example, *al-Dustur*, August 11, 2002, and *The Guardian*, July 10, 2002.

14. See, for example, *The Boston Globe*, October 10, 2002, and *The Washington Post*, September 23, 2002.

15. *The Star* (Amman), February 1, 2003.

16. Author interview with former Prime Minister 'Abd al-Salam al-Majali. Amman, Jordan. May 11, 2005.

17. Author interview with a former foreign minister of Jordan. Amman, Jordan. May 2005.

18. Author interview with a former foreign minister of Jordan. Amman, Jordan. May 2005.

19. Brand, "The Effects of the Peace Process on Political Liberalization in Jordan," 52–67.

20. On the 1989, 1993, and 1997 elections see Ryan, "Elections and Parliamentary Democratization in Jordan," 194–214. On Jordan's political liberalization, see also Brynen, "Economic Crisis and Post-Rentier Democratization in the Arab World: The Case of Jordan," 69–97; Mufti, "Elite Bargains and the Onset of Political Liberalization in Jordan," 100–129; and Robinson, Defensive Democratization in Jordan," 387–410.

21. Brand, "The Effects of the Peace Process on Political Liberalization in Jordan," 52–67.

22. Schwedler, "Don't Blink: Jordan's Democratic Opening and Closing."

23. Scham and Lucas, "'Normalization' and 'Anti-Normalization' in Jordan," 141–64.

24. Quoted in Lynch, "Jordan's King Abdallah in Washington."

25. Agence France Presse, October 11, 2002.

26. BBC Monitoring Middle East / Associated Press, August 7, 2002.

27. See Schwedler, "Occupied Maan: Jordan's Closed Military Zone."

28. "Black Masks Amid the Devout: Crackdown in Jordan," *The Economist*, November 14, 2002. See also, Center for Strategic Studies, *Ma'an: Azma Maftuhah* (Ma'an: An Open-ended Crisis). The November 2002 raid and military deployment in Ma'an followed the October 2002 assassination of American diplomat Lawrence Foley. Foley had been shot to death outside his home in Amman. Jordanian forces since that time attempted to round up the militants responsible. But whether the domestic military operation in Ma'an was truly aimed at religious fundamentalists or secular leftists, at criminal smuggling syndicates or foreign militants, the appearance in a Jordanian town of soldiers, tanks, and helicopter gunships invoked the same images as the unrest of 1989, 1996, and 1998. Jordanians drew comparisons not just to these earlier events within Jordan, but also to Israeli repression in the intifadah.

29. Author interviews with Jordanian policymakers. Amman, Jordan. May 2005.

30. Muasher interviewed by Agence France-Presse. See also Hala Boncompagni, "Jordan fears Israel could use Iraq war to deport Palestinians to Jordan," *Jordan Times*, October 12, 2002.

31. In her 2005 visit to Jordan, U.S. Secretary of State Condoleeza Rice specifically cited Jordan as a "frontline state" in her press conference at the Jordanian Foreign Ministry. "Remarks by US Secretary of State Condoleeza Rice and Jordan Foreign Minister Farouq Qasrawi after their meeting," June 19, 2005. U.S. Department of State, Office of the Spokesman, Amman, Jordan.

32. Author interview in Amman, Jordan. May 2005.

33. Author interview with Dr. Jawad al-'Anani, former senator, deputy prime minister, minister of industry and trade, minister of supply, and chief of the Royal Hashimite Court. Amman, July 13, 2001.

34. Author interview with former Prime Minister Fayez Tarawnah. Amman, Jordan. May 16, 2005.

35. Francesca Sawalha, "EU pledges to help Jordan in case of war—Awadallah," *Jordan Times*, February 28, 2003.

36. Author interview with a former foreign minister of Jordan. Amman, Jordan. May 2005.

37. *Al-Quds al-'Arabi*, December 31, 2004.

38. "Talabani: al-'alaqat al-Urduniyya al-Iraqiyya Istratijiyya wa Mumtaza," *al-Ra'y*, May 9, 2005.

39. But, as Greenwood has argued, this strategy seems to be aimed also at mollifying and co-opting key constituencies such as Transjordanians and the (largely Palestinian) business community. Greenwood, "Jordan's 'New Bargain.'"

40. For an analysis of liberalization and the 2003 elections, see Ryan and Schwedler, "Return to Democratization or New Hybrid Regime?: The 2003 Elections in Jordan," 138–51. The 2003 national parliamentary elections were the first since 1997, the first since the dissolution of parliament in 2001, and the first in the reign of King Abdullah II. The elections took place in the context of electoral laws that introduced a new system of magnetic voting cards, reduced the voting age from 19 to 18, and increased the number of parliamentary seats to 110 (including a new quota of six seats to guarantee minimal representation for women). The new laws also maintained the pattern of uneven electoral districts, tilting representation toward more conservative rural areas and away from urban centers of Palestinian or Islamist strength. Not surprisingly, the poll results yielded a parliament dominated by a clear majority of tribal and pro-regime candidates. There was, however, at least minimal representation for the opposition, which had returned to electoral participation after having boycotted the 1997 elections. For example, seventeen parliamentary seats went to the Islamic Action Front and four to independent Islamists.

41. For particularly devastating critiques along these lines, see Stephen Glain, "Letter from Jordan," *The Nation*, May 30, 2005, and Scott Wilson, "Jordan acts to curb rising chorus of critics," *The Washington Post*, September 30, 2004.

42. Lynch, *Voices of the New Arab Public: Iraq, al-Jazeera, and Middle East Politics Today.*

43. Francesca Sawalha and Khalid Dalal, "PM: Jordan to launch offensive to stop war," *Jordan Times* March 24, 2003.

44. Sawalha and Dalal, "PM," *Jordan Times*, March 24, 2003; Ian Fisher, "Protests continue as Jordan defends U.S. presence in border region," *New York Times*, March 24, 2003.

Chapter 13. Regime Security and Shifting Arab Alliances

1. Waltz, *Theory of International Politics.*

2. Walt, *The Origins of Alliances*; Walt, "Alliance Formation and the Balance of World Power," *International Security*, 3–43; and Walt, "Testing Theories of Alliance Formation," *International Organization*, 275–316.

3. Brand, *Jordan's Inter-Arab Relations.*

4. Lynch, *State Interests and Public Spheres,* and Barnett, *Dialogues in Arab Politics.*

5. David, *Choosing Sides.*

Bibliography

Interviews

Most interviews were kept anonymous at the interviewee's own request. The anonymous interviews, therefore, are documented in the endnotes by referring to the person's general position, such as government minister, member of parliament, journalist, or policymaker. Other interviews are listed below. Most interviews were conducted in Amman, Jordan, during fieldwork in 1992–1993, 1997, 1999, 2001, 2005, and 2006.

Abu 'Awdah, Adnan. Former senator, political advisor in the royal court, and Jordanian representative to the United Nations.

Abu Jaber, Kamel. Former foreign minister and president of Jordan's Institute for Diplomacy.

'Anani, Jawad al-. Former senator, deputy prime minister, and minister for planning and for supply.

'Arabiyyat, 'Abd al-Latif. Former speaker of the House of Deputies and leader of the Islamic Action Front.

Badran, Mudar. Former prime minister, senator, and director of Jordanian intelligence.

Barari, Hasan al-. Policy Analyst, Center for Strategic Studies, University of Jordan.

Bataynah, Safwan al-. Economic advisor at the Prime Ministry.

Braizat, Fares. Researcher and Deputy Director of the Center for Strategic Studies, University of Jordan.

Hamarneh, Mustafa. Director of the Center for Strategic Studies, University of Jordan.

Hassanat, Abdullah. Former editor of the *Jordan Times* newspaper.

Hindawi, Asim al-. Official at the Ministry of Industry and Trade.

Hourani, Hani. Director of the al-Urdun al-Jadid Research Center.

Khamash, Lt. General 'Amr. Former general in the Jordanian armed forces and advisor to King Hussein.

Khatib, 'Abd-al Illah al-. Former foreign minister of Jordan.

Kilani, Sa'ida. Co-Director of the Arab Archives Institute.

Lawzi, Ahmad al-. Former prime minister and speaker of the senate.

Majali, 'Abd al-Salam al-. Former prime minister and deputy speaker of the senate.

Masri, Muhammad al-. Researcher at the Center for Strategic Studies, University of Jordan.

Masri, Tahir al-. Former prime minister, foreign minister, and speaker of the Chamber of Deputies.

Qasim, Marwan al-. Former chief of the royal court and foreign minister.

Qudah, Iyad. Official at the Ministry of Planning.

Rifa'i, Zayd al-. Former prime minister and current Speaker of the Senate.

Safadi, Ayman. Former journalist for the *Jordan Times*, press officer for Crown Prince Hasan, press officer for H.M. King Abdullah II, and editor of *al-Ghad* newspaper.

Sharaf, Layla. Senator and former minister of culture and of information.

Tarawnah, Fayez. Former prime minister, chief of the Royal Hashimite Court, and deputy speaker of the senate.

Tell, Nawaf. Researcher at the Center for Strategic Studies and Director of the Negotiations Coordination Bureau of the Ministry of Foreign Affairs.

'Ubaydat, Ahmad. Former prime minister, senator, and director of Jordanian intelligence.

Zu'aby, Salih. Former secretary general of the parliament.

Books and Articles

'Abdalat, Marwan Ahmad Sulayman al-. *Kharita al-Ahzab al-Siyasiyya al-Urduniyya* (Map of Jordanian Political Parties). Amman: Dar al-'Ubra, 1992.

'Abdalla, Nazem. "Impact of the Gulf Crisis on Developing Countries." Amman: ES-CWA/UNDP Informal Background Paper, June 1991.

Abu Jaber, Kamel S. "Jordan and the Gulf War." In *The Gulf War and the New World Order*, edited by Tareq Y. Ismael and Jacqueline S. Ismael, 366–82. Gainesville: University Press of Florida, 1994.

Abu Jaber, Kamel S., Matthes Buhbe, and Mohammad Smadi, eds. *Income Distribution in Jordan*. Boulder: Westview Press, 1990.

Abu Jaber, Kamel S., and Schirin H. Fathi. "The 1989 Jordanian Parliamentary Elections." *Orient* 31 (1990): 67–86.

Abu Jaber, Raouf S. *Pioneers Over Jordan: The Frontiers of Settlement in Transjordan, 1860–1914*. London: I. B. Tauris, 1989.

Abu Khusa, Ahmad. *al-Dimuqratiyya wa al-Ahzab al-Siyasiyya al-Urduniyya* (Democracy and Jordanian Political Parties). Amman: Middle East Publishing Company, 1991.

Abu Odeh, Adnan. *Jordanians, Palestinians, and the Hashemite Kingdom in the Middle East Peace Process*. Washington, D.C.: United States Institute of Peace Press, 1999.

Abu Ruman, Hussein, ed., *'Aqd Min al-Dimuqratiyya fi al-Urdun* (A Decade of Democracy in Jordan). Amman: al-Urdun al-Jadid Research Center, 1999.

Adeola, Francis O. "Military Expenditures, Health, and Education: Bedfellows or Antagonists in Third World Development?" *Armed Forces and Society* 22, no. 3 (Spring 1996): 441–67.

Ajami, Fouad. *The Arab Predicament: Arab Political Thought and Practice Since 1967*. New York: Cambridge University Press, 1981.

———. "The End of Pan-Arabism." *Foreign Affairs* 57 (Winter 1978/79): 355–73.

Albrecht, Kirk. "Where is all the Business? Jordanian-Israeli Economic Ties Start Slowly." *Middle East Insight* 12, no. 2 (1996): 13–15.

Amawi, Abla. "The 1993 Elections in Jordan." *Arab Studies Quarterly* 16, no. 3 (Summer 1994): 15–27.

Anani, Jawad al-. "Adjustment and Development: The Case of Jordan." In *Adjustment Policies and Development Strategies in the Arab World*, edited by Said al-Naggar, 124–48. Washington, D.C.: International Monetary Fund, 1987.

———. "Falsafa al-Iqtisad al-Urduni bayn al-Fikr wa al-Tatbiq Khilal Nisf al-Qarn al-Maadi" (Jordanian Economic Philosophy Between Thought and Application During the Last Half Century). In *al-Iqtisad al-Urduni: al-Mushkilat wa al- Ifaq*, edited by Mustafa Hamarnah, 92–96. Amman: Center for Strategic Studies, 1994.

Anderson, Lisa. "Absolutism and the Resilience of Monarchy in the Middle East." *Political Science Quarterly* 106, no. 1 (1991): 1–15.

———. "Policy-Making and Theory-Building: American Political Science and the Islamic Middle East." In *Theory, Politics and the Arab World: Critical Responses*, edited by Hisham Sharabi, 52–80. New York: Routledge, 1990.

Andoni, Lamis. "Arab Cooperation Council: Allaying Fears." *Middle East International* 17 (February 1989): 8.

———. "Jordan: Badran's skillful game." *Middle East International* 15 (December 1989): 8–9.

———. "Jordan: First Test Case for Kabariti." *Middle East International* 522 (1996): 10–12.

Andoni, Lamis, and Jillian Schwedler. "Bread Riots in Jordan." *Middle East Report* 201 (October-December 1996): 40–42.

'Aqd Min al-Dimuqratiyya fi al-Urdun (A Decade of Democracy in Jordan). Amman: Konrad Adenauer Shiftung and the al-Urdun al-Jadid Research Center, 2001.

"Arab Cooperation: Getting Together, in Bits." *Economist* (February 25, 1989): 38–41.

'Arabuti, Khalid Ibrahim al-. *Fikr al-Husayn fi al-Mizan* (Hussein's Thought in the Balance). Amman: Wakala al-Na'im Li al-'Alaqat al-'Am, 1992.

Astorino-Courtois, Allison. "Transforming International Agreements into National Realities: Marketing Arab-Israeli Peace in Jordan." *Journal of Politics* 58, no. 4 (1996): 1035–54.

Ayoob, Mohammed. "Perspectives From the Gulf: Regime Security or Regional Security?" In *Asian Perspectives on International Security*, edited by Donald Hugh Millen, 92–116. New York: St. Martin's Press, 1984.

———. "The Security Problematic of the Third World." *World Politics* 43, no. 2 (1991): 257–83.

———. *The Third World Security Predicament: State Making, Regional Conflict, and the International System*. Boulder: Lynne Rienner, 1995.

Ayubi, Nazih. *Political Islam: Religion and Politics in the Arab World*. London: Routledge, 1991.

Azar, Edward E., and Chung-in Moon, eds. *National Security in the Third World: The Management of Internal and External Threats*. College Park, Maryland: Center for International Development and Conflict Management, University of Maryland Press, 1988.

Bailey, Clinton. *Jordan's Palestinian Challenge, 1948–1983: A Political History*. Boulder: Westview Press, 1984.

Baldwin, David A., ed. *Neorealism and Neoliberalism: The Contemporary Debate.* New York: Columbia University Press, 1993.

Ball, Nicole. *Security and Economy in the Third World.* Princeton: Princeton University Press, 1988.

Baram, Amatzia. "Baathi Iraq and Hashemite Jordan: From Hostility to Alignment." *Middle East Journal* 45, no. 1 (1991): 51–70.

———. "No New Fertile Crescent: Iraqi-Jordanian Relations, 1968–92." In *Jordan in the Middle East: The Making of a Pivotal State, 1948–1988,* edited by Joseph Nevo and Ilan Pappe, 119–60. Ilford: Frank Cass & Co. Ltd., 1994.

Barari, Hassan A. *Jordan and Israel: Ten Years Later.* Amman: Center for Strategic Studies, University of Jordan, 2004.

Barnett, Michael N. *Dialogues in Arab Politics: Negotiations in Regional Order.* New York: Columbia University Press, 1998.

———. "High Politics Is Low Politics: The Domestic and Systemic Sources of Israeli Security Policy, 1967–1977." *World Politics* 42, no. 2 (1990): 529–62.

———. "Institutions, Roles, and Disorder: The Case of the Arab States System." *International Studies Quarterly* 37 (1993): 271–96.

Barnett, Michael N., and Jack S. Levy. "Domestic Sources of Alliances and Alignments: The Case of Egypt, 1962–73." *International Organization* 45, no. 3 (1991): 369–96.

Bates, Robert H., and Da-Hsiang Donald Lien. "A Note on Taxation, Development, and Representative Government." *Politics and Society* 14, no. 1 (1985): 53–70.

Beblawi, Hazem, and Giacomo Luciani, eds. *The Rentier State.* London: Croom Helm, 1987.

Bennis, Phyllis, and Michel Moushabeck, eds. *Beyond the Storm: A Gulf Crisis Reader.* Edinburgh: Cannongate, 1992.

Boulby, Marion. *The Muslim Brotherhood and the Kings of Jordan, 1945–93.* Landham, Md.: University Press of America, 1999.

Braizat, Musa. *Jordan's Diplomacy: Balancing National Survival with Nation's Renewal.* Amman: University of Jordan Center for Strategic Studies, 1995.

Brand, Laurie A. "Economic and Political Liberalization in a Rentier Economy: The Case of the Hashemite Kingdom of Jordan." In *Privatization and Liberalization in the Middle East,* edited by Iliya Harik and Denis J. Sullivan, 167–88. Bloomington: Indiana University Press, 1992.

———. "Economics and Shifting Alliances: Jordan's Relations with Syria and Iraq, 1975–1981." *International Journal of Middle East Studies* 26, no. 3 (1994): 393–413.

———. "The Effects of the Peace Process on Political Liberalization in Jordan." *Journal of Palestine Studies* 28, no. 2 (1999): 52–67.

———. "'In the Beginning was the State . . .': The Quest for Civil Society in Jordan." In *Civil Society in the Middle East,* edited by Augustus Richard Norton, vol. 1. Leiden: E. J. Brill, 1995.

———. *Jordan's Inter-Arab Relations: The Political Economy of Alliance Making.* New York: Columbia University Press, 1994.

———. "Liberalization and Changing Political Coalitions: The Bases of Jordan's 1990–91 Gulf Crisis Policy." *Jerusalem Journal of International Relations* 13, no. 4 (1991): 1–46.

———. "Palestinians and Jordanians: A Crisis of Identity." *Journal of Palestine Studies* 96 (1995): 54–60.

———. *Palestinians in the Arab World: Institution Building and the Search for State.* New York: Columbia University Press, 1988.

Bratton, Michael. "Beyond the State: Civil Society and Associational Life in Africa." *World Politics* 41 (1989): 407–30.

Brookes, Stephen. "Two New Blocs Amid Shifting Sands." *Insight* 5, no. 11 (March 13, 1989): 36.

Brynen, Rex. "Economic Crisis and Post-Rentier Democratization in the Arab World: The Case of Jordan." *Canadian Journal of Political Science* 25, no. 1 (1992): 69–97.

———. "The Politics of Monarchical Liberalization: Jordan." In *Political Liberalization and Democratization in the Arab World,* edited by Bahgat Korany, Rex Brynen, and Paul Noble, 71–100. Boulder, Colorado: Lynne Rienner Publishers, 1998.

Brynen, Rex, Bahgat Korany, and Paul Noble, eds. *Political Liberalization and Democratization in the Arab World,* Vol. 1, *Theoretical Perspectives.* Boulder, Colorado: Lynne Rienner Publishers, 1995.

Buzan, Barry. *People, States and Fear: An Agenda for International Security Studies in the Post-Cold War Era.* 2nd ed. Boulder: Lynne Rienner Publishers, 1991.

Buzan, Barry, Ole Waever, and Jaap de Wilde. *Security: A New Framework for Analysis.* Boulder: Lynne Rienner, 1998.

Carey, Roger, and Salmon, Trevor C., eds. *International Security in the Modern World.* New York: St. Martin's Press, 1992.

Center for Strategic Studies. *Ma'an: Azma Maftuhah* (Ma'an: An Open-ended Crisis). Amman: Center for Strategic Studies, University of Jordan, 2003.

———. *Unemployment in Jordan—1996: Preliminary Results & Basic Data.* Amman: Center for Strategic Studies, University of Jordan, 1997.

Chatelus, Michel. "Rentier or Producer Economy in the Middle East? The Jordanian Response." In *The Economic Development of Jordan,* edited by Bichara Khader and Adnan Badran, 204–20. London: Croom Helm, 1987.

Chelkowski, Peter J., and Robert J. Pranger, eds. *Ideology and Power in the Middle East: Studies in Honor of George Lenczowski.* Durham, N.C.: Duke University Press, 1988.

Christensen, Thomas J., and Jack Snyder. "Chain Gangs and Passed Bucks: Predicting Alliance Patterns in Multipolarity." *International Organization* 44, no. 2 (1990): 137–68.

Clark, Janine. *Islam, Charity, and Activism: Middle-Class Networks and Social Welfare in Egypt, Jordan, and Yemen.* Bloomington: Indiana University Press, 2003.

Coffey, Joseph I., and Gianni Bonvicini, eds. *The Atlantic Alliance and the Middle East.* Basingstoke: MacMillan, 1989.

Cordesman, Anthony H. *Jordanian Arms and the Middle East Balance.* Washington, D.C.: The Middle East Institute, 1983.

Cottam, Richard W. "Levels of Conflict in the Middle East." In *The Atlantic Alliance and the Middle East,* edited by Joseph I. Coffey and Gianni Bonvicini, 17–41. Basingstoke: MacMillan, 1989.

Coulam, R., and R. Smith, eds. *Advances in Information Processing in Organizations: Research on Public Organizations.* Greenwich, Conn.: JAI Press, 1985.

"Dalil al-Hayat al-Hizbiyya fi al-Urdun: Hizb Jabha al-'Amal al-Islami" (Guide to Party Life in Jordan: Islamic Action Front Party). Amman: al-Urdun al-Jadid Research Center, 1993.

Dallas, Roland. *King Hussein: A Life on the Edge.* London: Profile Books, 1999.

Dann, Uriel. *King Hussein and the Challenge of Arab Radicalism, 1955–1967.* New York: Oxford University Press, 1989.

———. *King Hussein's Strategy of Survival.* Washington, D.C.: The Washington Institute for Near East Policy, 1992.

———. *Studies in the History of Transjordan, 1920–1949: The Making of a State.* Boulder, Colo.: Westview Press, 1984.

Darwish, Adel, and Mariam Shahin. "The End of an Epoch." *The Middle East* (March 1999): 4.

David, Stephen R. *Choosing Sides: Alignment and Realignment in the Third World.* Baltimore: Johns Hopkins University Press, 1991.

———. "Explaining Third World Alignments." *World Politics* 43, no. 2 (1991): 233–56.

Dawisha, Adeed. "Arab Regimes: Legitimacy and Foreign Policy." In *The Arab State*, edited by Giacomo Luciani, 284–99. Berkeley: University of California Press, 1990.

Dawn, Ernest C. *From Ottomanism to Arabism: Essays on the Origins of Arab Nationalism.* Urbana, Ill.: University of Illinois Press, 1973.

Day, Arthur. *East Bank/West Bank: Jordan and the Prospects for Peace.* New York: Council on Foreign Relations, 1986.

Devlin, John F. "The Purposes and Effect of the Arab Cooperation Council." *Geopolitics of Energy* (August 1989): 4–7.

Ecktein, Harry. "Case Study in Theory and Political Science." In *Handbook of Political Science: Strategies of Inquiry*, edited by Fred L. Greenstein, 80–137. Reading, Mass.: Addison Wesley Publishing Company, 1975.

Economic and Social Commission for Western Asia (ESCWA). *The Impact of the Gulf Crisis on the Jordanian Economy.* Amman: ESCWA, December 1990.

Economist Intelligence Unit. *Jordan: Country Profile 1991.* London: Economist Intelligence Unit, 1991.

Economist Intelligence Unit. *Jordan: Quarterly Economic Report*, no. 1 (1989).

Economist Intelligence Unit. *Jordan: Quarterly Economic Report*, no. 2 (1989).

Economist Intelligence Unit. *Jordan: Quarterly Economic Report*, no. 3 (1989).

Economist Intelligence Unit. *Jordan: Quarterly Economic Report*, no. 1 (1990).

Economist Intelligence Unit. *Jordan: Quarterly Economic Report*, no. 4 (1990).

Enayat, Hamid. *Modern Islamic Political Thought.* Austin: University of Texas Press, 1982.

Escude, Carlos. *International Relations Theory: A Peripheral Perspective.* Buenos Aires, Argentina: Universidad Torcuato Di Tella, Programa di Estudios Internacionales, 1993.

Esposito, John L. *Unholy War: Terror in the Name of Islam.* New York: Oxford University Press, 2002.

Faddah, Mohammad Ibrahim. *The Middle East in Transition: A Study of Jordan's Foreign Policy*. London: Asia Publishing House, 1974.

Faour, Muhammad. *The Arab World After Desert Storm*. Washington, D.C.: United States Institute of Peace, 1993.

Farah, Tawfiq. *Pan-Arabism and Arab Nationalism: The Continuing Debate*. Boulder, Colo.: Westview Press, 1987.

Fathi, Schirin H. *Jordan—An Invented Nation? Tribe-State Dynamics and the Formation of National Identity*. Hamburg, Germany: Deutsches Orient Institut, 1994.

Feiler, Gil. "Jordan's Economy, 1970–90: The Primacy of Exogenous Factors." In *State, Society, and Land in Jordan*, edited by Joseph Fishbach. Leiden: Brill, 2000.

Fishbach, Michael, ed. *State, Society, and Land in Jordan*. Leiden: Brill, 2000.

Freij, Hanna Y., and Leonard C. Robinson, "Liberalization, the Islamists, and the Stability of the Arab State: Jordan as a Case Study." *The Muslim World* 86, no. 1 (1996): 1–32.

Fromkin, David. *A Peace to End All Peace: The Fall of the Ottoman Empire and the Rise of the Modern Middle East*. New York: Henry Holt, 1989.

Garfinkle, Adam M. *Jordan and Israel in the Shadow of War: Functional Ties and Futile Diplomacy in a Small Place*. New York: St. Martin's Press, 1992.

Garnham, David. "Explaining Middle Eastern Alignments During the Gulf War." *The Jerusalem Journal of International Relations* 13, no. 3 (1991): 63–83.

Gause, F. Gregory III. "Balancing What? Threat Perception and Alliance Choice in the Gulf." *Security Studies* 13, no. 2 (2003/4): 273–305.

———. *Oil Monarchies*. New York: Council on Foreign Relations Press, 1994.

———. *Saudi-Yemeni Relations: Domestic Structures and Foreign Influence*. New York: Columbia University Press, 1990.

———. "Sovereignty, Statecraft, and Stability in the Middle East." *Journal of International Affairs* 45 (Winter 1992): 441–67.

———. "Systemic Approaches to Middle East International Relations." *International Studies Review* 1, no. 1 (1999): 11–31.

George, Alexander L. "Case Studies and Theory Development: The Method of Structured, Focused Comparison." In *Diplomacy: New Approaches in History, Theory and Policy*, edited by Paul Lauren, 43–68. New York: Free Press, 1979.

George, Alexander L., and Timothy McKeown. "Case Studies and Theories of Organizational Decision Making." In *Advances in Information Processing in Organizations: Research on Public Organizations*, edited by R. Coulam and R. Smith, 21–58. Greenwich, Conn.: JAI Press, 1985.

Gerges, Fawaz. *The Far Enemy: Why Jihad Went Global*. Cambridge: Cambridge University Press, 2005.

Ghadbian, Najib. "The New Asad: Dynamics of Continuity and Change in Syria." *Middle East Journal* 55, no. 4 (2001): 624–41.

Gorvett, Jon. "Facing a Dilemma." *The Middle East* (September 1998): 15–16.

Graz, Liesl. "Iraqi Sabers Rattle in the Gulf." *Middle East International* 3 (August 1990): 3–5.

Greenstein, Fred L., ed. *Handbook of Political Science: Strategies of Inquiry*. Reading, Mass.: Addison Wesley Publishing Company, 1975.

Greenwood, Scott. "Jordan's 'New Bargain': The Political Economy of Regime Security." *Middle East Journal* 57, no. 2 (2003): 1-21.

Gubser, Peter. "Jordan: Balancing Pluralism and Authoritarianism." In *Ideology and Power in the Middle East: Essays in Honor of George Lenczowski*, edited by Peter J. Chelkopwski and Robert J. Pranger. Durham, N.C.: Duke University Press, 1988.

———. *Jordan: Crossroads of Middle Eastern Events*. Boulder, Colo.: Westview Press, 1983.

Haley, P. Edward, and Lewis W. Snider, eds. *Lebanon in Crisis: Participants and Issues*. Syracuse: Syracuse University Press, 1979.

Halliday, Fred. *The Middle East in International Relations: Power, Politics and Ideology*. New York: Cambridge University Press, 2005.

———. "State and Society in International Relations: A Second Agenda." *Millennium: Journal of International Studies* 16, no. 2 (1982): 215–27.

Hamarneh, Mustafa, ed. *al-Iqtisad al-Urduni: al-Mushkilat wa al-Ifaq* (The Jordanian Economy: Problems and Prospects). Amman: Center for Strategic Studies, 1994.

Hamarneh, Mustafa B. "Jordan Responds to the Gulf Crisis." In *Beyond the Storm: A Gulf Crisis Reader,* edited by Phyllis Bennis and Michel Moushabeck, 228–40. Edinburgh: Cannongate, 1992.

———. "Jordan's Political Developments and Foreign Policy: A Brief Historical Overview." Unpublished Manuscript: Center for Strategic Studies, University of Jordan, November 1992.

Hamarneh, Mustafa, Rosemary Hollis, and Khalil Shikaki. *Jordanian-Palestinian Relations: Where To? Four Scenarios for the Future*. London: Royal Institute of International Affairs, 1997.

Hammad, Khalil. "The Role of Foreign Aid in the Jordanian Economy, 1959–1983." In *The Economic Development of Jordan*, edited by Bichara Khader and Adnan Badran. London: Croom Helm, 1987.

Harik, Iliya and Sullivan, Denis, eds. *Privatization and Liberalization in the Middle East*. Bloomington: Indiana University Press, 1992.

Harknett, Richard and Jeffrey Vandenberg. "Alignment Theory and Interrelated Threats: Jordan and the Persian Gulf Crisis." *Security Studies* 6, no. 3 (1997): 112–53.

Hashimite Kingdom of Jordan. *Economic and Social Development Plan 1993–1997*. Amman: Ministry of Planning, 1993.

———. *The Economic, Trade and Investment Agreements held between the Hashemite Kingdom of Jordan and Foreign Countries*. Volume 1. Amman: Directory of Economic Cooperation and Export Promotion, Ministry of Industry and Trade, 1988.

———. *Five Year Plan for Economic and Social Development 1986–1990*. Amman: Ministry of Planning, 1986.

———. *Majlis al-Qawmi li al-Takhtit: Khita al-Tanmiya al-Iqtisadiya wa al-Ijtima'iya, 1981–1985* (Command Council for Planning. Economic and Social Development Plan, 1981–1985). Amman: Ministry of Planning, 1981.

———. *Majmu'ah al-Itifaqiyat al-Iqtisadiya wa al-Tijariya bayn al-Mamlaka al-Urduniya al-Hashimiya wa al-Duwal al-'Arabiya* (Compendium of Economic and Trade Agreements Between the Hashimite Kingdom of Jordan and the Arab States). Volume One. Amman: Ministry of Industry and Trade, 1985.

———. *Majmu'ah al-Itifaqiyat al-Iqtisadiya wa al-Tijariya bayn al-Mamlaka al-Urduniya al-Hashimiya wa al-Duwal al-'Arabiya* (Compendium of Economic and Trade Agreements Between the Hashimite Kingdom of Jordan and the Arab States). Volume Two. Amman: Ministry of Industry and Trade, 1985.

———. *Mamlaka al-Urduniyya al-Hashimiyya: al-Withaq al-Watani al-Urduni* (Hashimite Kingdom of Jordan: Jordan National Charter). Amman: Government of the Hashimite Kingdom of Jordan, 1991.

———. *White Paper: Jordan and the Gulf Crisis, August 1990–March 1991.* Amman: Government of the Hashimite Kingdom of Jordan, August 1991.

Hawatmeh, George, ed. *The Role of the Media in a Democracy: The Case of Jordan.* Amman: Center for Strategic Studies, 1995.

Herb, Michael. *All in the Family: Absolutism, Revolution, and Democracy in the Middle Eastern Monarchies.* Albany: State University of New York Press, 1999.

Herbst, Jeffrey. "Responding to State Failure in Africa." *International Security* 21, vol. 3 (Winter 1996/97): 145–76.

Herz, John. *Political Realism and Political Idealism.* Chicago: University of Chicago Press, 1951.

Herzog, Chaim. *The Arab-Israeli Wars.* New York: Vintage Books, 1984.

Hewedy, Amin. *Militarization and Security in the Middle East: Its Impact on Development and Democracy.* New York: St. Martin's Press, 1989.

Heydemann, Steven, ed. *War, Institutions, and Social Change in the Middle East.* Berkeley: University of California Press, 2000.

Hinnebusch, Raymond A. "The Foreign Policy of Syria." In *The Foreign Policies of Middle East States,* edited by Raymond Hinnebusch and Anoushiravan Ehteshami, 141–65. Boulder: Lynne Rienner, 2002.

———. "Revisionist Dreams, Realist Strategies: The Foreign Policy of Syria." In *The Foreign Policies of Arab States: The Challenge of Change,* edited by Bahgat Korany and Ali E. Hilal Dessouki, 374–409. Boulder: Westview Press, 1991.

Hinnebusch, Raymond, and Anoushiravan Ehteshami, eds. *The Foreign Policies of Middle East States.* Boulder: Lynne Rienner, 2002.

Hourani, Albert. *Arabic Thought in the Liberal Age, 1793–1939.* London: Oxford University Press, 1962.

———. *A History of the Arab Peoples.* Cambridge: Harvard University Press, 1991.

Hourani, Hani, Hussein Abu Rumman, and Nasser Ahmad Kamel. *Who's Who in the Jordanian Parliament, 2003–2007.* Amman: al-Urdun al-Jadid Research Center, 2004.

Hourani, Hani, Hussein Abu-Rumman, and George Musleh, eds. *The Democratic Process in Jordan: Where To?* Amman: al-Urdun al-Jadid Research Center, 1996.

Hourani, Hani, Hamed Dabbas, and Mark Power-Stevens, eds., translated by George Musleh, *Who's Who in the Jordanian Parliament 1993–1997.* Amman: al-Urdun al-Jadid Research Center, 1995.

Hourani, Hani, et al. *Al-Ahzab al-Siyasiyya Al-Urduniyya* (The Jordanian Political Parties). Amman: al-Urdun al-Jadid Research Center, 1993.

Hourani, Hani, et al. *al-Mujtama'a al-Madani wa al-Hukm fi al- Urdun* (Civil Society and Authority in Jordan). Volume One. Amman: al-Urdun al-Jadid Research Center, 2004.

———. *al-Mujtama'a al-Madani wa al-Hukm fi al-Urdun* (Civil Society and Authority in Jordan). Volume Two. Amman: al-Urdun al-Jadid Research Center, 2004.

———. *Dirasat fi al-Intakhabat al-Niyabiyya al-Urduniyya* (Studies in the 1997 Representative [Parliamentary] Elections). Amman: al-Urdun al-Jadid Research Center, 2002.

Hourani, Hani, George Musleh, and Jillian Schwedler, eds. *Islamic Movements in Jordan.* Amman: al-Urdun al-Jadid Research Center, 1997.

Hourani, Hani, Sadeq Ibraheem Odeh, and George Musleh, eds. *Professional Associations and the Challenges of Democratic Transformation in Jordan.* Amman: al-Urdun al-Jadid Research Center, 2000.

Hourani, Hani, Ayman Yassin, Lola Keilani, Lana Habash, and Terre Lore. *Who's Who in the Jordanian Parliament 1997–2001.* Amman: al-Urdun al-Jadid Research Center, 1998.

Hudson, Michael C. *Arab Politics: The Search for Legitimacy.* New Haven and London: Yale University Press, 1977.

Human Rights Watch. *Clamping Down on Critics: Human Rights Violations in Advance of the Parliamentary Elections.* New York: Human Rights Watch, 1997.

Hunter, Shireen T., ed. *The Politics of Islamic Revivalism: Diversity and Unity.* Bloomington: Indiana University Press, 1988.

Hussein, Ibn Talal. *Uneasy Lies the Head: The Autobiography of His Majesty King Hussein I of the Hashemite Kingdom of Jordan.* New York: Bernard Geis Associates, 1962.

Ibrahim, Saad Eddin. *The New Arab Social Order: A Study of the Social Impact of Oil Wealth.* Boulder, Colo.: Westview Press, 1982.

———. "Oil, Migration and the New Arab Social Order." In *Rich and Poor States in the Middle East: Egypt and the New Arab Order,* edited by Malcolm H. Kerr and El Sayed Yassin, 17–70. Boulder: Westview Press, 1982.

Imana al-'Am li Majlis al-Ta'awun al-Arabi. *Majlis al-Ta'awun al-Arabi: Nasus al-Itifaqiyat wa al-Qararat al-Muqa'a Khilal al-Am al-Awal 1989–1990* (General Secretariat of the Arab Cooperation Council, Text of the Agreements and Decisions Signed During the First Year). Amman: Arab Cooperation Council, 1990.

International Monetary Fund. *Direction of Trade Statistics Yearbook.* Washington, D.C.: International Monetary Fund, 1991.

International Monetary Fund. *Government Finance Statistics Yearbook.* Washington, D.C.: International Monetary Fund, 1990.

International Monetary Fund. *International Financial Statistics Yearbook.* Washington, D.C.: International Monetary Fund, 1991.

Ismael, Tareq Y. *International Relations of the Contemporary Middle East: A Study in World Politics.* Syracuse: Syracuse University Press, 1986.

Ismael, Tareq Y., and Jacqueline S. Ismael, eds. *The Gulf War and the New World Order.* Gainesville, Florida: University Press of Florida, 1994.

Israeli, Raphael. "Is Jordan Palestine?" *Israel Affairs* 9, no. 3 (2003): 49–66.

"It's Reckoning Time for Jordan." *The Middle East* (June 1989): 26.

Iyad, Ranad al-Khatib. *al-Tayarat al-Siyasiyya fi al-Urdun wa Nas al-Mithaq al-Watani al-Urduni* (Political Tendencies in Jordan and Text of the Jordanian National Charter). Amman, 1991.

Jackson, Robert. *Quasi-States: Sovereignty, International Relations, and the Third World.* Cambridge: Cambridge University Press, 1990.

Jackson, Robert and Carl Rosberg. "Why Africa's Weak States Persist: The Empirical and the Juridical in Statehood." *World Politics* 35, no. 1 (October 1982): 1–24.

Ja'fari, Bishar al-. *al-Siyasa al-Kharijiyya al-Suriyya 1942–1982* (Syrian Foreign Policy). Damascus: Tlas, 1987.

Jervis, Robert. "Cooperation Under the Security Dilemma." *World Politics* 30, no. 2 (January 1978): 167–214.

———. *Perception and Misperception in International Politics.* Princeton: Princeton University Press, 1977.

Job, Brian L., ed. *The Insecurity Dilemma: National Security of Third World States.* Boulder: Lynne Rienner Publishers, 1992.

Jureidini, Paul A., and R. D. McLaurin. *Beyond Camp David: Emerging Alignments and Leaders in the Middle East.* Syracuse: Syracuse University Press, 1981.

———. "The Hashemite Kingdom of Jordan." In *Lebanon in Crisis: Participants and Issues,* edited by P. Edward Haley and Lewis W. Snider, 147–160. Syracuse: Syracuse University Press, 1979.

Kamrava, Mehran. "Conceptualizing Third World Politics: The State-Society See-Saw." *Third World Quarterly* 14, no. 4 (1993): 703–16.

———. *Democracy in the Balance: Culture and Society in the Middle East.* New York: Chatham House, 1998.

———. "Frozen Political Liberalization in Jordan: The Consequences for Democracy." *Democratization* 5, no. 1 (1998): 138–57.

———. *Politics and Society in the Third World.* London: Routledge, 1993.

Karawan, Ibrahim A. "Arab Dilemmas in the 1990s: Breaking Taboos and Searching for Signposts." *The Middle East Journal* 48, no. 3 (Summer 1994): 433–54.

Karl, Terry Lynn. *The Paradox of Plenty: Oil Booms and Petro-States.* Berkeley: University of California Press, 1997.

Kedourie, Elie. *Politics in the Middle East.* Oxford: Oxford University Press, 1992.

Kepel, Gilles. *Jihad: The Trail of Political Islam.* Cambridge: Harvard University Press, 2002.

———. *Muslim Extremism in Egypt: The Prophet and Pharoah.* Berkeley: University of California Press, 1984.

Kerr, Malcolm. *The Arab Cold War: Gamal Abd al-Nasir and His Rivals, 1958–70.* London: Oxford University Press, 1970.

Kerr, Malcolm H., and El Sayed Yassin, eds. *Rich and Poor States in the Middle East: Egypt and the New Arab Order.* Boulder: Westview Press, 1982.

Khader, Bichara and Adnan Badran, eds. *The Economic Development of Jordan.* London: Croom Helm, 1987.

Khalidi, Rashid, Lisa Anderson, Muhammad Muslih, and Reeva Simon, eds. *The Origins of Arab Nationalism*. New York: Columbia University Press, 1991.

Khatib, Fawzi. "Foreign Aid and Economic Development in Jordan: An Empirical Investigation." In *Politics and the Economy in Jordan*, edited by Rodney Wilson, 60–76. New York: Routledge, 1991.

Khulayfat, Sashban. *Al-Dimuqratiyya fi al-Urdun* (Democracy in Jordan). Amman: Dar Afaq, 1993.

Khuri, Tariq. *Mustaqbal al-Urdun: al-Dimuqratiyya, al-Huwiyya, al-Tahdiyyat* (The Future of Jordan: Democracy, Identity, Challenges). Amman, 1990.

Kienle, Eberhard. *Ba'th v Ba'th: The Conflict Between Syria and Iraq 1968–1989*. London: I.B. Taurus & Co., Ltd., 1990.

———. ed. *Contemporary Syria: Liberalization Between Cold War and Cold Peace*. New York: St. Martin's Press, 1994.

Kiernan, Peter. "Special Report: Jordan." *The Middle East* (September 1998): 29–31.

Kilani, Sa'eda. *Black Year of Democracy in Jordan: The 1998 Press and Publications Law*. Copenhagen: Euro-Mediterranean Human Rights Network, 1998.

Klieman, Aharon. "Israel's 'Jordanian Option': A Post-Oslo Reassessment." In *The Middle East Peace Process*, edited by Ilan Peleg. Albany, N.Y.: SUNY Press, 1998.

Knopf, Jeffrey W. "Beyond Two-Level Games: Domestic-International Interaction in the Intermediate-range Nuclear Forces Negotiations." *International Organization* 47, no. 4 (Autumn 1993): 599–628.

Korany, Bahgat. "National Security in the Arab World: The Persistence of Dualism." In *The Arab World Today*, edited by Dan Tschirgi, 161-178. Boulder, Colo.: Lynne Rienner Publishers, 1994.

Korany, Bahgat, and Ali E. Hillal Dessouki, eds. *The Foreign Policies of Arab States: The Challenge of Change*. Boulder: Westview Press, 1991.

Korany, Bahgat, Rex Brynen, and Paul Noble, eds. *The Many Faces of National Security in the Arab World*. New York: St. Martin's Press, 1993.

———. *Political Liberalization and Democratization in the Arab World*. Vol. 2, *Comparative Experiences*. Boulder, Colorado: Lynne Rienner Press, 1998.

Kumaraswamy, P.R. "Israel, Jordan and the Masha'al Affair." *Israel Affairs* 9, no. 3 (2003): 111–28.

Kuniholm, Bruce R. *The Persian Gulf and U.S. Policy*. Claremont, Calif.: Regina Books, 1984.

Lauren, Paul, ed. *Diplomacy: New Approaches in History, Theory and Policy*. New York: Free Press, 1979.

Lawson, Fred. "Domestic Conflict and Foreign Policy: The Contribution of Some Undeservedly Neglected Historical Studies." *Review of International Studies 21 (October 1985): 275-299.*

———. "Neglected Aspects of the Security Dilemma." In *The Many Faces of National Security in the Arab World*, edited by Bahgat Korany, Rex Brynen, and Paul Noble, 100–126. New York: St. Martin's Press, 1993.

———. *The Social Origins of Egyptian Expansionism During the Muhammad 'Ali Period.* New York: Columbia University Press, 1992.

———. *Why Syria Goes to War: Thirty Years of Confrontation.* Ithaca: Cornell University Press, 1996.

Layne, Linda. *Home and Homeland: The Dialogics of Tribal and National Identities in Jordan.* Princeton: Princeton University Press, 1994.

Levy, Jack S. "Domestic Politics and War." *Journal of Interdisciplinary History* 18, no. 4 (Spring 1988): 653–73.

Lewis, Norman N. *Nomads and Settlers in Syria and Jordan, 1800–1980.* Cambridge: Cambridge University Press, 1987.

Liska, George. *Nations in Alliance: The Limits of Interdependence.* Baltimore: The Johns Hopkins University Press, 1962.

Little, Douglas. "A Puppet in Search of Puppeteer? The United States, King Hussein, and Jordan, 1953–1970." *International History Review* 17, vol. 3 (1995): 512–44.

Lucas, Russell E. *Institutions and the Politics of Survival in Jordan: Domestic Responses to External Challenges, 1988–2001.* Albany: State University of New York Press, 2005.

Luciani, Giacomo, ed. *The Arab State.* Berkeley: University of California Press, 1990.

Lukacs, Yehuda. *Israel, Jordan, and the Peace Process.* Syracuse: Syracuse University Press, 1997.

Lunt, James. *Hussein of Jordan.* London: Macmillan, 1989.

Lust-Okar. "The Decline of Jordanian Political Parties: Myth or Reality?" *International Journal of Middle East Studies* 33, vol. 4 (November 2001): 545–69.

Lynch, Marc. "Jordan's King Abdallah in Washington." *Middle East Report Online* (May 8, 2002). http://www.merip.org/mero/mero050802.html.

———. *State Interests and Public Spheres: The International Politics of Jordan's Identity.* New York: Columbia University Press, 1999.

———. "Taking Arabs Seriously." *Foreign Affairs* 82, vol. 5 (2003): 81–94.

———. *Voices of the New Arab Public: Iraq, al-Jazeera, and Middle East Politics Today.* New York: Columbia University Press, 2006.

Maddy-Weitzman, Bruce. *The Crystallization of the Arab State System, 1945–1954.* Syracuse: Syracuse University Press, 1993.

Madfai, Madiha Rashid al-. *Jordan, the United States and the Middle East Peace Process, 1974–1991.* New York: Cambridge University Press, 1993.

Marashdeh, Omar. *The Jordanian Economy.* Amman: Al-Jawal Corporation, 1995.

Markaz Dirasat al-Wahda al-'Arabiyya. *Al-Urdun . . . Ila Ayna? Al-Huwiyya al-Watani-yya wa al-Istihqaqat al-Mustaqbaliyya* (Jordan . . . Where to? National Identity and Future Rights). Beirut: Center for Arab Unity Studies, 2004.

———. *Azmat al-Khalij wa Tada'iyatiha 'ala al-Watan al-'Arabi* (The Gulf Crisis and its Challenges to the Arab Nation). Beirut: Center for Arab Unity Studies, 1991.

Massad, Joseph A. *Colonial Effects: The Making of National Identity in Jordan.* New York: Columbia University Press, 2001.

Massis, Maher J. "Jordan: A Study of Attitudes Toward Democratic Changes." *Arab Studies Quarterly* 20, vol. 3 (Summer 1998): 37–63.

Mathews, Jessica Tuchman. "Redefining Security." *Foreign Affairs* (Spring 1989): 162–77.

Mazur, Michael P. *Economic Growth and Development in Jordan*. London: Croom Helm, 1979.

McKeown, Timothy J. "The Limits of 'Structural' Theories of Commercial Policy." *International Organization* 40, vol. 1 (1986): 43–64.

Middle East Economic Survey 32, 19 (13 February 1989): B1.

Middle East Economic Survey 32, 20 (20 February 1989): A8, C2.

Middle East Economic Survey 32, 26 (3 April 1989): C3.

Middle East Economic Survey 32, 38 (26 June 1989): A7.

Migdal, Joel. *Strong Societies and Weak States: State-Society Relations and State Capabilities in the Third World*. Princeton: Princeton University Press, 1988.

The Military Balance 1993–94. London: The International Institute for Strategic Studies, 1993.

Millen, Donald Hugh, ed. *Asian Perspectives on International Security*. New York: St. Martin's Press, 1984.

Milton-Edwards, Beverly and Peter Hinchcliffe. *Jordan: A Hashemite Legacy*. London: Routledge, 2001.

Mishal, Shaul. *West Bank/East Bank: The Palestinians in Jordan, 1949–1967*. New Haven, Conn.: Yale University Press, 1978.

Moore, Peter W. "The Newest Jordan: Free Trade, Peace, and an Ace in the Hole." *Middle East Report Online* (June 26, 2003). http://www.merip.org/mero/mero062603.html.

———. "What Makes Successful Business Lobbies? Business Associations and the Rentier State in Jordan and Kuwait." *Comparative Politics* 33, no. 2 (2001).

Moore, Peter W., and Bassel Salloukh. "Struggles under Authoritarianism: Regimes, States, and Professional Associations in the Arab World." *International Journal of Middle East Studies* 39, no. 1 (February 2007): 53–76.

Morganthau, Hans. *Politics Among Nations*. New York: Alfred Knopf, 1967.

Morrow, James D. "Arms Versus Allies: Trade-offs in the Search for Security." *International Organization* 47, no. 2 (1993): 207–33.

Mufti, Malik. "The 1978–1979 Syrian-Iraq Unification Plan." Paper presented at the 1991 meeting of the Middle East Studies Association, Washington, D.C.

———. "Elite Bargains and the Onset of Political Liberalization in Jordan." *Comparative Political Studies* 32, no. 1 (1999): 100–129.

———. *Sovereign Creations: Pan-Arabism and Political Order in Syria and Iraq*. Ithaca: Cornell University Press, 1995.

Mutawi, Samir. *Jordan in the 1967 War*. Cambridge: Cambridge University Press, 1987.

Naggar, Said El-, ed. *Adjustment Policies and Development Strategies in the Arab World*. Washington, D.C.: International Monetary Fund, 1987.

———. *Privatization and Structural Adjustment in the Arab Countries*. Washington, D.C.: International Monetary Fund, 1989.

Nasrallah, Fida. "The ACC and Arab Regional Problems." *Middle East International* 25 (August 1989): 19–20.

Nevo, Joseph. "Syria and Jordan: The Politics of Subversion." In *Syria Under Assad*, edited by Moshe Ma'oz and Avner Yaniv, 140–56. London: Croom Helm, 1986.

Nevo, Joseph, and Pappe, Ilan, eds. *Jordan in the Middle East: The Making of a Pivotal State, 1948–1988*. Ilford: Frank Cass & Co. Ltd., 1994.

Nimri Aziz, Barbara. "Iraq and Jordan—A Partnership Restored." *Middle East International* (May 2, 1997): 18–19.

Noble, Paul C. "The Arab System: Pressures, Constraints, and Opportunities." In *The Foreign Policies of Arab States: The Challenge of Change*, edited by Bahgat Korany and Ali E. Hillal Dessouki, 49–102. Boulder: Westview Press, 1991.

North, Andrew. "Another Defection." *Middle East International* (March 29, 1996): 13.

———. "Confusion on Iraq." *Middle East International* (March 15, 1996): 10–11.

Nye, Joseph S., and Sean Lynn-Jones. "International Security Studies: A report of a Conference on the State of the Field." *International Security* (Spring 1988): 5–27.

O'Donnell, Guillermo. *Modernization and Bureaucratic-Authoritarianism: Studies in South American Politics*. Berkeley: University of California Press, 1973.

O'Donnell, Guillermo, and Philippe C. Schmitter. *Transitions from Authoritarian Rule: Tentative Conclusions about Uncertain Democracies*. Baltimore: The Johns Hopkins University Press, 1986.

Owen, Roger. *State, Power and Politics in the Making of the Modern Middle East*. London: Routledge, 1992.

Peleg, Ilan, ed. *The Middle East Peace Process: Interdisciplinary Perspectives*. Albany, N.Y.: SUNY Press, 1998.

Perthes, Volker. *The Political Economy of Syria Under Asad*. London: I.B. Tauris, 1995.

Pfiefer, Karen, Marsha Pripstein-Posusney, Djavad Salehi-Isfahani, and Steve Niva. "Reform or Reaction? Dilemmas of Economic Development in the Middle East." *Middle East Report* (Spring 1999): 14–16.

Piro, Timothy J. "The Domestic Bases of Jordan's Foreign Policy: State Structures, Domestic Coalitions, and the National Interest." Paper Presented at the 1993 Annual Meeting of the Middle East Studies Association, Research Triangle Park, N.C.

———. *The Political Economy of Market Reform in Jordan*. Lanham, Maryland: Rowman and Littlefield, 1998.

Piscatori, James P., ed. *Islam in the Political Process*. Cambridge: Cambridge University Press, 1983.

Porath, Yehoshua. *In Search of Arab Unity*. London: Frank Cass, 1986.

Putnam, Robert D. "Diplomacy and Domestic Politics: The Logic of Two-Level Games." *International Organization* 42, no. 3 (1988): 427–60.

Rath, Katherine. "The Process of Democratization in Jordan." *Middle Eastern Studies* 30, no. 3 (1994): 530–57.

Reed, Stanley. "Jordan and the Gulf Crisis." *Foreign Affairs* 69, no. 5 (1990): 21–35.

Reich, Bernard, ed. *The Powers in the Middle East: The Ultimate Strategic Arena*. New York: Praeger Publishers, 1987.

Richards, Alan and John Waterbury, *A Political Economy of the Middle East: State, Class, and Economic Development*. Boulder: Westview Press, 1990.

Riedel, Tim. *Who is Who in Jordanian Parliament 1989–1993*. Amman, Jordan: Friedrich Ebert Shiftung, 1993.

Roberts, John. "Prospects for Democracy in Jordan." *Arab Studies Quarterly* 13, no. 3–4 (1991): 119–38.

Robinson, Glenn E. "Can Islamists be Democrats? The Case of Jordan." *Middle East Journal* 51, no. 3 (1997): 373–87.

———. "Defensive Democratization in Jordan." *International Journal of Middle East Studies* 30, no. 3 (1998): 387–410.

Rodenbeck, Max. "Egypt: Alignments." *Middle East International* 17 (February 1989): 8–9.

Rogan, Eugene, and Tariq Tell, eds. *Village, Steppe and State: The Social Origins of Modern Jordan*. London: British Academic Press, 1994.

Rothchild, Donald, and Naomi Chazan, eds. *The Precarious Balance: State and Society in Africa*. Boulder: Westview Press, 1988.

Ryan, Curtis R. "Between Iraq and a Hard Place: Jordanian-Iraqi Relations." *Middle East Report* 215 (2000): 40–42.

———. "Elections and Parliamentary Democratization in Jordan." *Democratization* 5, no. 4 (1998): 194–214.

———. "Hashemite Kingdom of Jordan." In *Government and Politics of the Middle East and North Africa*, 5th edition, edited by Mark Gasiorowski, David Long, and Bernard Reich, 246–66. Boulder: Westview, 2007.

———. "Jordan and the Rise and Fall of the Arab Cooperation Council." *Middle East Journal* 52, no. 3 (1998): 386–401.

———. "'Jordan First': Jordan's Inter-Arab Relations and Foreign Policy Under King Abdullah II." *Arab Studies Quarterly* 26, no. 3 (Summer 2004): 43–62.

———. "Jordan in the Middle East Peace Process: From War to Peace with Israel." In *The Middle East Peace Process*, edited by Ilan Peleg, 161–77. Albany, N.Y.: SUNY Press, 1998.

———. *Jordan in Transition: From Hussein to Abdullah*. Boulder: Lynne Rienner Press, 2002.

———. "Jordan: The Politics of Alliance and Foreign Policy." In *Small States in World Politics: Explaining Foreign Policy Behavior*, edited by Jeanne A. K. Hey, 135–55. Boulder: Lynne Rienner Press, 2003.

———. "Jordan's Changing Relations." *Middle East Insight* 15, no. 6 (November/December 2000): 83–87.

———. "The Odd Couple: Ending the Jordanian-Syrian 'Cold War.'" *Middle East Journal* 60, no. 1 (Winter 2006): 33–56.

———. "Peace, Bread, and Riots: Jordan and the International Monetary Fund." *Middle East Policy* 6, no. 2 (1998): 54–66.

———. "Political Liberalization and Monarchical Succession in Jordan." *Israel Affairs* 9, no. 3 (2003): 129–40.

———. "Political Strategies and Regime Survival: The Case of Egypt." *Journal of Third World Studies* 18, no. 2 (Fall 2001): 25–46.

Ryan, Curtis R., and David L. Downie. "From Crisis to War: Origins and Aftermath

Effects of the 1990–91 Persian Gulf Crisis." *Southeastern Political Review* 21, no. 3 (1993): 491–510.

Ryan, Curtis R., and Jillian Schwedler. "Return to Democratization or New Hybrid Regime? The 2003 Elections in Jordan." *Middle East Policy* 11, no. 2 (2004): 138–51.

Sadowski, Yahya M. *Scuds or Butter? The Political Economy of Arms Control in the Middle East*. Washington, D.C.: The Brookings Institution, 1993.

Sakijha, Bassem and Sa'eda Kilani, eds. *Towards Transparency in Jordan*. Amman: Arab Archives Institute, 2000.

Salibi, Kamal. *The Modern History of Jordan*. New York: I. B. Tauris, 1998.

Satloff, Robert. *From Abdullah to Hussein: Jordan in Transition*. Oxford: Oxford University Press, 1994.

———. *They Cannot Stop Our Tongues: Islamic Activism in Jordan*. Washington, D.C.: Washington Institute for Near East Policy, 1986.

———. *Troubles on the East Bank: Challenges to the Domestic Stability of Jordan*. New York: Praeger Press, 1986.

Sayigh, Yezid. "Arab Military Industrialization: Security Incentives and Economic Impact." In *The Many Faces of National Security in the Arab World*, edited by Bahgat Korany, Rex Brynen, and Paul Noble, 214–38. New York: St. Martin's Press, 1993.

Scham, Paul L., and Russell E. Lucas. "'Normalization' and 'Anti-Normalization' in Jordan: The Public Debate." *Israel Affairs* 9, no. 3 (2003): 141–64.

Schueftan, Dan. "Jordan's 'Israeli Option.'" In *Jordan in the Middle East, 1948–1988: The Making of Pivotal State*, edited by Joseph Nevo and Ilan Pappe, 254–82. Portland: Frank Cass, 1994.

Schwedler, Jillian. "Don't Blink: Jordan's Democratic Opening and Closing." *MERIP Press Information Note* (July 3, 2002). http.//www.merip.org/mero/mero070302.html.

———. *Faith in Moderation: Islamist Parties in Jordan and Yemen*. Cambridge: Cambridge University Press, 2006.

———. "Islamic Identity: Myth, Menace, or Mobilizer?" *SAIS Review* 21, no. 2 (2001): 1–17.

———. "Occupied Maan: Jordan's Closed Military Zone." *Middle East Report Online* (December 3, 2003). http://www.merip.org/mero/mero120302.html.

———. ed. *Toward Civil Society in the Middle East? A Primer*. Boulder: Lynne Rienner, 1995.

Seale, Patrick. *Asad: The Struggle for the Middle East*. Berkeley: University of California Press, 1988.

———. *The Struggle for Syria: A Study of Post-War Arab Politics 1945–1958*. Oxford: Oxford University Press, 1965.

Secretary General of the Arab Cooperation Council. *Majlis al-Ta'awun al-Arabi: Nasus al-Itifaqiyat wa al-Qararat al-Muqa'a Khilal al-Am al-Awal, 1989–1990* (Arab Cooperation Council: Text of the Agreements and Decisions Signed During the First Year, 1989–1990). Amman: Arab Cooperation Council, 1990.

Sela, Avraham. *The Decline of the Arab-Israeli Conflict*. Albany: State University of New York Press, 1998.

Shahin, Mariam. "Jordan: Not Yet a Comfortable Partnership." *The Middle East*, no. 243 (1995): 8–9.

———. "The Man Who Would be King." *The Middle East* (September 1998): 11–12.

Shlaim, Avi. *Collusion Across the Jordan: King Abdullah, the Zionist Movement, and the Partition of Palestine*. New York: Columbia University Press, 1988.

Singer, J. David and Melvin Small. "Alliance Aggregation and the Onset of War." In *Quantitative International Politics: Insights and Evidence*, David Singer, ed., 247-286, New York: The Free Press, 1968.

Sivan, Emmanuel. *Radical Islam: Medieval Theology and Modern Politics*. New Haven: Yale University Press, 1985.

Siverson, Randolph M., and Harvey Starr. "Regime Change and the Restructuring of Alliances." *American Journal of Political Science* 38, no. 1 (1994): 145–61.

Sluglett, Marion Farouk, and Peter Sluglett. *Iraq Since 1958: From Revolution to Dictatorship*. London: I.B. Tauris & Co., 1987.

Snow, Peter. *Hussein: A Biography*. London: Barrie and Jenkins, 1972.

Snyder, Glenn H. *Alliance Politics*. Ithaca: Cornell University Press, 1997.

———. "Alliance Theory: A Neorealist First Cut." *Journal of International Affairs* 44, no. 1 (1990): 103–23.

———. "Alliances, Balance, and Stability." *International Organization* 45, no. 1 (1991): 121–42.

———. "Process Variables in Neorealist Theory." Unpublished Manuscript, 1994.

———. "The Security Dilemma in Alliance Politics." *World Politics* 36, no. 4 (1984): 461–95.

Snyder, Glenn H., and Paul Diesing. *Conflict Among Nations: Bargaining, Decision-Making, and System-Structure in International Crises*. Princeton: Princeton University Press, 1977.

Snyder, Jack. *Myths of Empire: Domestic Politics and International Ambition*. Ithaca: Cornell University Press, 1991.

Sonderman, Fred A. "The Concept of the National Interest." *Orbis* (Spring 1977): 121–38.

Spalding, Nancy Jackson. "State-Society Relations in Africa: An Exploration of the Tanzanian Experience." *Polity* 29, no. 1 (Fall 1996): 65–96.

Stein, Janice Gross. "The Security Dilemma in the Middle East: A Prognosis for the Decade Ahead." In *The Many Faces of National Security in the Arab World*, edited by Bahgat Korany, Rex Brynen, and Paul Noble, 56–75. New York: St. Martin's Press, 1993.

Stephens, Robert. "Jordan and the Powers." In *The Shaping of an Arab Statesman: Abd al-Hamid Sharaf and the Modern Arab World*, edited by Patrick Seale. London: Quartet Books, 1983.

Susser, Asher. *Jordan: A Case Study of a Pivotal State*. Washington, D.C.: Washington Institute for Near East Policy, 2000.

Sways, Sulayman. "Kharita al-Ahzab al-Siyasia fi al-Urdun" (A Map of Political Parties in Jordan). *Al-Urdun Al-Jadid* (1990): 122–41.

Taheri, Amir. "Jordan's Choice: Taking the Right Side this Time," *National Review,* February 3, 2003. http://www.nationalreview.com/script/printpage.p?ref=/comment/comment-taheri020303.asp.

Tal, Lawrence. "Dealing with Radical Islam: The Case of Jordan." *Survival* 37, no. 3 (1995): 139–56.

Taylor, Alan R. *The Arab Balance of Power.* Syracuse: Syracuse University Press, 1982.

Terrill, W. Andrew. "Saddam's Closest Ally: Jordan and the Gulf War." *Journal of South Asian and Middle Eastern Studies* 9, no. 2 (1985): 43–54.

Thomas, Caroline. *In Search of Security: The Third World in International Relations.* Boulder: Lynne Rienner Publishers, 1987.

———. "Third World Security." In *International Security in the Modern World,* edited by Roger Carey and Trevor C. Salmon, 90–114. New York: St. Martin's Press, 1992.

Tibi, Bassam. *Arab Nationalism: Between Islam and the Nation-State.* New York: St. Martin's Press, 1997.

Ullman, Richard H. "Redefining Security." *International Security* (Summer 1983): 129–53.

Wahby, Mohammad. "The Arab Cooperation Council and the Arab Political Order." *American-Arab Affairs* 28 (1989): 61–66.

Walt, Stephen M. "Alliance Formation and the Balance of World Power." *International Security* 9 (1985): 3–43.

———. *The Origins of Alliances.* Ithaca: Cornell University Press, 1987.

———. "Testing Theories of Alliance Formation: The Case of Southwest Asia." *International Organization* 42 (1988): 275–316.

Waltz, Kenneth N. *Theory of International Politics.* New York: Random House, 1979.

Ward, Michael Don. *Research Gaps in Alliance Dynamics.* Denver: Graduate School of International Studies, University of Denver, 1982.

Wedeman, Ben. "Jordan's 'Siamese Twins' Agonize Over National Identity: Prospects for a Palestinian Entity Renews Old Debate." *Middle East Insight* 10, no. 3 (1994): 35–40.

Wendt, Alexander. "Anarchy is What States Make of it: The Social Construction of Power Politics." *International Organization* 46, no. 2 (1992): 391–425.

———. *Social Theory of International Politics.* New York: Cambridge University Press, 2000.

Wiktorowicz, Quintan. "Civil Society as Social Control: State Power in Jordan." *Comparative Politics* (2000): 43–61.

———. "The Limits of Democracy in the Middle East: The Case of Jordan." *Middle East Journal* 53, no. 4 (1999): 606–20.

———. *The Management of Islamic Activism: Salafis, the Muslim Brotherhood, and State Power in Jordan.* Albany: State University of New York Press, 2000.

Wilson, Mary. *King Abdullah, Britain, and the Making of Jordan.* New York: Cambridge University Press, 1987.

Wilson, Rodney, ed. "The Economic Relations of the Middle East: Toward Europe or Within the Region?" *The Middle East Journal* 48, no. 2 (Spring 1994): 268–87.

———. *Politics and the Economy in Jordan.* New York: Routledge, 1991.

Wolfers, Arnold. "'National Security' as an Ambiguous Symbol." *Political Science Quarterly* 67 (December 1952): 481–502.

World Bank. *World Development Reports 1995.* Oxford University Press, 1995.

Yapp, Malcolm E. *The Making of the Modern Near East 1792–1923.* New York: Longman, 1987.

Yorke, Valerie. *Domestic Politics and Regional Security: Jordan, Syria and Israel: The End of an Era?* Aldershot: Gower/The International Institute for Strategic Studies, 1988.

Zakaria, Fareed. "Realism and Domestic Politics: A Review Essay." *International Security* 17, no. 1 (1992): 177–98.

Zeine, Zeine N. *The Emergence of Arab Nationalism.* Delmar, N.Y.: Caravan, 1958.

Zunes, Stephen. "The Israeli-Jordanian Agreement: Peace or Pax Americana?" *Middle East Policy* 3, no. 4 (1995): 57–68.

Index

external security concerns and, 147–52;
Jordan and Israel, 145–46, 162–64; PLO
and Israel, 148–50; political economy and,
156–58
Perception of threat to regimes, 18, 30–33. *See
also* External security concerns
Peres, Shimon, 161
PLO: Egyptian-Israeli process and, 105;
Jordan and, 63–64, 65, 71, 78, 170; Lebanese
civil war and, 88; peace accord with Israel,
148–50; as representative of Palestinian
people, 82, 106; Syria and, 170
Policymakers, influences on, 8
Political economy: Arab Cooperation Council
and, 121–24; disparity, dependence, and insecurity in, 53–59; during Gulf crisis, 140–42;
ideology and, 58–59; Iraq-Jordan alliance
and, 109–10; Israel, peace accord with, and,
156–58; militarization and, 34; October War
coalition and, 79–81; Syria-Jordan alliance
and, 91–92; Syria-Jordan Cold War and,
175–78; Second U.S.-Iraq War and, 195–98
Political opposition, 37–40, 191–95
Political tool, Arabism as, 48–50, 52, 59–60
Porath, Yoshua, 6
Post-colonial states: authoritarian, 15–16,
36 40, 58; legacies of, 25; regime security
approach and, 13; security threats in, 26–27;
theories and studies of, 9; Western-centric
concepts and, 7–8
Pragmatic trend in Arab politics, 46, 182–83
Public opinion in Jordan: alliance with Iraq
and, 105–6, 107, 108–9; Arab Cooperation
Council and, 120–21; current, 201; during
Gulf crisis, 130, 134, 136–38; peace accord
with Israel and, 153–56, 159–60

Qadhafi, Mu'ammar al-, 39, 72
Al-Qa'ida, 184, 200
Qasim, Marwan al-, 62, 104, 129–30, 131, 133
Qatar, 197

Rabin, Yitzhak, 145, 161
Raghib, Ali Abu al-, 175, 202, 203
Ramadan War. *See* October 1973 war
Realignments, explanations of, 17–19
Realist approach, 18. *See also* Gause, F.
Gregory

Redundancy of pressures, 195–96
Reform, regime resistance to, 39. *See also*
Liberalization
Refugees from Iraq, 194
Regime security approach: arms racing, mili-
tarization, and, 32; choices of alignments
and, 17–19; empirical evidence for, 207–9;
overview of, 10, 11–14, 19–22, 204–7; trade-
offs and, 15–17; value of alignments, 14. *See
also* Domestic politics; External security
concerns; Political economy
Rejection Front, 102
Rentier states, 35–36, 217–39, 220–11. *See also*
Gulf states
Revolutionary republic, Syria as, 84–85
Rifa'i, Zayd al-: Arab Cooperation Council
and, 117; Iraq, Iran, and, 108; riots and, 123;
sacking of, 119; Syria and, 85–86, 88, 90,
92, 174
Riots in response to austerity program, 119,
122–23, 135

Sadat, Anwar, 3, 45, 56, 72–73, 99–101
Sanctions against Iraq, 141–42, 179, 187
Saudi Arabia: Arab Cooperation Council and,
117; defense expenditures of, 34; Egypt and,
56–57; in Gulf crisis, 3; Islamism in, 51; Jordan and, 65, 79, 80, 109, 110, 198; Trilateral
Alliance and, 71–73. *See also* Fahd Ibn 'Abd
al-'Aziz Al Sa'ud
Schwedler, Jillian, 191
Seale, Patrick, 6
Second Gulf War (1st U.S.-Iraq War). *See*
Gulf crisis
Security: in Arab political context, 24–28;
meaning of, in Middle East, 7; regimes as
obsessed with, 11–12, 18. *See also* Regime
security approach
Security dilemma: in Arab political context,
24–28; arms racing, militarization, and,
30–34; classic form of, 23–24, 206–7; costs
of, 34–35, 37–40, 41; exceptions to, 35–36;
multiple, as facing Arab regimes, 28–30
Sela, Avraham, 6
September 11 attacks, 184
Sharaf, 'Abd al-Hamid, 93
Sharaf, Layla, 180
Shubaylat, Layth, 160, 192–93

Curtis R. Ryan is an Associate Professor of Political Science at Appalachian State University in North Carolina. He specializes in international and Middle East politics, with particular interests in inter-Arab relations, Islam and politics, alliances, democratization, and international security. He is the author of *Jordan in Transition: From Hussein to Abdullah*.